India's Foreign Policy

Changing Perspective (With Special Reference to SAARC Countries)

INDIA'S FOREIGN POLICY
CHANGING PERSPECTIVE (WITH SPECIAL REFERENCE TO SAARC COUNTRIES)

Dr. Sanjay Kumar Singh

PRASHANT PUBLISHING HOUSE
DELHI-110094

Published by :
Prashant Publishing House
C-34, 28 Foota Road, Gali-3,
West Karwal Nagar, Delhi-110094
Phone : 011-22963970, Mob. : 9810396373
e-mail.: prashantpublishinghouse@gmail.com

India's Foreign Policy: Changing Perspective (With Special Reference to SAARC Countries)

First Published 2015

ISBN 978-93-80565-52-1

PRINTED IN INDIA
Published by Mr. R.K. Jha M/s Prashant Publishing House and Published at H.S. Offset House Press, Delhi.

Preface

The foundations of India's foreign policy were laid during the freedom movement when our leaders, even when fighting for independence, were engaged with the great causes of the time. The principles of India's foreign policy, that emerged then, have stood the test of time: a belief in friendly relations with all countries of the world, the resolution of conflicts by peaceful means, the sovereign equality of all states, independence of thought and action as manifested in the principles of Non-alignment, and equity in the conduct of international relations.

Since the new millennium, relations between India and China have been characterised by 'hot economics and cold politics' or 'cooptetion'—economic cooperation and political competition. In recent years, tensions between the two countries have increased due to the border dispute.

The enduring Indo-Pakistan rivalry is well known. The Kashmir conflict and cross-border terrorism have historically led to tensions between the two countries. The beheading of an Indian soldier along the Line of Control (LoC) in January this year and incessant ceasefire violations since have vitiated relations between the two countries. LSE Professor Sumantra Bose avers that "cross-border incidents as well as terrorist incidents are symptoms of the deeply conflictual nature of the India-Pakistan relationship.

India and Afghanistan have mutual economic and strategic interests—as Professor Bharat Karnad at the Centre for Policy Research, New Delhi, puts it: "India needs natural resources, access to Central Asia through Chabahar Port (in Iran), and the mineral-rich Hajigak region as a base for intelligence operations and, if needed, to squeeze Pakistan. Kabul needs Indian capital, technical assistance, development aid, and military assistance."

The most significant initiative made by the Narendra Modi government is the focus on neighbouring countries and major Asian powers coupled with emphasizing on the two decades old Look East Policy. Asia being the major focus area of his foreign policy, Modi and his foreign minister chose several Asian countries for their initial bilateral visits. He has made state visits to Bhutan and Nepal and Japan within the first 100 days of his government and also hosted Asia leaders like Chinese President Xi Jinping and Australian Prime Minister Tony Abbott apart form inviting SAARC leaders in his inauguration ceremony. External Affairs Minister Swaraj has also made official visits to Dhaka, Bangladesh, Kathmandu, Nepal, Naypidaw, Myanmar, Singapore, Hanoi, Vietnam, Manama, Bahrain, Kabul, Afghanistan, and Dushanbe, Tajikistan.

The South Asian Association for Regional Cooperation (SAARC) was established in 1985. This organization has a key focus on economic and developmental issues. SAARC has eight members: Afghanistan, Bangladesh, Bhutan, India, Maldives, Nepal, Pakistan, and Sri Lanka. Additionally, there are some nations with observer status, including the United States, Australia, Japan, and China. Myanmar (Burma) also has the status of an observer, but is keen to become a full member. This country shares more than 1,600 kilometers of borders with India. Owing to geographical and political realities for this discussion, Myanmar is thus considered as a part of SAARC.

This book contains the fundamental and basic information of the subject.

—Editor

Contents

Preface

1. India's Foreign Policy Challenges in 2014 1
2. Foundations of India's Foreign Policy 53
3. India's SAARC Satellite Proposal and Policy 87
4. India's Foreign Policies in South Asia 124
5. India's Relationship with Her Neighbors! 188
6. India Relations and Policy of China and Bhutan 228
7. Indian Foreign Policy in the 21st Century 264
8. Foreign Policy, Diplomacy and National Consensus 301

Bibliography 333

Index 335

1

India's Foreign Policy Challenges in 2014

China

Since the new millennium, relations between India and China have been characterised by 'hot economics and cold politics' or 'cooptetion'—economic cooperation and political competition. In recent years, tensions between the two countries have increased due to the border dispute. According to Dr Harsh Pant at King's College London, "the lingering border dispute between India and China continues to be the single-most important impediment, though increasingly the larger context of this relationship is undergoing a transformation. As the balance of power in Asia changes and India strives to manage the rise of China with its own blend of internal and external balancing, this will assume a bigger profile in Sino-Indian bilateral ties." It is highly unlikely that relations between the two rising giants will improve in 2014, and will continue to be characterised by 'cooptetion' and military confrontation in the medium term.

Pakistan

The enduring Indo-Pakistan rivalry is well known. The Kashmir conflict and cross-border terrorism have historically led to tensions between the two countries. The beheading of an Indian soldier along the Line of Control (LoC) in January this year and incessant ceasefire violations since have vitiated relations between the two countries. LSE Professor Sumantra Bose avers that "cross-border incidents as well as terrorist incidents are symptoms of the deeply conflictual nature of the India-Pakistan relationship. The Kashmir dispute is real and important, but has simply provided a focal point for a multifaceted and deeply rooted antagonism." The emphasis on security obscures other aspects of the relationship, including a growing appetite on both sides of the border for increased bilateral trade. In the context of increasingly adverse domestic political environments in both countries – the jingoistic right-wing in India and Pakistan's irredentist military – hindering the diplomatic process, there is an even greater need to re-think India- Pakistan relations in 2014.

Afghanistan

India and Afghanistan have historically enjoyed friendly relations. According to Dr Shanthie D'Souza at the National University of Singapore, the most significant aspect of the India-Afghanistan relationship is that the "long history of cultural and civilisation linkages have been further strengthened by a decade of development assistance, capacity building initiatives and economic opportunities." India and Afghanistan have mutual economic and strategic interests—as Professor Bharat Karnad at the Centre for Policy Research, New Delhi, puts it: "India needs natural resources, access to Central Asia through Chabahar Port (in Iran), and the mineral-rich Hajigak region as a base for intelligence operations and, if needed, to squeeze Pakistan. Kabul needs Indian capital, technical assistance, development aid, and military assistance."

However, terrorism and resulting regional instability pose a serious challenge to the relationship. The "challenge remains in terms of establishing regional trade, transit and connectivity by making Afghanistan a land bridge connecting South with Central Asia from which both Afghanistan and Pakistan would derive tremendous economic benefits," adds Dr D'Souza.

United States

On the eve of Prime Minister Manmohan Singh's meeting with President Obama in Washington on 27 September, 2013, the media painted a gloomy picture of India-US relations. There were assertions that the relationship between the two largest democracies in the world was 'oversold' and experiencing a 'drift'. Indeed, there is no paucity of disagreements between the two countries: Pakistan, Afghanistan, UN reforms, permanent membership for India of the UN Security Council, and economic challenges such as India's unwillingness to open its markets. Professor Brahma Chellaney at the Centre for Policy Research underlines that the "India-US strategic partnership is somewhat lopsided and unbalanced because of India's structural and strategic limitations." In the new year, Dr Pant believes that "New Delhi and Washington will face the challenge of maintaining stable ties as the United States prepares to leave Afghanistan with help from the Pakistan military. But on larger strategic issues, there is a convergence between the two states that is as striking as it is potent. The relations are likely to only improve over the long term."

Iran

India has long pursued a careful balancing act between its relationships with Iran and the United States. In recent years, India and Iran have been trying to manage their economic, energy and political cooperation in the shadow of US and European Union sanctions. A potential US-Iran rapprochement will likely ease existing diplomatic and economic pressure on India in this context.

Iran under President Hassan Rohani is expected to enhance cooperation with India in the areas of energy, connectivity, trade, and on the issue of Afghanistan. Both countries also seek to enhance connectivity through the International North South Transport Corridor (INSTC) and the Chabahar Port. However challenges remain in the bilateral relationship. "The biggest challenge for India Iran relations is that India does not have a clearly articulated foreign policy strategy towards Central Asia or the Gulf," explains Professor Lawrence Sáez at SOAS. "At a bilateral level, India does not engage directly with Iran, partially as a result of US pressure and mostly as a result of India's own inertia and strategic incompetence. At an international institutional level, India has shown little enthusiasm for including Iran as an active participant in SAARC."

Sri Lanka

India and Sri-Lanka have had cordial relations in the new millennium. LSE's Dr Rajesh Venugopal explains that "security cooperation, trade and investment, China and the Tamil situation are important factors in India-Sri Lanka relationship." Human right violations against Tamils and rehabilitation of Tamils in the national mainstream in Sri Lanka after the end of the civil war have strained diplomatic relations between the two countries. Ceteris paribus, Dr Venugopal believes that "relations are unlikely to improve in the next year simply because India will enter into election mode, and every party will be under pressure to attack Sri Lanka in order to win the Tamil Nadu vote." However, defence ties between the two countries would continue as usual through joint training, sharing of warfare expertise and military exchanges.

Bangladesh

Since Sheikh Hasina and her Awami League came to power five years ago, there has been tremendous goodwill for India in Bangladesh. There is a wide consensus that Sheikh Hasina has largely delivered on Indian security concerns by cracking down on terrorism directed against India from Bangladeshi soil. However, contentious issues remain in the bilateral relationship: the division of common river waters, the land corridor that India wants through Bangladesh to connect West Bengal to the north-eastern states, the continuing influx of undocumented migrants from Bangladesh through the porous border and the continuing presence of anti-India forces in Bangladesh despite the recent crackdown. "India's giant size and Bangladesh's smallness mean that it is difficult to negotiate equally to reach fair outcomes between the two countries," says LSE's Professor David Lewis. "The long border means Bangladeshis feel encircled and enclosed by India, leading to distrust and border tensions."

Nepal

In recent years, the increasing dominance of Maoism in Nepal's domestic politics, along with the strengthening economic and political influence of China, has led the Nepalese government to gradually distance itself from India. Nepal has also become a haven for terrorists and separatists operating in India: the recent arrests of two high profile terrorists – Abdul Karim Tunda and Mohammed Ahmed Sidibappa – have brought the India-Nepal border into sharp focus. India has been seeking Nepal's cooperation in managing the border through several bilateral mechanisms. However due to domestic political turmoil, lack of political will and a resource crunch, Nepal has been unable to effectively cooperate with India. But that could change if Nepal sees increasing political stability in 2014.

Burma

Political developments in Burma over the last two years have opened a new chapter in India-Burma relations. Burma, like Vietnam, is an important pillar in India's 'Look East' policy. Burma's internal political dynamics will determine the course of bilateral relations: Burma's transition from authoritarianism to democracy, communal and ethnic violence and implementation of bold reform initiatives presents immense challenges as well as opportunities for India. Challenges include the long-running border problems (compounded by the diplomatic row over pillar number 76 in the north-eastern Indian state of Manipur), Indian support for pro-democratic forces, China's influence and active role in state building in Burma and the uninterrupted flow of weapons from Burma for the rebels in north-east India among others. On the commercial front, India would like to gain access to Burma's oil and gas reserves but faces competition from other countries especially China. But given the limitations of Indian public sector investment in Burma due to bureaucratic hurdles, private-sector investment would have to increase in the new year in order to consolidate ties.

Vietnam

Bilateral ties between India and Vietnam have improved significantly in recent years. Due to its antagonistic relations with China, Vietnam is a key component of India's 'Look East' policy. Although the two countries have enhanced their political and security cooperation, there is still a need to strengthen commercial and economic ties. Both countries need to think creatively about expanding investment opportunities, especially in the energy, steel and pharmaceutical sectors. This can be done by establishing stronger institutional mechanisms that review and develop the economic relationship on a regular basis. The burgeoning relationship between the India and Vietnam raises concerns in China and may have repercussions on Sino-Indian relations in 2014 and onwards.

INDIA'S FOREIGN POLICY OPPORTUNITIES AND CHALLENGES IN MID-2014

India's foreign policy opportunities and challenges in mid-2014 under the leadership of India's new Prime Minister Narendra Modi will expectedly acquire bold and audacious contours dispelling the earlier ten years of appeasement and timidity.

India's foreign policies in the 2004-2014 periods failed to exploit the strategic leverages that were being bestowed on India, internationally and regionally, in recognition of India's emerging major power potential in the process of crystallising till mid-2004.

Perceptionaly, what is evident in mid-2014 is the debris of collateral damages of obsessive Pakistan-centric and China-centric Indian foreign policy with no gains visible for indulging in appeasement of these two prominent India's military adversaries.

Perceptionaly again, India during the preceding ten years seemed to have outsourced and mortgaged its foreign policy directions to Washington which was more sensitive to Pakistan's and China's sensitivities than Indian national security interests.

Prime Minister Modi's opening move even before oath-taking as PM was South Asia-centric and not Pakistan-centric as was being made out by the Indian media. PM Modi made a significant and imaginative political outreach to the SAARC Nations when he invited their leaders for his oath-taking ceremony. That all of them came was a measure of the Indian Prime Minister's personal leadership waiting to unfold and his underlying objective of attaching first priority to India's SAARC neighbours. They all came despite the very negative propaganda and demonization of Mr Modi indulged in by India's then ruling Congress Party from 2002-2014.

PM Modi's opening foreign policy act was therefore well conceived by him as in light of the above negative campaign it gave an opportunity to SAARC leaders to personally size-up PM Modi and vice versa.

In a further act of reinforcing his India's neighbourhood-priorities policy it has been announced today that PM Modi's first foreign visit would be to Bhutan, a nation strategically important for India because looming large over it is China. Nepal having been lost to China by the flawed policies of the previous Government, India cannot afford to let Bhutan slip under China's influence likewise because of Indian insensitivities.

Now moving to the larger canvas of India's opening moves under the new leadership of PM Modi, one would like to advocate that India's foreign policy initiatives to be classified in two major categories.

Category I nations would be those nations which present promising "Opportunities" to India in terms of evolution of more robust and substantial partnerships and in which their past record does not carry any baggage of discord or tensions with India. Such nations would also be those nations which in the contemporary global security environment enjoy strategic convergences with India and can hopefully be strategic assets in India's ascendant power trajectory.

Category II Nations would be those nations which are not likely to shape or emerge as "Opportunities" for India but would always be "Challenges" for India's foreign policy decision makers. Such countries have a record of discord, strategic distrust of India and many irritants exist in their relationships with India. They cannot be wished away but nor can India afford to allocate disproportionate time and effort to win them over.

In Category I Nations for Indian foreign policy attention I would like to include Japan, Vietnam, Indonesia, Israel and France and possibly Germany.

In Category II Nations I would primarily classify and include USA, Russia, China, and Pakistan. These nations do not present opportunities for India to ascend the power-trajectory and more often than not would impede that process.

So as PM Modi starts planning his diplomatic calendar of foreign visits, it is the Category I Nations that should figure first.

Japan should be PM Modi's' first foreign visit as both countries enjoy significant strategic convergences on Asian and Indo Pacific security and stability. A strong Strategic Partnership exists between the two nations and these need to be reinforced significantly, by Japan being PM Modi's first port of call. Needless to state that in Asia there are only three major powers, namely, China, Japan and India. China is not willing to cede or share strategic space in Asia neither to Japan nor India. Further China is in a conflictual relationship with both Japan and India.

Vietnam has long and historic ties with India and also a Strategic Partnership with India. Geostrategically located, it is also a significant geopolitical player in South East Asia and ASEAN region. Combining his visit to Japan with a visit to Vietnam on the return leg would be a significant step for India and Asian security.

France also has been a good friend of India and has been a reliable and trusted supplier of arms and armaments to India, besides a substantial Strategic Partnership. The Indian Ministry of Defence has for far too long sat on and impeded the126 MRCA Rafael Fighter aircraft. This has seriously affected India's cutting edge defensive and offensive aerial combat capabilities. PM Modi with his dynamic style should prod the Indian Defence Ministry to finalise the deal within three months as it stood finalised a number of years back but for some nit-picking by the previous Government.

The United States has been placed in Category II because its intentions' and approaches to India have always been ambiguous and at times contentious. Its National Security Strategy in the past has included references to prevention of rise of hegemonic nations in Asia including India. Except for the short span of 2-3 years in the md-2000s the record is not of substantive support to Indians national security interests despite a much-touted Strategic Partnership. United States has still not forsaken playing balance-of- power games in the Indian Sub-Continent by balancing Pakistan against India. Too many trade irritants also exist. India would be well advised to go-slow in rushing head-long into a resuscitation of the Strategic Partnership and let it be reinforced by the pressure of the unfolding international power-dynamics.

Russia too has been placed in Category II because Russia in terms of Asian security still persists in giving weightage to China strategically over India. Gone are the days when Russia stood as a bulwark in India's favour as a countervailing power. India can afford to wait till geopolitically the Russia-China strategic nexus wears thin.

Lastly one comes to India's military adversaries namely China and Pakistan. No Nobel Peace Prizes await any Indian Prime Minister for a breakthrough in their adversarial relationships and postures against India. Without wasting disproportionate time on both of them, India should follow the policy of "Congagement" with Pakistan and China. 'Strategic Distrust' would continue to predominate for a long time to come until their domestic political dynamics bring about radical transformations in their political cultures.

PM Modi can be expected to bring about a radical transformation in India's military capabilities and higher defence structure endowing an inclusive role to India's military hierarchy in national security affairs. This would make India's defence capabilities that much stronger and enable India to withstand any military coercion or destabilisation by China or Pakistan besides making Indian foreign policy that much more robust.

Concluding, one can only refer to the pointers that are coming where China is making the first moves to establish contacts and dialogues with the new Modi Government in India and Pakistan would follow suit. Pakistan is not India's long term threat. It is China that is India's long term and potent threat and this strategic reality should not be wished away in our foreign policy making.

In terms of systemic changes in India's foreign policy structures, PM Modi should dispense with the system of Special Envoys system (a slot for retired IFS diplomats), Track II initiatives and so many other Tracks which foul up the foreign policy making structures. Let institutionalised foreign policy be the rule and if dramatic results are to be achieved it should be the prerogative and be coming from the dynamism of PM Modi himself. With so much on the plate to be handled in terms f India's foreign policy by Prime Minister Modi as he sets out to map India's foreign policies, it is incumbent that India's foreign policy objectives be prioritised and be categorised into "Opportunities" and "Challenges" in relation to India's national security interests. In the field of foreign policy formulation "Opportunities" are always fleeting and need to be grasped instantly. "Challenges" will always abound and must wait till geopolitical dynamics offer leverages to convert challenges into opportunities.

NARENDRA MODI NUANCES FOREIGN POLICY APPROACH AHEAD OF BRICS SUMMIT

Prime Minister Narendra Modi today nuanced his government's foreign policy approach seeking an aggressive Indian engagement on global issues to address regional crises and security threats for restoring global peace and stability while advancing economic stability.

Modi, who arrived here amidst light drizzle for an overnight halt en route to Brazil for participation in the sixth summit of the five-nation grouping BRICS, said in his departure statement in Delhi that he also hoped that negotiations at the summit would lead to establishment of the BRICS Development Bank.

Modi was received at the airport by Indian Ambassador to Germany Vijay Gokhale and senior officials from the German Foreign Ministry.

Berlin was preferred to Frankfurt for a transit halt on Germany's request for a possible bilateral meeting with Chancellor Angela Merkel but their team's entry into the FIFA World Cup has rendered it a mere stopover for sleeping off jet lag.

Merkel is in Brazil to watch the World Cup final. Usually, Indian Prime Ministers transit through Frankfurt for further journeys across the Atlantic.

Modi's departure statement appeared to be giving a new thrust to India's foreign policy approach when he spoke of New Delhi's engagement on global issues. "I look at the BRICS summit as an opportunity to discuss with BRICS Partners how we can contribute to international efforts to address regional crises, address security threats and restore a climate of peace and stability in the world.

"I also look forward to our discussions to further advance intra-BRICS economic cooperation and our collective efforts to advance global economic stability and prosperity. In particular, I look forward to the successful conclusion of major BRICS initiatives like the New Development Bank and the Contingent Reserve Arrangement, which have seen significant progress since their launch in New Delhi in 2012," Modi said.

"These initiatives will support growth and stability in BRICS and also benefit other developing countries," he said.

The BRICS Development Bank with an initial corpus of USD 100 billion was decided in principle at the Durban summit last year. India and China are said to be vying for getting the headquarters of the bank in New Delhi or Shanghai.

Preparing for his first multilateral engagement with world leaders, Modi said they were meeting at a time of political turmoil, conflict and humanitarian crisis in several parts of the world and persisting weakness and risks in the global economy.

WITH BRICKS AND MORTAR, MODI PUTS A FOREIGN POLICY IN PLACE

Two months ago Prime Minister Narendra Modicancelled a summit with Japan because he wanted a substantive visit. On Monday, Japan and India ramped up ties in a significant way, laying the way for India's economic development and transformation. It also gives a good peek into what Modi's foreign policy is really like.

Since the moment Narendra Modi invited the Saarc heads of state to attend his swearing-in ceremony, the new NDA government has opened up foreign policy into a veritable hive of activity. Most Indian commentators believed Modi was turning soft on Pakistan after the evident bonhomie during the meeting.

While 100 days is really no time to assess a new regime's foreign policy, recent developments give a fair idea of where he wants to go with it.

First, it can best be described as a 'hub-and-spoke' approach to foreign policy. At the core is the growth and development of India. This is the paramount principle governing all Modi's foreign policy. The second concentric circle, tied closely to the first, is the South Asian neighbourhood. Modi is a believer in the truth, first articulated by former PM IK Gujral, that India's development will be incomplete if its neighbours don't tread the same path. The spokes would be the countries India will engage intensively which would assist the development of his core principles.

These would be Japan, Israel, Germany, Singapore, Canada and the US, not always in that order. These are countries that India will invite to help transform India, its economy, its skill-sets, its cities and its technology. The Japan visit is a big step in that direction despite the possible disappointment of a failed nuclear deal.

Placed in this context, Modi's big bang beginning makes complete sense. His first visits to Bhutan and Nepal too are clearly part of the same vision. Foreign minister Sushma Swaraj made Bangladesh her first port of call, making way for a possible Modi visit by year-end.

Modi has started reaching out to Mamata Banerjee in West Bengal, indicating his readiness to work out a political deal with the Bengal chief minister to take the Bangladesh relationship forward perhaps with the land boundary agreement.

Sri Lanka will pose a slightly different challenge, but bilateral ties now are currently on cruise control. India has refused visas to UN investigators seeking to interview people in Sri Lanka regarding the UNHRC resolution, which India abstained in March.

When Modi abruptly called off foreign secretary talks with Pakistan, the government took a lot of flak on what seems like a see-saw Pakistan policy. But there are several indications that India's approach to other South Asian neighbours will not be replicated in Pakistan. Nawaz Sharif's decision to come, despite the strictures against meeting the Hurriyat then did not go down well with the Pakistan army, but sent a positive signal to Modi.

What did not, was the ISI-LeT attack on the Indian consulate in Herat, Afghanistan. Coming a couple of days before his swearing in, the incident showed the dangers that underlay the apparent bonhomie.

Why did Modi draw a red line on the Hurriyat meeting? For conversations with many familiar with developments, Modi's approach to Pakistan will be guided by a couple of things – first, a tough stand on the border and LOC, which has been evident for the past few weeks. For the second time in as many weeks, Pakistan has complained about Indian firing on the border. The "sentinels on the border" as the MEA calls them, have been ordered to give back more than they get.

That does not mean Modi will cut off diplomatic contact, though it's very clear Modi's interest in Pakistan as a nation is minimal, unlike his predecessor. If Nawaz Sharif survives his current crisis and makes it to New York for the UN general assembly, Modi and Sharif may well sit down for a chat. India will make trade concessions to Pakistan to sweeten a stalled trade deal, but that's it. Inside Kashmir, Modi has a very different vision – the elections in November will be the first time Modi-Shah combine will test their policy. A state government, not opposed to the centre, more nationalistic in tone than before, can alter ground situations more than any conversation between India and Pakistan.

In 100 days, one thing is clear. Modi is not enamoured of either the foreign minister, or the foreign office. While MEA officials are scrambling, they are frequently being ticked off for lack of ideas and even preparation. The old-fashioned diplomatese that MEA dishes out in high-level briefings is leaving Modi cold. He wants crisp output from MEA in tune with his vision.

Foreign minister Sushma Swaraj is competent and hands-on minister and wants to keep her ministry away from the PMO marauders. She may not succeed, particularly if Modi appoints a foreign policy adviser as many have speculated. At this point though, Sushma can claim several successes, including evacuating Indians from troubled spots in the Middle East. But the disconnect between the MEA and PMO is real.

"Modi's vision is bigger than we all imagine it to be," said a source who is believed to be close to the PM. "What we don't know is how successful he will be."

BRIC in Future

The list of 22 selected countries by nominal GDP from year 2006 to 2050: BRICs, G7 and Next Eleven. The bottom chart list the same 22 countries by nominal GDP per capita (the rankings for this bottom chart do not reflect the GDP per capita for all the world's countries). BRIC countries are highlighted and labelled in bold. Figures reflect data published in 2007.

BRIC Summits

The BRIC countries met for their first official summit on 16 June 2009, in Yekaterinburg, Russia, with Luiz Inacio Lula da Silva, Dmitry Medvedev, Manmohan Singh, and Hu Jintao, the respective leaders of Brazil, Russia, India and China, all attending.

The core focus of the summit was related to improving the current global economic situation and discussing how the four countries can better work together in the future, as well as a more general push to reform financial institutions.

There was also discussion surrounding how developing nations, such as those members of BRIC, could be better involved in global affairs in the future. In the aftermath of the summit the BRIC nations suggested that there was a need for a new global reserve currency that is 'diversified, stable and predictable'.

The statement that was released stopped short of making a direct attack on the perceived 'dominance' of the US dollar, something which the Russians have been critical of; however, it still led to a fall in the value of the dollar against other major currencies.

The foreign ministers of the BRIC countries had met previously on May 16, 2008 also in Yekaterinburg.

One week prior to the summit, Brazil offered $10 billion to the International Monetary Fund. It was the first time that the country had ever made such a loan. Brazil had previously received loans from the IMF and this announcement was treated as a significant demonstration of how Brazil's economic position had changed. China also announced plans to invest a total of $50. 1 billion and Russia planned to invest $10 billion.

Summit	Date	Host country	Host leader	Location held
1st	June 16, 2009	Russia	Dmitry Medvedev	Yekaterinburg
2nd	April 16, 2010	Brazil	Luiz Inacio Lula da Silva	Brasilia
3rd	TBA	China	Hu Jintao	Beijing

The BRIC Term

Various sources refer to a purported "original" BRIC agreement that predates the Goldman Sachs thesis. Some of these sources claim that President Vladimir Putin of Russia was the driving force behind this original cooperative coalition of developing BRIC countries. However, thus far, no text has been made public of any formal agreement to which all four BRIC states are signatories. This does not mean, however, that they have not reached a multitude of bilateral or even quadrilateral agreements. Evidence of agreements of this type are abundant and are available on the foreign ministry websites of each of the four countries. Trilateral agreements and frameworks made among the BRICs include the Shanghai Cooperation Organization (member states include Russia and China, associate members include India) and the IBSA Trilateral Forum, which unites Brazil, India, and South Africa in annual dialogues. Also important to note is the G-20 coalition of developing states which includes all the BRICs.

Also, because of the popularity of the Goldman Sachs thesis "BRIC", this term has sometimes been extended whereby "BRICK" (K for South Korea), "BRIMC" (M for Mexico), "BRICA" (GCC Arab countries – Saudi Arabia, Qatar, Kuwait, Bahrain, Oman and the United Arab Emirates) and "BRICET" (including Eastern Europe and Turkey) have become more generic marketing terms to refer to these emerging markets.

Marketing

The BRIC term is also used by companies who refer to the four named countries as key to their emerging markets strategies. By comparison the reduced acronym IC would not be attractive, although the term "Chindia" is often used. The BRIC's study specifically focuses on large countries, not necessarily the wealthiest or the most productive and was never intended to be an investment thesis. If investors read the Goldman's research carefully, and agreed with the conclusions, then they would gain exposure to Asian debt and equity markets rather than to Latin America. According to estimates provided by the USDA, the wealthiest regions outside of the G6 in 2015 will be Hong Kong, South Korea and Singapore. Combined with China and India, these five economies are likely to be the world's five most influential economies outside of the G6.

On the other hand, when the "R" in BRIC is extended beyond Russia and is used as a loose term to include all of Eastern Europe as well, then the BRIC story becomes more compelling. At issue are the multiple serious problems which confront Russia (potentially unstable government, environmental degradation, critical lack of modern infrastructure, etc.), and the comparatively much lower growth rate seen in Brazil. However, Brazil's lower growth rate obscures the fact that the country is wealthier than China or India on a per-capita basis, has a more developed and global integrated financial system and has an economy potentially more diverse than the other BRICs due to its raw material and manufacturing potential. Many other Eastern European countries, such as Poland, the Czech Republic, Slovakia, Hungary, Romania, Bulgaria, and several others were able to continually sustain high economic growth rates and do not experience some of the problems that Russia experiences or experience them to a lesser extent. In terms of GDP per capita in 2008, Brazil ranked 64th, Russia 42nd, India 113th and China 89th. By comparison South Korea ranked 24th and Singapore 3rd.

Brazil's stock market, the Bovespa, has gone from approximately 9, 000 in September 2002 to over 70, 000 in May 2008. Government policies have favored investment (lowering interest rates), retiring foreign debt and expanding growth, and a reformulation of the tax system is being voted in the congress. The British author and researcher Mark Kobayashi-Hillary is editing a new book titled 'Building a Future with BRICs' for European publisher Springer Verlag that examines the growth of the BRICs region and its effect on global sourcing. Contributors to the book include Nandan Nilekani, and Shiv Nadar, with publication scheduled for October 2007.

Criticism

A criticism is that the BRIC projections are based on the assumptions that resources are limitless and endlessly available when needed. In reality, many important resources currently necessary to sustain economic growth, such as oil, natural gas, coal, other fossil fuels, and uranium might soon experience a peak in production before enough renewable energy can be developed and commercialized, which might result in slower economic growth than anticipated, thus throwing off the projections and their dates. The economic emergence of the BRICs will have unpredictable consequences for the global environment. Indeed, proponents of a set carrying capacity for the Earth may argue that, given current technology, there is a finite limit to how much the BRICs can develop before exceeding the ability of the global economy to supply.

Academics and experts have suggested that China is in a league of its own compared to the other BRIC countries. As David Rothkopf wrote in *Foreign Policy*, "Without China, the BRICs are just the BRI, a bland, soft cheese that is primarily known for the whine that goes with it. China is the muscle of the group and the Chinese know it. They have effective veto power over any BRIC initiatives because without them, who cares really? They are the one with the big reserves. They are the biggest potential market. They are the U. S. partner in the G2 (imagine the coverage a G2 meeting gets vs. a G8 meeting) and the E2 (no climate deal without them) and so on. " Deutsche Bank Research said in a report that "economically, financially and politically, China overshadows and will continue to overshadow the other BRICs. " It added that China's economy is larger than that of the three other BRIC economies (Brazil, Russia and India) combined. Moreover, China's exports and its official for ex-reserve holdings are more than twice as large as those of the other BRICs combined.

Another criticism is the understatement of GDP growth in China over the next 45 years; which predicts growth falling far below normal development. This contradicts the rapid economic growth that has already taken place in the country and the experience of countries like South Korea catching up with western

GDP per capita, which China has been growing faster than in a similar period of development. There are many uncertainties and assumptions in the BRIC thesis that could mean that any or all of these four countries will not live up to their promise. The pre-eminence of China and India as major manufacturing countries with unrealised potential has been widely recognised, but some commentators state that China's and Russia's disregard for human rights and democracy could be a problem in the future. , as is the possibility of conflict over Taiwan in the case of China. Likewise, the population of Russia is steadily aging, and Brazil's and China's populations will begin to decline in several decades, and with their demographic windows closing in several decades as well. This may have implications for those countries' future, for there might be a decrease in the overall labour force and a negative change in the proportion of workers to retirees.

Brazil's economic potential has been anticipated for decades, but it had until recently consistently failed to achieve investor expectations. Only in recent years has the country established a framework of political, economic, and social policies that allowed it to resume consistent growth. The result has been solid and paced economic development that rival its early 70's "miracle years", as reflected in its expanding capital markets, lowest unemployment rates in decades, and consistent international trade surpluses-that led to the accumulation of reserves and liquidation of foreign debt (earning the country a coveted investment grade by the S&P and Fitch Ratings in 2008). How long such positive factors will stay in place remains to be seen.

Finally, India's relations with its neighbour Pakistan have always been tense. In 1998, there was a nuclear standoff between Pakistan and India. Border conflicts with Pakistan, mostly over the long held dispute over Kashmir, has further aggravated any economic ties. The BRIC countries have enormous populations of extremely impoverished people. This impedes progress by limiting government finances, increasing social unrest, and limiting potential domestic economic demand. Factors such as international conflict, civil unrest, unwise political policy, outbreaks of disease and terrorism are all factors that are difficult to predict and that could have an effect on the destiny of any country.

Other critics suggest that BRIC is nothing more than a neat acronym for the four largest emerging market economies, but in economic and political terms nothing else (apart from the fact that they are all big emerging markets) links the four. Two are manufacturing based economies and big importers (China and India), but two are huge exporters of natural resources (Brazil and Russia). *The Economist,* in its special report on Brazil, expressed the following view: "In some ways Brazil is the steadiest of the BRICs. Unlike China and Russia it is a full-blooded democracy; unlike India it has no serious disputes with its neighbors. It is the only BRIC without a nuclear bomb. " The Heritage Foundation's "Economic Freedom Index", which measures factors such as protection of property rights and free trade ranks Brazil ("moderately free") above the other BRICs ("mostly unfree").

It is also noticed that BRIC countries have undermined qualitative factors that is reflected in deterioration in Doing Business ranking 2010 and other several human indexes.

In a not-so-subtle dig critical of the term as nothing more than a shorthand for emerging markets generally, critics have suggested a correlating term, CEMENT (Countries in *E*merging *M*arkets *E*xcluded by *N*ew *T*erminology). Whilst they accept there has been spectacular growth of the BRIC economies, these gains have largely been the result of the strength of emerging markets generally, and that strength comes through having BRICs and CEMENT.

Brimck

Mexico and South Korea are currently the world's 13th and 15th largest by nominal GDP, just behind the BRIC and G7 economies, while both are experiencing rapid GDP growth of 5% every year, a figure comparable to Brazil from the original BRICs. Jim O'Neill, expert from the same bank and creator of the economic thesis, stated that in 2001 when the paper was created, it did not consider Mexico, but today it has been included because the country is experiencing the same factors that the other countries first included present. While South Korea was not originally included in the BRICs, recent solid economic growth led to Goldman Sachs proposing to add Mexico and South Korea to the BRICs, changing the acronym to BRIMCK, with Jim O'Neill pointing out that Korea "is better placed than most others to realize its potential due to its growth-supportive fundamentals.

A Goldman Sachs paper published later in December 2005 explained why Mexico and South Korea weren't included in the original BRICs. According to the paper, among the other countries they looked at, only Mexico and South Korea have the potential to rival the BRICs, but they are economies that they decided to exclude initially because they looked at them as already more developed. However, due to the popularity of the Goldman Sachs thesis, "BRIMC" and "BRICK" are becoming more generic marketing terms to refer to these six countries.

In their paper "BRICs and Beyond", Goldman Sachs stated that "Mexico, the four BRIC countries and South Korea should not be really thought of as emerging markets in the classical sense", adding that they are a "critical part of the modern globalised economy" and "just as central to its functioning as the current G7". The term is primarily used in the economic and financial spheres as well as in academia. Its usage has grown specially in the investment sector, where it is used to refer to the bonds emitted by these emerging markets governments.

Mexico

Primarily, along with the BRICs, Goldman Sachs argues that the economic potential of Brazil, Russia, India, Mexico and China is such that they may become (with the USA) the six most dominant economies by the year 2050. The thesis was proposed by Jim O'Neill, global economist at Goldman Sachs. These countries are forecast to encompass over forty percent of the world's population and hold a combined GDP (PPP) of 14. 951 trillion dollars. On almost every scale, they would be the largest entity on the global stage.

Goldman Sachs did not argue that these five countries are a political alliance (such as the European Union) or any formal trading association, like ASEAN. Nevertheless, they have taken steps to increase their political cooperation, mainly as a way of influencing the United States position on major trade accords, or, through the implicit threat of political cooperation, as a way of extracting political concessions from the United States, such as the proposed nuclear cooperation with India. Due to Mexico's rapidly advancing infrastructure, increasing middle class and rapidly declining poverty rates it is expected to have a higher GDP per capita than all but three European countries by 2050, this new found local wealth also contributes to the nation's economy by creating a large domestic consumer market which in turn creates more jobs.

INDIAN FOREIGN POLICY UNDER NARENDRA MODI

The likely defeat of the Congress Party in India's 16th general election has prompted considerable debate about the impact a change of guard in Delhi will have on foreign policy. What would India's foreign policy look like in the event of the Hindu nationalist Bharatiya Janata Party (BJP) government coming to power, either on its own or with the support of allies?

Many in India and abroad believe that India's foreign policy is poised for a "sea change" under a BJP government, especially one headed by the strident Narendra Modi.

According to Sreeram Chaulia, professor and dean at the Jindal School of International Affairs in Sonipat, India, foreign policy under Modi-led government will see greater emphasis on commercial diplomacy, "more assertive actions in response to [Pakistan backed] cross-border terrorism," greater attention to long-term policy planning with a view to formulating grand strategy for scenarios in 2020 and beyond, "a bigger role for the military in shaping India's national security and formulating doctrines," and a greater say for the states in the government's formulation and execution of foreign policy.

Not much is known of Modi's foreign policy thinking. Even the BJP's election manifesto, which is said to carry his "definite imprint," sheds little light; just a over a page of the 52-page document is devoted to foreign policy.

A controversial and polarizing figure, Modi has often poured scorn on the Congress-led United Progressive Alliance (UPA) government's "soft" response to terrorist attacks emanating from Pakistan and to Chinese incursions into Indian territory. This has contributed to a widely held perception that he will be tough in his response to Pakistan-backed terrorism and would not baulk at the use of force. Modi is also expected to take a tougher stand in dealing with India's territorial disputes with Pakistan and China.

What "tough" might mean in practice is unclear at this point, and how far Modi will go is hotly debated. Some have even argued that he may reserve the right to use tactical nuclear weapons against Pakistan in response to a major terrorist attack. Most, of course, don't go that far.

According to Chaulia, in dealing with terrorism emanating from Pakistan, Modi could go for "clinical counter-strikes" and covert operations, including targeted assassinations of key figures in the Pakistan-based, anti-India terrorist network. But he "will try to avoid war with Pakistan at all costs because of the obvious danger of nuclear exchange," he says.

While agreeing that Modi will appear tough with Pakistan, T P Sreenivasan, a former diplomat who spent 37 years with the Indian Foreign Service, argues that "this toughness will not go beyond a point" as he will realize soon that with "war not an option anymore, a tough approach will go only so far."

In fact, foreign policy under Modi, Sreenivasn says, "will not change in any significant way." It would be "continuity rather than change, because former diplomats would be advising Modi, foreign policy not being his forte." Changes if any will be in nuance and not fundamental in nature.

Indeed, a striking feature of India's foreign policy is its continuity. Certainly there have been shifts, but as Manjari Chatterjee Miller points out in a recent article in *Foreign Affairs*, "the broad shape of Indian foreign policy has remained the same for nearly five decades." Even when shifts do occur, they are not "sudden," "have rarely, if ever, been political," and "have had little to do with the prime minister's political ideology."

It is in emphasis and style rather than substance that the Modi government's foreign policy will differ from that of the UPA. Modi will be less patient with Pakistan and can be expected to base his relations with all of India's neighbors (and not just Pakistan and China) on reciprocity.

But like another BJP prime minister, Atal Bihari Vajpayee (1998-2004), Modi would try to reach a final settlement with Pakistan on Kashmir, Chaulia says.

In fact, Modi is reported to have already reached out to Pakistan by sending his emissaries to confer with its leadership.

Vajpayee was assertive in his conduct of foreign policy. Within three months of coming to power, his government conducted a string of nuclear tests, declared India to be a nuclear weapon state, and abandoned the decades-old policy of nuclear ambiguity. His government's relations with Pakistan were often tense; the two countries fought a near-war at Kargil in 1999 and tensions soared repeatedly over major terrorist attacks in India. Following a terrorist attack on India's parliament in 2001, the Vajpayee government ordered a massive, year-long mobilization of the security forces along the India-Pakistan border to push Pakistan to dismantle the anti-India terrorist network on its soil.

This toughness notwithstanding, Vajpayee also set in motion a peace process with Pakistan, engaged in dialogue with it at the highest level, reached a ceasefire agreement that remains in force and initiated a direct bus service between the two countries.

So will Modi mix toughness with talks in dealing with Pakistan as did Vajpayee?

Modi's critics point out that unlike Vajpayee he is not liberal in his outlook and has not demonstrated the vision that would be required to pursue a lasting peace.

What could force Modi to moderate his positions, however, is the priority he is expected to give economic development at home. That will require regional stability if it is to succeed and could force Modi to tone down his confrontationist approach and reach out to India's neighbors.

Sreenivasan says that Modi's emphasis on economic matters will require him to adopt a "soft policy towards the rich countries." In this, the U.S. will be of "primary interest" to the Modi government, he says. Indeed, shared economic interests will see Modi and the U.S. put aside past differences – since 2005, the U.S. has denied Modi a visa over his complicity in the Gujarat riots of 2002 – and do business with each other.

However, it is with Asian powers such as Japan, China and Singapore that Modi's economic diplomacy will be the most energetic. Having established strong economic ties with these countries as chief minister of Gujarat, he is likely to build on this foundation. In this Japan will hold special appeal to Modi. Not only is it a rich non-Western country in Asia, and thus more acceptable to the BJP's thinking, but Japanese Prime Minister Shinzo Abe's own nationalistic and militaristic policies will strike a chord with Modi.

Modi's efforts to attract foreign investment to Gujarat are revealing of his likely economic diplomacy as prime minister. As chief minister he built a strong relationship with China, visited it at least four times and successfully attracted Chinese investment into Gujarat. Neither his nationalist outlook nor national security concerns stood in the way of his wooing of Beijing. As prime minister, he can be expected to court China for investment, setting aside the "expansionist attitude" with which he has labelled Beijing.

Modi is expected to allow state governments a greater say in the formulation and execution of foreign policy. He has said that states that have special links with other countries, whether due to shared borders, historical links, or cultural commonalities should be consulted in framing policies and crafting strategies with that country. He has spoken of India's 30 states as partners in his government's execution of foreign policy and of wanting to entrust them with "the task of forging beneficial foreign relations with at least 30 corresponding partner countries."

However, it is doubtful that Modi would treat non-BJP state governments, especially those of the Congress, as partners in his foreign policy execution. He may cede to demands from non-BJP regional parties in power in the states that are his allies in government. For instance, should the All-India Anna Dravida Munetra Kazhagam, the party in power in Tamil Nadu, join his government, Modi could be expected to allow its views to prevail in the crafting of India's policy to Sri Lanka. But much will depend on how dependent he is on the AIADMK.

Overall, Modi is likely to be comfortable with federalizing foreign policy only with regard to the states courting foreign investment. On other matters it will be his government that calls the shots.

Of course, all this assumes that Modi will be able to form a government, on its own or with allies. Should that assumption prove false, then India may well end up with a coalition of regional and national parties. Such a coalition is very likely to be unstable, with little in common among its constituents. Preoccupied with survival and pulling in different directions, expect Indian foreign policy to be somewhat chaotic, lacking the robustness or purpose that could be expected of a strong BJP government.

A MODI FOREIGN POLICY: THE KNOWNS AND UNKNOWNS

Change is in the air in Indian politics, with Narendra Modi, prime ministerial candidate of the center-right Bharatiya Janata Party (BJP), headed toward leading India's next government. His administration will replace the longest-serving Indian government since 1977 and will—unusually for India—be led by an individual who has been chief minister of a state for nearly a dozen years. With the BJP having won a majority on its own, it will be able to form the first non-Congress-party non-coalition government in India's history. What change might this bring in Indian foreign policy? First and foremost, it is important to say that there is a lot we don't know. There is a better sense of Modi's priorities and preferences when it comes to economic policy, but not as much known about his foreign policy preferences. This is complicated by the fact that who will form his core national security and foreign policy team—the national security advisor, as well as the political and bureaucratic leaderships in the foreign, defense, home and finance ministries—is not yet known.

The structural and ideological basis of Indian foreign policy and the existence of a permanent bureaucracy mean that there will be continuity in many areas, but there is likely to be change on a few fronts. Modi is likely to double down on the theme of foreign policy as foreign economic policy, with India's economic imperatives driving its international interactions. Diplomats might be expected to serve as force multipliers for Indian economic policy rather than business serving such a function for Indian foreign policy. There is also a possibility of institutional reform of India's foreign, energy and trade policymaking apparatus—something Modi has discussed—though the feasibility of this is unknown. There has been talk of capacity increases, bringing in outside experts to a greater extent, as well as institutional reorganization. In addition, it'll be interesting to see whether and how Modi brings in the states and the diaspora into his foreign policy approach – also something he has talked about on a number of occasions. Furthermore, there might be specific changes in India's relationships with particular partners, for example, a new Indian government might bring relations with Israel more out into the open.

Pakistan: The Wild Card

What about interactions with other key countries? The relationship with Pakistan is perhaps the biggest wild card. It is not known whether Modi will essentially take the line that India needs stability in its neighborhood to ensure economic growth and development, which is the primary and perhaps sole objective for which he will have a clear public mandate. Such an assessment could mean Modi would reach out to Pakistani Prime Minister Nawaz Sharif and take confidence-building measures further, especially in the economic realm. There are some who think he'll go further—in the Nixon-going-to-China vein. They point to the precedent of the last BJP Prime Minister Atal Bihari Vajpayee reaching out to the Pakistani leadership. However, it is important to keep in mind that that initiative materialized only after the Indian nuclear tests had proved that BJP-led coalition government's security credentials. Furthermore, the fact that the Kargil conflict between the two countries erupted just a few months after Vajpayee traveled to Lahore has not been forgotten.

There's a possibility that Modi will take a more hawkish line instead. This is especially likely if, in the first six months or so of his government, there is a major terrorist attack in India or on Indians abroad that can be traced to elements in Pakistan. This is not a far-fetched scenario—terrorist groups might see the period of political transition as an opportunity to derail any chance for peace. And in the event of such an attack it is unlikely that any Indian government will sit back and do nothing or essentially act in a post-Mumbai-like manner—especially if there is little cooperation from the Pakistani government.

China: Economic Opportunity and Security Concern

On India's other major neighbor—China—there are two Modis. One, the economic-minded leader who wants to do business with and in that country. This is the Modi who had traveled to China as Gujarat's chief minister, seeking investment and opportunities for Gujarati business there. We'll probably see more of this Modi at the upcoming BRICS summit in Brazil—likely to be one of his first overseas visits—where he will meet Chinese president Xi Jinping. The other Modi is the security-minded leader who has run on a tougher-on-national-security platform and publicly criticized China as having an "expansionist mindset"—making it a point to do so in territory that China claims. Absent a border crisis, the new Indian government is likely to try to reconcile these two instincts, balancing economic engagement with preparation for a more assertive China.

In the last few weeks, Chinese officials and scholars have, publicly at least, welcomed the prospect of a Modi government. Yet they might come to look with concern at a couple of other potential elements of a Modi foreign and security policy. First, the continued modernization of the Indian military and the upgrading of India's border infrastructure. Second, the deepening of India's political and economic ties with countries in East and Southeast Asia, especially Japan, Singapore, South Korea and Vietnam. A third element—a potential rise in nationalism in India—might also become a subject of concern, with implications not just for India's relations with China, but also its approach toward Pakistan, multilateral issues and the United States.

The U.S.: Will Modi Look Back or Move Forward?

There are two schools of thought on how a Modi government might deal with the United States. Some analysts argue that his (and his advisors') resentment of the American attitude toward him over the last decade will dominate this dynamic; that he will pay back the lack of official engagement with him since 2005 with an approach that will hold the U.S. at arms length. Others believe that given Modi's priorities (economic growth, meeting energy needs, balancing against China) and the depth of the India-U.S. relationship, the U.S. will continue to be an essential partner for India under a Modi government even though it might not be warm. Which trajectory the bilateral relationship takes will partly depend on what the U.S.—both the administration and Congress—does on India policy over the next few months, both in terms of style and substance.

Modi has recently commented on each of these three relationships. On Pakistan, he's put the ball in Islamabad's court, stressing it needs to take action on the counter-terrorism front to build trust with India. However, he's also identified a shared goal—fighting poverty and unemployment. On China, he has stated that it is possible for the two countries to resolve their differences and take the Sino-Indian relationship "to another level." On the U.S., Modi has asserted that he will take the relationship—one that involves "natural allies" and mutual interest—forward.

We will have to wait and see whether Modi's foreign policy actions matches his recent rhetoric; whether "good days lie ahead"—Modi's "morning-in-America"-like promise to India—for India's relations with certain countries or not. How a Modi government's foreign policy will play out will also depend on how other countries approach India. Furthermore, it will depend on what kind of crises the government will face and how it will react. Finally, much—including Modi's foreign policymaking space—will depend on domestic factors, including economic growth, social stability and the state of play in Indian politics.

ASIAN FOREIGN POLICY OF NARENDRA MODI GOVERNMENT

The most significant initiative made by the Narendra Modi government is the focus on neighbouring countries and major Asian powers coupled with emphasizing on the two decades old Look East Policy. Asia being the major focus area of his foreign policy, Modi and his foreign minister chose several Asian countries for their initial bilateral visits. He has made state visits to Bhutan and Nepal and Japan within the first 100 days of his government and also hosted Asia leaders like Chinese President Xi Jinping and Australian Prime Minister Tony Abbott apart form inviting SAARC leaders in his inauguration ceremony. External Affairs Minister Swaraj has also made official visits to Dhaka, Bangladesh,Kathmandu, Nepal, Naypidaw, Myanmar, Singapore, Hanoi, Vietnam, Manama, Bahrain, Kabul, Afghanistan, and Dushanbe, Tajikistan.

Asian Century

Time and again Modi emphasized his believe on 21st century being the Asian century and also asked whether it would be the Indian Century. China, Japan and India being the first, second and third largest Asian economy respectively are among the most likely candidate to lead the strategically important Asia in the later part of this century. But China's increasingly assertive postures in the region recent years have raised concerns in the respective quarters. It seems Modi's foreign policy is focused on improving bilateral relations to higher levels with strategically located Asian countries like Japan, Vietnam, Australia without forging any formal security alliance in the Indo-Pacific region to avoid direct confrontation with China. India, due to its good relation with both Russia and United States, is often considered to be the swing state in the race for strategic dominance in Asia between the democratic alliance of Japan and US and China-Russia club on the other hand.

Relations within the Indian subcontinent

Even before becoming the Prime Minister Narendra Modi hinted that his foreign policy will actively focus on improving ties with India's immediate neighbours which is being termed as neighbourhood first policy in the media and he started well by inviting all heads of state/heads of government of South Asian countries in his inauguration and on the second day on office he held bilateral talks with all of them individually which was dubbed as a mini SAARC summit by the media. Later during a launch event at ISRO he has asked Indian scientists to take the endeavour to develop a dedicated SAARC satellite to share the fruits of the technology like tele-medicine, e-learning etc. with the people across South Asia to complement the currently operating Indian Technical and Economic Cooperation Programme program in the region.

Bhutan

Narendra Modi made his first foreign visit to Bhutan following an invitation by King Jigme Khesar Namgyel Wangchuck and Tobgay. The visit was called by the media as a "charm offensive" that would also seek to check Bhutan-China relations that had recently been formalised. He also sought to build business ties, including a hydro-electric deal, and inaugurated the India-funded Supreme Court of Bhutan building. While talking about the visit, Modi said that Bhutan was a "natural choice" for his first foreign destination because of the "unique and special relationship" the two countries shared. He added that he was looking forward to nurture and further strengthen India's special relations with Bhutan. His entourage included Foreign Minister Sushma Swaraj, National Security Adviser Ajit Doval and Foreign Secretary Sujatha Singh. He was further set to discuss the insurgency in Northeast India, and China.

Nepal

Modi arrived for a two-day visit to Nepal on 3 August. The last visit of an Indian prime minister to Nepal was 17 years ago in 1997 by I. K. Gujral. The talks with Nepal were focused on reviewing the 1950's Treaty of Peace and Friendship, India-funded 'hydroelectricity projects' in Nepal and other infrastructure projects in Nepal, although the much anticipated Indo-Nepal power trade agreement (PTA) could not get signed due to technical problem in the draft agreement. Following Jana Andolan, that marked the beginning of constitutional democracy in 1990, Modi became the first foreign leader to address the Parliament of Nepal. The Western media read it as a shift in foreign affairs for India, as well as a Nepal policy shift. He did *puja* at the fifth century Hindu Pashupatinath temple (where he donated Rs. 25 crores and the head priest, Mool Bhatta Ganesh Bhatta, said: "I told him that we see him as a mascot for Hinduism, and appreciate his efforts in saving Hindu culture"). Further he pledged not to interfere in Nepal's internal affairs (following controversy of appointment of Indian priests at a Nepali temple), Modi announced a credit assistance programme of US$1 billion to Nepal and said "Nepal can free India of its darkness with its electricity. But [*sic*] we don't want free electricity, we want to buy it. Just by selling electricity to India, Nepal can find a place in the developed countries of the world." He also told Nepali MPs he wanted to turn India's "hostile borders benign and ultimately gateways for free trade and commerce...borders must be bridges not barriers." The *Kathmandu Post*reacted in writing: "Modi mantra warms Nepal's hearts." The *New York Times* also suggested the lack of a meeting with former King Gyanendra signified that India would not support a return to monarchy despite the lack of a new constitution of Nepal. The commonality of a majority Hindu heritage was also played up.

Prior to Modi's visit, Swaraj made a three day visit to Nepal from 27 July 2014 and co-chaired the Indo-Nepal Joint Commission meeting and also prepared the ground for Modi's scheduled visit. The last visit by a foreign minister of India to Nepal was made 23 years before this.

Bangladesh

There was scepticism during election campaign about Bangladeshi illegal immigrants in India which raised concern in Bangladesh but it was Prime Minister Sheikh Hasina who made a remark: "I am delighted to see a great friend of Bangladesh leading an extremely friendly country, India, in the coming days." following Modi's victory in the general election. And the new Indian govt too were quick to realize the immense geo-strategic importance of Bangladesh in India's security paradigm and therefore Foreign Minister Sushma Swarajchose Dhaka for her first stand-alone foreign visit on 26–27 June 2014, where she met her counterpart Abul Hassan Mahmood and also called on Sheikh Hasina. Discussions were held regarding the land boundary agreement (LBA), the proposed Teesta water sharing pact, cooperation in eliminating extremist groups from North-East taking refuge in Bangladesh and illegal immigration. And taking a lesson from the previous UPA govt experience Swaraj had discussed contentious issues of Bengal with Chief Minister Mamata Banerjee before leaving for Dhaka, indicating a federal style of foreign policy.

Afghanistan

The first challenge before the new govt had come from Herat, Afghanistan where the Indian consulate was attacked by the ISI backed terrorist organisation days before Modi's inauguration. Visiting the war-torn country on 10 September Swaraj called "India Afghanistan's first strategic partner". and has committed to play a greater role in capacity building by strengthening the Afghan National Army but sighed away from possibility of sending troops or direct export of military hardware from India instead according to an arrangement made earlier India would pay for purchase of arms and ammunitions from Russia.

Potential re-emergence of the Taliban and al-Qaeda in the subcontinent following NATO withdrawal from the country by end of 2014 and the deadlock over the US-Afghan bilateral security agreement (BSA) have raised concerns among Indian security establishments.

India is also in the process of reviving an old agreement for modernising the Chabahar Port in Iran. This is to provide an alternative sea access to Afghanistan which will help further the Indian investment in the country and bilateral trade which is so far restricted by Pakistan's hostile transit policy through Karachi Port.

Sri Lanka

Despite India being Sri Lanka's only neighbour the India-Sri Lanka relations faced stagnation in recent decades due to several reasons including the large scale civilian casualties in civil war in the Tamil dominated north of the island country and a growing Chinese influence in Sri Lanka. In fact there were hardly any high level visits between the two therefore inviting President Mahinda Rajapaksato the inauguration in Delhi, overcoming domestic pressures from Tamil Nadu based political parties, helped set the ball rolling. At the same time the Sri Lankan President announced the release of Indian fishermen jailed in Sri Lanka in a goodwill gesture. But when the two leaders met in Delhi Modi had reportedly asked for Rajapaksa's commitment for fast implementation of thirteenth amendment to the constitution giving more self-rule to the Sri Lankan Tamil people in Jafna.

However the Indian govt is in favor of a good relationship as part of a greater 'neighbourhood first' policy and now Modi is scheduled to visit Colombo in January 2015 and will be the first Indian prime minister to address the Sri Lankan Parliament in 35 years.

Pakistan

Modi has long been considered as a hardliner nationalist against enemy forces across the border sponsoring terrorist attacks in India while he was Chief Minister of Gujarat, a state bordering Pakistan, but post-election things have changed substantially when he decided to invite Nawaz Sharif in the swearing-in ceremony.

Foreign Secretary level talk scheduled on 25 August in Islamabad was called off last minute by India following a meeting with secessionist leaders from Jammu & Kashmir at the Pakistani high commission in Delhi. Later External Affairs Minister Swaraj averted the question of whether Prime Minister will meet Nawaz Sharif in New York on the sidelines of UNGA by saying that "there is no full stop in diplomacy".

Relations with East and Southeast Asia

From the very beginning the Modi led govt made it ample clear that India would focus more and more on improving relation with ASEAN and other East Asian countries as per India's Look East Policy which was formulated during Narasimha Rao's govt in 1992 for better economic engagement with its eastern neighbours but successive govt later successfully turned it into a tool for forging strategic partnership and security cooperation with countries in that region in general and Vietnam and Japan in particular. In her recent visit to Hanoi, Vietnam Sushma Swaraj has stressed on the need for an Act East Policy that she said should replace India's over two decade-old Look East Policyemphasizing a more proactive role for India in this region.

Japan

Japan occupies a very important place in Modi's Asian strategy, as India is looking toward Japan, at a time when it is becoming 'normal state' amending decades old pacifist constitution, to forge a security alliance to balance an increasingly assertive China in the Indo-Pacific region. Maritime cooperation is most likely and bilateral naval exercises are on the cards. Significantly in 2014 Japan participated in the Malabar, a primarily bilateral naval exercise between India and US, held in Sea of Japan. Negotiations progressed recently for selling of US 2 amphibious aircraft to Indian Navy and the long pending civil nuclear agreements which would eventually help strengthen the strategic partnership.

Modi visited Japan on a five day official trip from 30 August to 3 September which was labelled as his fist bilateral state visit outside thesubcontinent also by the media. His 2014 visit further strengthened the ties between the two countries and resulted in several key agreements, including the elevating the already established strategic partnership to the "Special Strategic Global Partnership". Business ties are stronger than ever with a commitment of US$33.5 billion Japanese investment in India in the next five year. India is in the process of importing Shinkansen technology form Japan as part of Modi's Diamond Quadrilateral project for introducing high-speed rail in India.

His visit to Kyoto supervised the signing of a cooperation agreement between Varanasi and Kyoto both regarded as heritage city and cultural centre in their respective country.

China

Prior to election Modi had expressed reservation over alleged Chinese 'expansionism' into India's frontiers as India and China locked into bitter territorial disputes over last fifty years. During his Japan trip, Modi has said eighteenth century mind-set of vistaar-vad or expansionism won't work and vikaash-vad or peaceful development is needed for sustainable peace and tranquillity in the world which was read by a portion of media as a subtle jibe on China. But he is also in favour of enhanced economic partnership with China.

Economic activity defines relation with China as it is India's biggest trading partner in goods. Soon after taking office commerce MinisterNirmala Sitharaman has already made two visits to China. The two countries have forged a mechanism called 'strategic and economic dialogue' (SED) to discuss the trade and other economic issues. Modi has publicly expressed his willingness to enhance trade and economic cooperation with China. Describing the newly found activism in bilateral relation Modi said India China relation moving "INCH (India-China) towards MILES(Millennium of Enhanced Synergy) ".

India sent National Security Adviser Ajit Doval as a special envoy of Prime Minister Modi to Beijing to negotiate the agenda and the schedule of the presidential visit to India which is appreciated by the top Chinese leadership who are known to be fond of diplomatic decorum. President Xi Jinping, only third Chinese President to visit India, arrived in Ahmedabad, Modi's hometown, on 17 September which coincides with Modi's birthday. China is expected to commit investment over US$100 billion in India's infrastructure projects including in high speed trains and dedicated Chinese industrial parks to balance the huge trade deficit exists in China's favour. The two leaders had earlier met in Brazil this year on the sidelines of BRICS summit.

Vietnam

Vietnam, strategically located in the South China Sea, plays an pivotal role in India's Southeast Asian policy and it is often referred as the important pillars of its 'Look East Policy' by the Indian diplomats. . Defence and security cooperation in recent years define the strategic partnership along with fast growing bilateral trade which stands at US$8 billion in FY 2013.

Visiting Indian President Pranab Mukherjee called Vietnam, "a trusted friend and an important pillar of India's Look East Policy" which emphasized the depth of their strategic partnership. The leaders reiterated their desire and determination to work together to maintain peace, stability, growth and prosperity in Asia. And the two side vouched for 'freedom of navigation' in the South China Sea, which China claims as its exclusive economic zone, and called the parties concerned to exercise restraint, avoid threat or use of force and resolve disputes through peaceful means in accordance with universally recognised principles of international law, including the United Nations Convention on the Law of the Sea-1982. .

India-Vietnamese defence cooperation has multiplied in recent years with emphasize on maritime security which includes training of Vietnamese naval personnel with Indian naval ships making frequent port-call in Vietnam in past few years. Recently it extended a US$100 m Line of Credit for purchase of Fast attack craft for Vietnamese navy from India. Vietnam is also interested in acquiring Brahmos supersonic missiles, a Indo-Russian joint venture project, Vietnam has friendly relation with both Russia and India a precondition for exporting the missile system and talks regarding the deal is believed to be in the advanced level.

Agreements signed in oil exploration cooperation between India and Vietnam as it earlier offered India to explore strategically located oil blocks in South China Sea, which is disputed by Chinese claims. On the following day Chinese Foreign Ministry through an official media statement expressed its objection to India's activity in what it refers its exclusive economic zone. External Affairs Minister earlier during her Hanoi trip said the state-owned ONGC Videsh will exploit the opportunity provided in Vietnam, a development China sees as an aggression into its backyard. Economic ties are fast growing with US$8 billion bilateral trade and the two sides emphasized the need of increasing people to people contact which is set to get a boost with upcoming launch of direct flight between Delhi and Ho Chi Minh City and using Bollywood to promote Vietnam to Indian audience.

Singapore

Singapore is amongst the top source countries of foreign direct investment (FDI) coming to India. Economic cooperation dominates the India Singapore relations given Singapore's strategic importance in India's 'Look East' policy. External Affairs Minister Swaraj visited Singapore on 16 August where she held talks with her counterpart Shanmugam and Prime Minister Lee Hsien Loong regarding Singapore's investment in India and their potential role in Modi's pet smart city project.

Earlier Modi played host to Singaporean Minister for Foreign and Law K. Shanmugam where he recalled his policies as Gujarat chief minister to expand cooperation between the two countries in, amongst others, public housing for the middle and lower classes based on Singapore's expertise.

Former Singaporean Prime Minister Goh Chok Tong visited India on 10 September and held several high level meetings with Prime Minister and other Ministers, later in conversation with a selected members from the media he referred former Indian Prime Minister Vajpeyee as Scholar but Modi is "Man of Action", while reassuring once again his countries full cooperation smart city project.

Australia

Australian Prime Minister Tony Abbott was the first head of government to make a state visit to India in Modi government which shows the importance both side attaches to their relations. The most significant event of his tour was the signing of a civil nuclear energy cooperation agreement for supplying uranium (Australia is believed to have one third of world's total uranium reserve) to India. The nuclear deal is a further step toward India achieving international acceptability for its nuclear programme despite not ratifying the nuclear non-proliferation treaty, and follows similar agreements with the United States and France. The two side also agreed to enhance Maritime security cooperation in the Indo-pacific region and future joint naval exercise in the Indian ocean. During the joint statement following the summit Australian PM Abbott referred India as a model citizen in terms of following International guidelines justifying the nuclear deal beyond the scope of NPT and called *India the emerging democratic superpower*".

Taiwan

As Modi has identified economic cooperation as a major thrust area in his foreign policy and coined slogans like Make in India to invite foreign direct investment (FDI) in manufacturing sector, Taiwan was one of the first to respond to his call. India Electronics and Semiconductor Association (IESA) and Taipei Computer

Association signed memorandum of understanding for local manufacturing of semiconductors and electronics, even there are plans to set up 'Taiwanese hardware park' in about 200-300 acres of land.

Although India was among the first few countries to recognize PRC therefore jeopardizing relation with the island but later developed an official relation with ROCwhich it maintains through "India-Taiwan Association" a De facto embassy in Taipei.

Relations with West Asia (Middle East)

Indian External Affairs Ministry refers the region as West Asia and not as Middle East which is a more popular attribution, particularly in the western countries.

The region plays a vital role in India's economy as it supplies nearly two third of India's total oil import, bilateral trade is also flourishing in recent years particularly with UAE and other gulf states. Over the years millions of Indian mostly working class have migrated to the gulf looking for jobs and they account for a sizeable share in the total remittances received from abroad.

Bahrain

Swaraj choose Manama, Bahrain for her first visit to the gulf. The visit marked the first high level exchange from Modi govt to any Arab states following apprehension of less priority given to the Indo-Arab relation under Modi administration. The island country with a significant population of Indian origin people has extensive trade and business ties with India. There addressing at a business meet the minister reiterated "Our government is firmly committed to bring back growth, have clear policies which will facilitate business environment, transparency and speed, well thought out decisions".

Israel

Israel is one of India's most important strategic partner and major source of its military hardware. Relation is expected to flourish with Modi govt as the ruling BJP is known for its pro-Israeli stands and in favour of strengthening ties with Israel. Sushma Swaraj, who was chairperson of the 'India-Israel parliamentary friendship group', visited Israel earlier and publicly expressed her admiration for former Israeli Prime Minister Golda Meir.

2014 Israel-Hamas Conflict

At the height of the tension between Israel and Hamas in July India in offered a rhetorical condemnation holding both sides responsible for erupting violence and asked Israel to stop "disproportionate use of force" in Gaza which was read by many as departure from tradition of more vocal supports for the Palestinian cause.

External Affairs Minister Swaraj insisted that "there is absolutely no change in India's policy towards Palestine, which is that we fully support the Palestinian cause while maintaining good relations with Israel. " clarifying India's current position on the issue. That might sound like fence-sitting, but it's a policy shared by all Indian governments of the past 20 years following the establishment of formal diplomatic relation in 1992.

Sushma Swaraj, a seasoned parliamentarian, had herself blocked the opposition demand in Rajya Sabha for passing a resolution condemning Israel for 2014 Israel-Gaza conflict by saying that "India has friendly relation with both Israel and Palestine and therefore any such move may impact its friendship negatively".

Although later in a symbolic gesture India joined others BRICS nations in voting at the United Nations Human Rights Council for a probe into the alleged human rights violation in Gaza. Which generated mixed response among media and analysts in India.

INDIA & US: SHAPING THE 21ST CENTURY

Fast-track diplomacy and smart development-centric diplomacy are the twin mantra of the new government in Delhi. Starting from hosting the leaders of South Asian neighbours to engaging key Asian partners, China and Japan, India's Prime Minister Narendra Modi is now headed for the US on a defining trip that is set to infuse "the defining partnership of the 21st century" with a new burst of energy and vitality. Spectacle, colour, high diplomacy, culture, commerce and creativity – all these varied elements are going to be fused into Prime Minister Modi's maiden voyage to America (Sept 26-30), which is poised to be a blockbuster diplomatic event.

New Horizons

There are several firsts to this prime ministerial trip: This will be not only the first visit of Narendra Modi as the Prime minister of India, but it will also be his first meeting with US President Barack Obama. Mr Modi will also become the first foreign leader to be given the largest-ever community reception in the heart of New York City - around 20,000-odd Indian-Americans will be listening in to the Indian leader at the Madison Square Garden, the iconic venue better known for celebrity rock stars and singers performing on its grand stage. This will also be the first time when an Indian leader's speech will be beamed live on giant screens at Time Square, the pulsating heart of Manhattan which is frequented by thousands of people every day. This is also the first time the US Senate has designated September 30 as the day of India-US Partnership, which has coincided with the day Prime Minister Modi will meet President Obama in Washington for full-spectrum talks.

In the run-up to the prime ministerial visits, senior figures of the US administration have visited India in the first 100 days of the Modi government, including US Secretary of State John Kerry, Defence Secretary Chuck Hagel, Commerce Secretary Penny Pritzker and Deputy Secretary of State William Burns. They held wide-ranging talks in New Delhi, which have firmed up an ambitious agenda for making the summit meeting between the leaders of the world's oldest and most populous democracies substantive and successful.

Raising the Bar

Many issues will be competing for the leaders' mind space, but one can safely say that their overarching focus will be to impart a renewed momentum to the India-US relationship, which was transformed after the path-breaking civil nuclear deal of 2008, converting the hitherto estranged democracies into engaged democracies. While the nuclear deal, also called the 123 agreement, remains a work in progress, proponents of stronger India-US relations say it's time for 456, indicating a common desire to raise the bar for the relationship which is seen as central to ongoing effort to shape an inclusive and pluralistic 21st century world order.

Business Diplomacy

With a business-friendly Prime minister in charge of Asia's third largest economy, the focus will be on business and widening the arc of co-prosperity to create new win-win opportunities for both sides. This will be reflected in Prime Minister Modi's interaction with top American CEOs, separately in New York and Washington. In these meetings, the Indian leader, armed with the largest parliamentary majority in the last three decades, is expected to make a robust pitch for attracting American investments and seek the participation of US capital and expertise to actualise his vision of making India a manufacturing powerhouse and building 100 smart cities. Sending positive signals to the global investor community, the FDI cap in the insurance sector has already been raised to 49 per cent. The defence sector has also been opened up to foreign investment. In return, India is expecting the US establishment to show some flexibility to accommodate India's interests and concerns vis-à-vis the IPR regime's application to life-saving generic drugs and visa fee for Indian IT professionals.

In the economic arena, the sky is virtually the limit, with the new government walking the talk on economic reforms. The US is India's largest trading partner. The two sides are now looking to multiply bilateral trade five-fold to $500 billion. The trade balance is in India's favour. The US is already the fifth largest source of foreign direct investments into India, with cumulative FDI inflows from the US from April 2000 to March 2014 amounting to about $ 11.92 billion. Indian companies have invested over US $ 17 billion in the US in the last few years.

Upswing in defence ties

The defence ties are on an upswing. In September 2013, the two sides signed a Joint Declaration on Defence Cooperation, which envisages qualitatively upgrading the defence relationship by simplifying technology transfer policies and exploring possibilities of co-development and co-production of defence systems. The two sides are expected to renew their defence framework agreement during the forthcoming visit.

Counter-terror cooperation

Against the backdrop of the unfolding transition in Afghanistan and the proliferation of terrorist threats in Iraq and the Middle East, counter-terror and security cooperation are expected to get a boost in the forthcoming talks. This will be reflected in the symbolic visit of Mr Modi to Ground Zero, the site of the World Trade Centre in New York which was targeted by barbaric terror strikes on September 11, 2001 and the newly-inaugurated 9/11 Museum and Memorial.

Global Partnership

With 36 bilateral dialogue mechanisms straddling diverse areas and a growing convergence of interests across the arc of the globe spanning from Africa to Afghanistan, this is the turning point for the multi-faceted India-US relations.

With an arc of instability widening around the world, one can expect some focussed discussions on a wide array of regional and global hotspots, including Afghanistan, Syria, Iraq and the volatile situation in the Middle East. This burgeoning cooperation on region global issues makes the India-US partnership truly global and strategic. In an interview to Fareed Zakaria of CNN, Mr Modi has underlined the global compass of the India-US cooperation.

"Relations between India and America should not be seen within the limits of just Delhi and Washington. It's a much larger sphere. The good thing is that the mood of both Delhi and Washington is in harmony with this understanding. Both sides have played a role in this." Underlining that India and the US are bound together, by history and culture, the Prime minister voiced confidence that "these ties will deepen further."

Mapping the way ahead

There is, therefore, strong political will on both sides to make this critically important relationship work, and acquire new energy and vibrancy in days to come. In countless ways, the narratives of the India Story and the American Dream are getting fused. Over 100,000 Indian students studying in various American universities and the 3-million strong Indian diaspora in the US exemplify the intertwining of the Indian and American dreams. Above all, where the India-US relations score is in the unparalleled scale of people-to-people contacts, with burgeoning linkages in the fields of education, research and innovation. And it is in these areas the action lies in the future.

Tradition, Talent, Tourism, Trade and Technology - these 5 Ts which Prime Minister Modi has spelt out as part of his long-term vision of revitalising Brand India and the India Story can get a boost from closer partnership with the US. The US, too, is looking at India as a burgeoning market, a hub of innovation and a rising Asian power. The situation is ripe for dreaming big, and making the defining partnership of the 21st century deliver new possibilities for 1.5 billion people of India and the United States of America.

THE LONG VIEW: ABCD OF INDIA-CHINA RELATIONS

A for Asia. B for Business. C for Culture. And D for Diplomacy and Development. This is the emerging alphabet of multi-faceted engagement between the two Asian powers which are forging a new vocabulary and semantics to script new pathways of cooperation and to reconfigure the evolving world order. The ABCD of India-China relations will find fuller articulation in the September 17-19 visit of Chinese President Xi Jinping to India, a potentially defining trip which could transform ties between the two Asian neighbours and create new opportunities for their 2.5 billion people, one third of the world's humanity.

Why Modi-Xi summit matters

When the leaders of India and China hold talks, the world will be watching closely, and not without reason. They are, after all, Asia's leading economies with a combined GDP of over $11 trillion and proactive stakeholders in crafting an inclusive international world order. This time round, there is a new configuration, which promises to invest the maiden full-spectrum summit between

India's Prime Minister Narendra Modi and China's Xi Jinping with an added resonance: on both sides, there are strong-willed leaders who are armed with an unambiguous mandate to take decisive initiatives and are crafting a new chapter in national resurgence of their respective countries.

Xi Jinping is widely seen as China's most powerful leader since Mao Zedong as he holds the triumvirate of positions within the Chinese establishment that confers him near absolute power: he is the General Secretary of the Communist Party of China, the president of the state and chairman of the Central Military Commission. Narendra Modi, on the other hand, is the first India head of government to command a clear parliamentary majority in the last quarter of a century, liberating him from the fret and fever of coalition politics.

Translated into simple terms, it means both leaders have the power to walk the talk. Prime Minister Modi's connection to China dates back to his days as Gujarat chief minister during which he travelled to China four times and managed to net investments running into millions of dollars into his state. The two leaders struck good equations when they first met on the sidelines of the BRICS summit in Fortaleza in July this year. And they are known to admire and hold each other in high regard. This personal chemistry, backed by a synergy of interests, gives both leaders space to build a lasting relationship between the two emerging Asian powers.

Pragmatism: Business & Development

Coming back to the ABCD, Business and Development will be the key highlights of the Modi-Xi summit meeting. The talks between the leaders of the world's two most populous countries will renew the focus on sustaining a new pragmatic model of relationship, which means not letting complex and difficult issues like the decades-old boundary dispute coming in the way of developing and expanding relationship in other areas, be it economic, military and cultural. This imaginative and flexible approach has yielded rich dividends: bilateral trade between India and China has exceeded $65 billion and the two countries are not leaving any stone unturned to scale it up to $100 billion in the not-too-distant future. The burgeoning economic relationship, however, has its flip side: a ballooning trade imbalance of over $30 billion. To bridge this trade imbalance, India is looking to get China to grant market access to Indian IT and pharma companies.

With India's infrastructure sector hungry for investment and expertise, China has an unprecedented opportunity to partner India in its developmental journey. China is looking to set up dedicated industrial parks in India catering to Chinese companies, help modernise Indian Railways and scale up investments in Asia's third largest economy.

Taking off from their strategic economic dialogue, the two countries are now aiming at structural transformation in their economic ties, from the buyer-seller model to a more enduring investment-driven model. Investments are currently abysmally low: China, which boasts of over $3 trillion in foreign exchange reserves, has invested less than a billion dollars into the emerging market of India. Against this backdrop, one can expect the unveiling of mega investment plans by the Chinese president, and at least two Chinese industrial parks in Gujarat and Maharashtra. China, which is known as the factory of the world, is expected to lend its expertise in assisting the transformation of India, the office of the world, into a manufacturing powerhouse, a key priority of the new government in New Delhi.

Building Trust

While big-ticket economic pacts look set to steal the limelight, the two leaders will also be looking to deepen strategic trust and widen the arc of understanding on issues that are central to their core interests. Maintaining peace and tranquillity on the un-demarcated boundary will be on top of the agenda. In the previous summit meetings, India had underlined that maintaining peace on the border is a prerequisite to building better relation and actualising the full potential of the India-China relations, which remain underleveraged largely due to a lingering trust deficit stemming from the unresolved boundary dispute. In October 2013, during the visit of India's then prime minister Manmohan Singh to Beijing, the two countries signed a landmark Border Defence Cooperation Agreement, and one can expect buttressing of this framework and additional confidence building measures to ensure friction-free frontiers. Taking a long-range view, the two leaders have an unrivalled opportunity to give a decisive push to boundary negotiations which remain stuck in Phase II, the most crucial and difficult part of the labyrinthine negotiations which will form the basis for the actual delineation of the boundary.

Building Trust: Hand-in-Hand

Looking ahead, pragmatism is the operative mantra in the evolving India-China relations, and looks set to stay that way. In the military sphere, the two Asian powers are now looking to build greater trust and intensify interaction between the top military brass. India and China have held three rounds of counter-terror exercise entitled Hand-in-Hand. The defence ministers of the two countries have developed a mechanism of annual dialogue and Indian ships make goodwill visits to Chinese ports.

Refreshingly, India and China have fashioned pragmatic cooperation in the international arena by closely cooperating on a range of cross-cutting issues like climate change and multilateral trade negotiations. They are influential members of leading multilateral bodies like the BRICS, the ASEAN Regional Forum, the East Asia Summit and G20 club of emerging economies.

A for Asian Century

Clearly, the simultaneous rise of India and China unfolding on the global stage hold the key to an emerging Asian century. With so much at stake in building a harmonious partnership, India and China are now banking on culture and creativity to act as connectors between people of the two countries. Travel, tourism and people-to-people contacts are poised for an upswing in 2014, which both countries have designated as the Year of India-China Friendship. Buddhism provides civilizational connect and Bollywood bonding is becoming stronger - a festival of Bollywood films was launched in China recently to much acclaim. The two countries are now looking to sign a pact on the joint production of films, which promises to build a new popular bridge between them and give Indian filmmakers access to the second largest market in the world after the US.

Skill, Speed and Scale

There will always be sceptics, but a journey of thousand miles begin with a small step, as a Chinese proverb says. Looking ahead, the two Asian giants look set to forge a more constructive and multi-pronged partnership and have accepted a pragmatic model of cooperation in which elements of competition and cooperation will co-exists, hopefully in a creative fusion. The new template of cooperative partnership will be underpinned by ABCD as well as the three S which Prime Minister Modi has spoken of. India needs Skill, Speed and Scale to compete with China, Modi has famously said. This receptivity to learn from each other's developmental experiences is reflected in a growing realisation in both New Delhi and Beijing that cooperation, rather than conflict, will bring more benefits and spur the rise of both India and China and help shape a balanced Asian century. Rhetorical quibbles apart, the Indian and Chinese dreams of national development and resurgence are entwined at deeper levels. It's time for the leaders of India and China to walk the talk of an Asian century and make the dreams of their two and a half billion people real.

INDIAN PM MODI AND CHINA'S XI JINPING: BUILDING A CLOSER DEVELOPMENTAL ORGANIZATION

President Xi Jinping's visit to India from September 17-19 provided a chance for both the leaderships to know each other's concerns and aspirations better and made incremental progress in the bilateral relations, specifically in the economic field while opening up several areas in the social sector.

The joint statement issued at the end of Xi's visit was termed as "building a closer developmental partnership", unlike the previous such statements as "vision" document (as in October 2013) or a "shared vision" (in 2008) or "principles for relations" (in 2003). The 2005 formulation on "strategic and cooperative partnership" has now been extended in today's statement to include "strategic and cooperative partnership for peace and prosperity". Semantics apart, this reflects the desire of the two leaderships to work in an atmosphere of peace and stability for achieving economic developmental goals each had visualized for their respective countries.

However, there are no radical departures in the current joint statement from the previous understandings between the two. Panchsheel principles were re-iterated twice. One China policy entered the joint statement through back door with the observation that both sides will "abide by the principles and consensus both had agreed to" in the previous engagements.

Major Achievements

There are some significant achievements during this round of discussions and the joint statement enlists these. In the economic field, two industrial parks will be set up with an investment from China to the tune of $20 billion in the next five years. After four years of high level interactions in which the un-sustainability of trade imbalance had been outlined by the Indian side, China finally relented with this measure, although scaled down the amount from the initial $100 billion estimate. India's cumulative trade deficit from 2007 to 2013 stood at $169 billion with China. Related to this is the agreement to develop further railway projects in India. The Strategic and Economic Dialogue – which was concluded three times between India and China and designed to discuss macro-economic issues – is set to intensify bilateral cooperation. Interestingly, the Bank of China was allowed to open a branch in Mumbai although the rupee-to-renminbi currency swap issues are yet to be discussed in a formal way.

Secondly, at the broader diplomatic level, the bilateral consultations on Afghanistan, West Asia, Africa, Central Asia and Counter-terrorism are acknowledged and it appeared that – in the light of the gradual withdrawal of the US-led forces from Afghanistan both New Delhi and Beijing are poised to enhance counter-terror missions in the region.

Another aspect is the revival of the idea of cooperating on civil nuclear issues, a sticking point after China backed the US 1172

Resolution in the Security Council criticising the Indian nuclear tests of 1998. While the 2006 joint statement of Manmohan Singh-Hu Jintao mentioned for the first time the possibility of engaging in civil nuclear programme, nothing concrete took place between the two so far. The current joint statement stated that both "will carry out bilateral cooperation in civil nuclear energy in line with their respective international commitments".

At a broader strategic level, both reiterated their support to the multipolar world and vowed to cooperate on climate change, Doha Development Round of WTO, energy and food security, reform of the international financial institutions and global governance. Interestingly, the joint statement stated that they uphold freedom of navigation and the Asia-Pacific region will uphold an "open, transparent, equal and inclusive framework of security and cooperation based on the observance of the basic principles of international law." In the light of the South China Sea disputes, this statement is significant.

India and China: New Balance of Power?

Overall, the meetings between Modi and Xi and the recent events indicate to a balance of power element in bilateral relations, despite references to ancient civilisational wisdom and the like. Both were trying hard to reconcile with mutual security concerns over Tibet, Indian Ocean Region, India-Japan-US relations, China's nuclear cooperation with Pakistan and investments in the Pakistan occupied Kashmir, trade deficits and the like to the enduring mutual interests on counter-terrorism, sustainable economic development (manufacture sector vs services) and the like.

Moreover, the kind of media coverage – more positive than negative – for China's President and his entourage at Ahmadabad and New Delhi – is unprecedented. The Indian media did contribute to the expansion of China's soft power in the region with live publicity given to the Chinese delegation. However, it is doubtful if a similar treatment will be given to Prime Minister Modi whenever he makes the official visit next. It is instructive to note that in 2009, the US President Obama wanted a live coverage of his speech in Shanghai, but was denied by the Chinese side.

There were as well polite but firm responses from either side indicating that neither wishes to cross a certain limit in the bilateral relations, although it is difficult to say whether a Cold war kind of situation prevails between them. These are in relation to the build-up on the disputed border areas at Chumar.

ASSESSING US-INDIA RELATIONS: A PERSPECTIVE FROM CHINA

Three US political heavyweights - Secretary of Commerce Penny Pritzker, Secretary of State John Kerry and Secretary of Defense Chuck Hagel - just visited India successively within a fortnight. Prime Minister Narendra Modi is expected to visit the US for the UN summit in September. The Obama administration has been making every effort to bring the US and India closer by covering significant grounds for bilateral cooperation. What are the reasons for this?

First, there seems to be a re-establishment of the US-India relationship. This bilateral relationship has not been developing smoothly since President Barack Obama assumed the office. In December 2013, just five months before the new BJP government was formed, the Khobragade incident occurred. In July this year, India publicly criticized US surveillance of the BJP, calling it 'unacceptable'. The recent US diplomatic endeavour can be seen as a remedial effort therefore to turn the unhappy page over and re-establish a working relationship with India.

Second is maintaining the US strategic interest in Asia. The US considers China an emerging threat, and it has historically attempted to make India its pawn in the Asia-Pacific 'rebalancing strategy'. Its long-term strategy therefore is to use India to contain the rise of China. The fundamental aim is to contain China by developing friendly but utilitarians foreign relations with India and maintaining its dominant role in the Asia-Pacific region. However, this is not going to be an easy task.

Third is the attempt to create a friendly atmosphere for Modi's visit in September. For a long time, the US-India bilateral relationship was neither hot nor cold, and the different policy orientations of the two countries caused suspicion that the mutual, relatively independent strategies of the two giants pushed each other further apart rather than closer. Against this background, US wants to reinforce its partnership with India and pave the way for future cooperation. Since Modi formed the new government, the Obama administration has extended an olive branch to India by inviting him to pay a visit to the US and actively engaging the Indian defence industry.

While the US needs India to be a part of its rebalancing strategy, India also considers China as an important partner at at least two levels. First, China is one of the most crucial trade partners of India and bilateral trade reached USD 65 billion in 2013. Cooperation in the areas of energy, telecommunications and infrastructural construction have become prominent. In addition, India and China have a common interest in South-South cooperation. The Brazil BRICS summit caught the world's attention, and the meeting between Indian Prime Minister Narendra Modi and Chinese President Xi Jinping was highlighted. Since the BRICS has become an important economic cooperation organisation and is posited to plays a key role in the world arena, mutual economic relations between these two countries will definitely be enhanced in the future.

Needless to say, India's independent strategic tradition will not let it get easily involved in any country's containment strategy. US-India relations are therefore of a dual nature. The two countries need each other for future developments in global politics, economic growth and military cooperation. The US worries that it will not be able to 'control' India in the future once it becomes too strong, and at the same time India doubts US strategic intentions in South Asia. This is another major limiting factor for the two countries.

Restricting the development of US-India relations further is that there is no common military threat for US and India, and therefore no possible foundation for a military alliance. Although the 'China threat' is somehow popular in India and the US, China has been actively promoting cooperation with the US and India in handling non-traditional security problems and its efforts have been quite fruitful. In the aspect of traditional security cooperation also, China maintains stable military relationship with the US and India. For instance, China joined the RIMPAC naval exercise with the US in 2014 for the first time and held the joint military exercise, 'Hand-In-Hand' in Chengdu in November 2014. Another joint military exercise is scheduled with India on counter-terrorism on the borders of Pakistan in November 2014.

Additionally, the visions of the two countries of the world order are conflicting. India wants a multipolar world in which it can become an important pole in the future. However, the US wants the status quo and since another emerging power can become too challenging. The attitude of the US on India have been swayed by considerations of gains and losses since the Cold War, and it is not easy for US to change its mind now and treat India as a real strategic partner.

The US is bound to remain an essential partner for India. However, the future development of the US-India bilateral relationship will not be very smooth, and cooperation and conflict will be the norm due to historical and current factors.

2

Foundations of India's Foreign Policy

A country's foreign policy, called the international relations policy, consists of strategies chosen by the state to safeguard its national interests and to achieve its goals in international relations. The approaches are strategically employed to interact with other countries. In the recent time, due to the deepening level of globalization and transnational activities, the states will also have to interact with non-state actors. The aforementioned interaction is evaluated and monitored in attempts to maximize benefits of multilateral international cooperation. Since the national interests are paramount, foreign policies are designed by the government through high-level decision making processes. National interests accomplishment can occur as a result of peaceful cooperation with other nations, or through exploitation. Usually, creating foreign policy is the job of the head of government and the foreign minister (or equivalent). In some countries the legislature also has considerable oversight.

The foundations of India's foreign policy were laid during the freedom movement when our leaders, even when fighting for independence, were engaged with the great causes of the time. The principles of India's foreign policy, that emerged then, have stood the test of time: a belief in friendly relations with all countries of the world, the resolution of conflicts by peaceful means, the sovereign equality of all states, independence of thought and action as manifested in the principles of Non-alignment, and equity in the conduct of international relations. Under the leadership of Jawaharlal Nehru, India was the founder member of the Non-aligned Movement. India has played an active role in strengthening the Movement and making it an effective voice in representing the collective aspirations and interests o the developing countries on such vital issues as development, peace and stability. India hosted the 7th NAM Summit in New Delhi in 1983g. In recent years, after the end of the Cold War, our foreign policy has been focused on strengthening the Movement by redefining its priorities in keeping with the changing times.

India has also been in the forefront of the world community in the struggle against colonialism. Indeed, the Independence of India itself played the role of a catalyst in removing the vestiges of colonialism in other parts of the developing world, particularly in Africa. India was also the first country to raise the question of racial discrimination in South Africa in 1946. It was at India's initiative that the AFRICA (Action for Resistance to Invasion, Colonialism and Apartheid) Fund was set up at the 8th NAM Summit in Harare in 1986. India was the Chairman of the AFRICA Fund Committee, which wound up in 1993.

A notable feature of Indian foreign policy has been its strong advocacy of general and complete disarmament, with nuclear disarmament being accorded the highest priority. Towards this end, India has taken several initiatives within the United Nations and outside. In 1988, India presented to the 3rd Session of the UN General Assembly devoted to Disarmament an Action Plan for Ushering in a Nuclear Weapons Free and Non-Violent World Order.

In order to highlight international concern about the unprecedented nuclear arms race, India was also a member of the Six-Nation Five-Continent joint Initiative in the 1980s. But while India has, and will, remain committed to nuclear disarmament, to be achieved in a time-bound framework, it has consistently and in a principled manner opposed such discriminatory treaties as the Nuclear non-Proliferation Treaty (NPT) and Comprehensive Nuclear Test Ban Treaty (CTBT) and has refused to give up its nuclear options until all countries in the world including nuclear weapon states embrace the idea of nuclear disarmament in a phased manner.

As a founder member of the United Nations, India has been firmly committed to the purposes and principles of the United Nations and has made significant contributions to its various activities, including peace-keeping operations. India has been a participant in all its peace-keeping operations including those in Korea, Egypt and Congo in earlier years and in Somalia, Angola and Rwanda in recent years. India has also played an active role in the deliberations of the United Nations on the creation of a more equitable international economic order. It has been an active member of the Group of 77, and later the core group of the G-15 nations. Other issues, such as environmentally sustainable development and the promotion and protection of human rights, have also been an important focus of India's foreign policy in international forums. Commensurate with national interests and security, the improvement of bilateral relations is an important component of any foreign policy, and India has succeeded in establishing a network of mutually beneficial relations with all countries of the world.

In particular, the improvement of relations with our neighbours has always been one of the pillars of India's foreign policy. India played an historic and unique role in the liberation of Bangladesh which emerged as a sovereign nation in 1971. Through the implementation of the 1964 and 1974 Agreements, the issues of the stateless people of Indian origin in Sri Lanka were resolved. In 1988, India helped preserve the integrity of Maldives by coming to the assistance of that country and preventing an attempted take over by armed mercenaries. The Indian government has taken recent initiatives to further strengthen ties with our neighbours, which have won international appreciation.

These initiatives are based on five clear principles: First, with neighbours like Bangladesh, Bhutan, Maldives, Nepal and Sri Lanka, India does not ask for reciprocity but gives all that it can in good faith and trust. Secondly, no South Asian country should allow its territory to be used against the interests of another country of the region. Thirdly, none will interfere in the internal affairs of another. Fourthly, all South Asian countries must respect each other's territorial integrity and sovereignty. And finally, they should settle all their disputes through peaceful bilateral negotiations. These tenets have paid rich dividends. A landmark Treaty has been signed with Bangladesh on the sharing of waters of the Ganga. With Bhutan and Nepal, major projects of economic collaboration have been advanced.

Our relations with Sri Lanka have shown steady improvement. With Pakistan, India ha consistently pursued a policy seeking to improve relations under the framework of the Simla Agreement signed in 1972 which provided for the resolution of outstanding issues peacefully and bilaterally and for establishing durable peace in the Sub-continent. Bilateral discussions with Pakistan have resumed recently and India would continue efforts to have good neighborly relations with Pakistan. An important achievement of India's foreign policy has been the strengthening of regional co-operation.

India is an active member of the South Asian Association for Regional Cooperation (SAARC) which was launched in December 1985. With India's full support, SAARC has recently taken significant steps in accelerating the pace of economic co-operation. The South Asian Preferential Trade Arrangement (SAPTA) became operational in December 1995. At the 9th SAARC Summit in Male in May 1997, which was chaired by India, a historical decision has also been taken to strive for a South Asian Free Trade Area (SAFTA) latest by the year 2001 AD. The emergence of the Indian Ocean Rim Association for Regional Co-operation (IOR-ARC) in March 1997, as a major instrument of cooperation in the larger region, has also had the active support of India.

India's foreign policy has always regarded the concept of neighbourhood as one of widening concentric circles, around a central axis of historical and cultural commonalties. From this point of view, it has always given due priority to the development of relations with South East Asia. In 1947, India organized the Asian Relations Conference. It chaired the International Control Commission in 1954 and was a major player in the organization of the Bandung Conference in 1955. Today, India is implementing a 'Look East' policy which is underpinned by important economic considerations. Some significant steps in the pursuance of this policy have been taken with the admission of India as a full dialogue partner of ASEAN and a member of the ASEAN Regional Forum, in 1996.

An attribute of a dynamic foreign policy is the ability to respond to changing developments. The emergence of the Central Asian Republics in the aftermath of the break up of the Soviet Union was one such recent development, and India, given the strategic and economic importance of this region, has been quick to strengthen its bilateral relations with each of these Republics. The shift in recent years by the countries of Central and East Europe to political pluralism and market-oriented structures has also seen India trying to build upon existing business and institutional linkages so as to further strengthen the traditional ties of friendship with the countries of this region. The countries of the Gulf have a political and strategic importance for India. The region is a major market for Indian exports. Three million Indians are employed in these countries. The strengthening of ties with this region, therefore, has been a priority of India's foreign policy.

With China the aim of Indian foreign policy has been of developing a relationship of friendship, cooperation and good neighbourliness, exploiting the potential for favourably growth wherever it exists, even as we seek to find a fair, reasonable and mutually acceptable solution to the outstanding border issue. Towards this aim, a series of high level visits have been exchanged, bilateral trade and economic cooperation is growing, and an Agreement on Confidence Building Measures, as part of a wider dialogue on security, has been signed.

INDIAN FOREIGN POLICY ORIENTATION IN THE TWENTY-FIRST CENTURY

It is a truism that the foreign policy of any major state will be predicated upon and shaped by its perception of what constitutes the core national interest as leavened by the principles and value systems that the state in question adheres to. The related extrapolation is that the national interest, desegregated into its principal constituent elements, viz: political, military and economic determinants, would have to be protected, nurtured and advanced, as the case may be, in a complex and on occasion contradictory manner. State itself as an entity is located in a definitive spatio-temporal context and this provides the backdrop against which individual states evolve distinctive foreign policies. The regional and global strategic systemic consequently becomes a referent that defines the contours of domestic foreign policy and the latter evolves in a dynamic manner. The temporal determinant acquires greater salience when we note that both the state and the systemic have their own transmutative trajectories in the long cycle of history.

This chapter seeks to examine the past evolution and current orientation of India's foreign policy (FP) and dwells in some detail on certain regions and countries. The chapter argues that there is an element of continuity and change that is discernible in India's FP and that this has been impelled by a combination of factors specific to the Indian experience. If FP is perceived as a 'strategy' to realize the larger national interest, a useful and succinct definition (for a word that has elicited a plethora of multi-disciplinary interpretations) is provided by John Lewis Gaddis who defines it as: "the process by which ends are related to means, intentions to capabilities, objectives to resources."

In relation to the process of evolving a FP, it may be added that the strategic culture of the state and its ruling/governing elite play a central role and this is very noticeable in the Indian case. India's strategic culture, as is the case of many other states, is a distillate of two ontological features-geography and history – filtered through the cultural impress of its ruling elite at any given point in time. As a civilizational-state (a characteristic it shares with China) there is an inherited, albeit burnished dominant narrative about the past even as it seeks to grapple with modernity in all its manifestations. To that extent, while independent India post 1947 sought to outline an appropriate FP, its genealogy goes back to the immediate and buried past – which in this case links the DNA of imperial British India with the tenets of the *Arthashastra* that goes back to circa 302 BC! Hence this chapter argues that there are certain elements of continuity by way of tangible objectives in India's FP that are inexorable and dictated by existential characteristics such as geographical location and size. These are further transmuted by contemporary politics and the constraints and opportunities exuded by the prevailing international strategic systemic.

This chapter is confined to the trends in the evolution of post-1947 Indian FP and its current orientation and the first significant articulation about India's objectives, interestingly, precede 1947. India which was coming out of the colonial yoke through the Gandhian path of 'ahimsa' (non-violence) had a set of nationalist leaders led by Pandit Nehru and in September 1946, while providing an outline of the interim government's objectives on the cusp of Indian independence, Nehru stated: "It is because of this expectation of an early realization of full independence that we have entered this Government and we propose to function so as progressively to achieve independence in action both in our domestic affairs and our foreign relations…as a free nation with our own policy and not merely as a satellite of another nation."

There is further elaboration of the Nehruvian vision of Indian FP and a few months after he became Prime Minister of independent India, he observed: "Foreign policies…are not just empty struggles on a chess board. Behind them lie all manner of things. Ultimately, foreign policy is the outcome of economic policy, and until India has properly evolved her economic policy, her foreign policy will be rather vague, rather inchoate, and will be groping."

There is a sense of prescience in Nehru's later articulation for the effectiveness of India's FP in the early decades – the objectives it may have set for itself – were not backed by adequate and appropriate national resources and capabilities. Hence many of the lofty aspirations were not realized, thereby resulting in the chequered nature of India's foreign policy effectiveness in the period 1947-62. However this paper argues that there is a core consistency by way of the security and strategic concerns that under grid foreign policy and in the Indian case, the linkages and departures with the policy of imperial British India are instructive. 19th century European geo-strategic rivalry among the major powers became the 'Great Game' (a la Arthur Conolly and not Rudyard Kipling) and the central objective of then ascendant Britain was to keep the Russian Bear from accessing the Indian Ocean through the Central Asian region. Historians aver that even the Mughal emperors had much the same unease about any Russian foray to the subcontinent and this geo-strategic chess-game informed much of the foreign policy of the then major powers.

Theoreticians introduced the 'heartland versus rim land' theory and the dictates of the continental power and the salience of maritime power. Post World War II, when the mantle of the dominant power had passed to the USA, the 'game' continued but with a different packaging – namely the containment of communism.

The former Soviet Union was the new 'bear' whose advance was to be resisted and the global systemic evolved along the grid of bipolarity. Here one may introduce the co-relation between the foreign policy of individual states and the manner in which it is shaped by the compulsions of the global systemic. The proposition is that very few states barring the hegemon have the ability to conduct truly autonomous or independent foreign policies and the thumb-rule for all other states – to the extent they are relevant to the systemic – is that their manoeuvrability and space is shaped by the power compulsions of the systemic.

Bipolarity was the flavour of the Cold War decades and most of the world was divided along the East-West axis and their related military alliances. India, under Nehru, which had already anticipated this power block divisiveness had made its fundamental choice Non alignment. In his December 1946 speech, Nehru had already asserted: "We propose, as far as possible, to keep away from the power politics of groups, aligned against one another, which have led in the past to world wars and which may again lead to disasters on an even vaster scale."

Consequently the existential force of bipolarity and the postures of the two superpowers shaped the choices for the rest of the world – including the non-aligned group. India, as a nascent post-colonial state had its own internal consolidation to address as a first priority but its foreign policy, this chapter argues, flowed from an innate sense of how best to manage its more relevant strategic space. This was most succinctly summed up by the British High Commissioner to India at the time (1951) in a secret cable to London elucidating India's security-foreign policy orientation. Sir Archibald Nye opined that the Indian policy could be perceived as "operating in three concentric circles, the principles governing each of which bear little or no relation to the principles followed in the others."

This has been further interpreted as the innermost circle of contiguous states – viz: Afghanistan, Ceylon (now Sri Lanka), Nepal, Tibet and Burma – where it was perceived that India had 'vital' interests. The second circle included the rest of the world minus the four major powers at that time, namely the USA, USSR, UK and PRC.

The second ring was prioritized as areas that were more relevant such as SE Asia to minimal relevance as say South America. Sir Nye added, even at that time, that Pakistan was a 'unique' case. The more detailed elucidation that followed suggested that the policies – security and foreign – followed by India were very different for each set of circles and that while the innermost elicited a kind of hard-nosed realpolitik approach *a la* Bismarck, while in the second circle, "Indian policy was characterized by anti-colonialism and support for nationalism, with perhaps a smattering of realism in Asian countries like Malaya and Iran, where India's interests were engaged." And with regard to the outermost circle, India's foreign and security policy posture was "to a great extent determined by her passionate desire to keep out of conflict and to stand aside from Great Power struggles."

This chapter argues that Indian FP was and is shaped by a set of three determinants – namely the external international systemic and the dominant strategic discourse and practice; the Indian perception about what constitutes the core national interest and the national resources and capabilities it can bring to bear to protect or advance this interest; and finally the cognitive perception of the ruling/governing elite at the time. Within this matrix, there is both continuity and change by way of specific trend lines and initiatives taken by India over a 60 year period – from 1946 to 2006.

I would further aver that this entire policy response trajectory is to be located within the domain of India's distinctive strategic culture – which has also been evolving over this period.

Broadly desegregated, the trends in Indian FP may be divided in the temporal periods 1947-1962; 1962-1991; 1991-1998; and 1998-mid 2006 and refereed along the three elements identified earlier. The early phase from 1947-1962 was a period when nascent India was seeking to consolidate its identity as a free and independent state with the attendant mix of aspirations and anxieties and to that extent the immediate priority was internal and domestic.

The aftermath of partition and the grapple with participative democracy when economic and fiscal resources were modest, consumed greater part of national funds and energy – but it would be fair to state that on the foreign policy front – the Nehruvian approach was followed. A degree of realism where India's vital interests were affected was one component, while issues such as de-colonization and support for freedom struggles comprised the other. On larger global issues such as nuclear weapons, a normative, humanistic approach was preferred and vis-à-vis the superpowers, nonalignment was the preferred stance. If the domestic ambiance and the persona of a leader like Nehru were two of the drivers, the ambiance of the external global strategic systemic as manifest in the early phase of the Cold war (post Cuban missile crisis in 1962, the author would argue, the Cold War entered a different techno-strategic phase) was the more significant determinant in shaping Indian FP.

The rationale for the creation of an independent Pakistan is beyond the scope of this chapter but suffice it to note that the reality of a Pakistan in August 1947 brought the Great Game DNA through the Cold War filter into the calculus of Indian FP. Pakistan's willingness to join the US-led military alliances such as the CENTO and SEATO during the 1950's and 1960's made it the problematic 'other' for India and a number of Indian FP initiatives including those relating to Kashmir were directly affected by this Cold War undercurrent. One may hypothetically aver that an undivided British India would have perhaps adopted a different kind of FP orientation for there were no fundamental divergences with the

US led Western alliance. Nehru himself had no special love for the ideology of communism so much so that India would have crossed over into the red camp in retrospect appear misplaced. On the international canvas, India acquired a certain profile that belied its nascent political pedigree and underdeveloped economic profile. This was evident in the Indian support to Japan immediately after Hiroshima, the Indonesian freedom struggle, the Korean and Indo-China wars, the mantle of Asian leadership et al. The brief 1962 Sino-India war punctured this self-image and is a major punctuation in the evolution of India's strategic culture, security perceptions and foreign policy orientation. Disillusionment and a rude awakening were the leit motifs of the trauma and humiliation of 1962 and this experience scarred Nehru personally and the Indian polity collectively.

Bitter recrimination followed about the great Chinese betrayal and the invalidity of Asian solidarity on one hand and a realization that India's inherent national resources and tangible capabilities – in this case military – were woefully inadequate to underwrite the foreign policy contours that had been earlier envisioned. To go back to Gaddis, there was a mismatch between the objectives and the availability of resources. Post 1962 was a period of consolidation for India and Nehru died a broken man in 1964.

His successors – Lal Bahadur Shastri briefly and later Indira Gandhi were wedded to the mantra of nonalignment on the global stage but introduced certain nuances in the practice of foreign policy. The external dynamic of the Cold War entered Asia through the Vietnam war and later the nettlesome issue of Cambodia. Both these events had considerable negative impact on India's relations with the USA and SE Asian nations– the focus of this chapter. In the post Nehru decades – that is from 1964 till the tragic assassination of Mrs. Indira Gandhi in 1984 – India engaged in two wars with Pakistan – in 1965 and 1971 – the latter leading to the birth of Bangladesh – and the 1974 Peaceful Nuclear Explosion, and here one notes a certain caution and assertiveness in Indian FP. The Indian disillusionment with the US and other western powers – such as UK (which in any case was becoming more and more dependent on the trans-Atlantic alliance and the US) in the aftermath of the 1962 war and the subsequent Chinese nuclear test in 1964 led to a gradual tilt towards the former USSR and in about a decade – from the mid 1960's onwards, the USSR emerged as India's major supplier of military inventory and a trusted friend over issues such as Kashmir when they came up in the UNSC.

This tilt had its corrosive impact on India's relations with the USA and its allies – leading to what is often described as the 'estrangement' between the world's oldest and largest democracies – ironically when the values that were being contested in the Cold war were freedom and the threat to democracy. Subsequently the Soviet occupation of Afghanistan in 1979 and the Iranian Revolution brought the Cold War closer to India on its western flank and the estrangement with the USA was further enhanced through India's muted response over Afghanistan and the call for the Indian Ocean as a Zone of Peace among other foreign policy responses.

The period 1984 till 1990 was one of further consolidation for India under the stewardship of Rajiv Gandhi (this was the period when India embarked upon its Peace Keeping Operation in Sri Lanka) and some significant regional FP initiatives were pursued including a thawing of relations with China (which had gone into the deep freeze after the 1962 war) and improved relations with the USA.

This was also a period when India's fiscal prudence was not as astute as it may have been and while on one hand there was a visible element of India's military capability being effectively enhanced – as perceived in the Indian Navy's expansion and the swift assistance to Maldives in November 1988 which was threatened by a renegade takeover – the macro economic and fiscal indicators were deteriorating. This was also a period of considerable internal turbulence for India and there was a quick succession of Prime Ministers and short-lived Central governments. Political instability was compounded by the terrorist assassination of Rajiv Gandhi and a very complex internal security environment. Apart from Jammu and Kashmir, the prosperous state of Punjab witnessed a rash of separatist violence that was finally quelled.

This was also the period when the Cold War was coming to an unintended end and Gorbachev's glasnost-perestroika and the rapprochement with the USA led to a dramatic turn of events. Overnight on December 8, 1991, the Soviet Union became 'former' and Russia emerged with a very different geography and political identity. Bipolarity was relegated to the pages of history and a very new global strategic systemic was born. Unipolarity – or so it seemed.

The USA which had just led a very successful coalition in early 1999 for in Gulf War I – the War for Kuwait, was perceived as the sole hegemon with no challenger in sight – China was still recovering from the opprobrium of Tiananmen. It is the contention of this chapter that while the end of the Cold War led to a complete review and re-orientation of the FP of most nations, for the global strategic grid was completely transformed, it was the equivalent of a double-whammy for India since the domestic situation was also undergoing considerable turbulence. PM Narasimha Rao assumed office in June 1991 succeeding two predecessors who had served for less than a year each. India's economic health was frail and the fiscal indicators were alarming with a balance of payment crisis looming. India's forex reserves were down to a few weeks. Thus the country was faced with an exigency wherein all three determinants that shape and influence FP were in a state of flux-namely the global systemic, national capabilities and resources, and a new leadership that was grappling with political, economic and social turbulence – the right-wing BJP party was gaining ground in India at the time.

India's major FP transformation came about in the Narashima Rao years (June 1991-May 1996) and much of it was impelled by the economic liberalization that Delhi was embarked upon. India's socialist command planning model and the license-raj permit economic and trade system gave way to a more liberalized approach and in many ways the Indian economy was freed from the politico bureaucratic shackles imposed upon it for decades. The macro-results were very favourable. The inflexible Hindu rate of growth suddenly accelerated and this was also enabled to a great extent by deft financial planning led by then Finance Minister Dr. Manmohan Singh and the global techno-commercial wave related to the computer and information revolution. As Baru has noted: "after recording virtually no growth in the first half of the 20th century, the (Indian) economy grew at an annual average rate of 3.5 percent in 1950-80 and 5.4 percent in 1980-90 and 6.2 percent in 1990-2000."

THE SHAPING OF INDIA'S NEW FOREIGN POLICY

P.V. Narashima Rao's predecessor Rajiv Gandhi tied India's nuclear disarmament with US and other nuclear powers. He was calling for total abolition of nuclear arms. But the world changed when Rao became the prime minister, he inherited an economy that was nearly broke, there was no Soviet Union to support, and the US fresh from its gulf war victory was strutting as the only super power of the world.

In 1992, the UN security council passed a resolution stating that proliferation of nuclear and other weapons of WMD is a threat to international peace and security. US and other western nations were warning India, the list topper among the countries likely to acquire nuclear weapons that it has to face the wrath of the entire international system if it did not fall in line. P.V. Narashima Rao and his principal secretary J.N. Dixit, understood that the moment of nuclear reckoning was at hand. They knew they had to summon all the intellectual guile to wriggle out of the situation. India could not have found diplomats more wily than these two. Bush senior asked India to join a conference of five nations with US, Russia, China and Pakistan to discuss nuclear nonproliferation in the subcontinent.

Negotiating framework proposed by Bush was deeply offensive to India's sense of standing. Not only would the conference concentrate on getting India and Pakistan to behave on the nuclear issue, but their conduct was going to be supervised by Washington, Moscow and Beijing sitting at a higher table. The ultimate insult was that China, which India saw as an equal, was to become a guarantor of peace and stability in the sub-continent. This was a China that, India knew, helped Pakistan acquire nuclear weapons. In no way was India going to accept such a set of negotiations.

In typical fashion, Narashima Rao was non-committal pointing to the political difficulties at home, he said that he would prefer to discuss the problem in detail with the United States bilaterally before he could join multilateral nuclear negotiations. It was agreed that bilateral nuclear talks would begin within few weeks.

Having found an escape route at a critical moment, Narashima Rao launched India on a two track policy-engage the Americans in a nuclear dialogue and prepare for conducting nuclear tests. The first was a visible track and the second invisible. Narashima Rao gave orders to the atomic energy establishment in Bombay to get ready for another round of nuclear test, but the scientists wanted time-at least 2 years. Meanwhile, the pressure from the United States was relentless. 'Buy me time' was the constant refrain from Narashima Rao to dixit. The foreign office bobbed and weaved and found every trick in the diplomatic book to avoid getting into multilateral negotiations on the nuclear issue. In the talks India invented arguments for expanding the multilateral negotiations framework to include every possible country from Israel to Japan. By December 1995 India was ready for Pokhran-II. Narashima Rao had achieved the impossible. He had managed to fob off the various international pressure on India to close its nuclear option. The economy, formerly the weakest element in the country's portfolio, had turned around and was now an attractive feature that created the basis for a different relationship with the world. In addition he was ready to conduct nuclear tests and hence put India in a different strategic pedestal.

It's a different story that US found India's preparation for a nuclear test and Rao had to pull the plug on the supposed tests in 1995. But Raja Mohan agrees that PVN was the one who prepared everything for India to cross the nuclear Rubicon.

INDIA'S LINGERING CONSTRAINTS

India faces several constraints at the international/regional, domestic and perceptual levels in achieving a global leadership role in the near term. At the international level, India's late arrival as an independent state in 1947 (two years after the post-World War II order was finalized in San Francisco), precluded a leading role in the UN system. The UN Security Council was set up then with five permanent members who were allies in the winning coalition of the War. That set up still continues because the leading powers in the Security Council are unwilling to alter the composition of the Council. No systemic event has yet to upset the post-WW II order in terms of the structure of international institutional governance. The Cold War rivalry caused India to avoid joining alliances, and led it to pursue a non-aligned policy which also allowed it to somewhat compensate for the immediate dearth of hard power resources. However, India's quasi-alliance with the Soviet Union during 1970s and 80s precluded Western support for it to gain a leading role.

Regionally, India has been constrained by the conflict with Pakistan and China and the need to bifurcate its military forces into two fronts. The off and on alliance that the US and Pakistan have formed and China's continuing balancing coalition with Pakistan have constrained India's power in the region. The conflict in Kashmir also took considerable amount of Indian attention, and it is still simmering. In recent years, India has been affected by the weak states populating its neighborhood, especially Afghanistan, Pakistan, Bangladesh, Nepal and Sri Lanka. All these states have internal conflicts that have affected India. Nepal has emerged as major source of security challenge to India, through the Maoists (Naxalites) who now form a corridor in India's tribal belts from North to the South. Large scale migration form Bangladesh has caused internal conflict in Assam and Tripura.

The external pressures have been accentuated by the weak state syndrome of India itself. The Indian state has strength in some areas, but it is often called a 'soft state' in dealing with pressing national problems. Many parts of India, especially in states such as Bihar, UP and Jharkhand are similar to Sub-Saharan Africa in terms of state control and governance. The ability of the state to provide public goods, and services, especially in the security area, has been in decline or stagnant, despite the fact that the State has acquired considerable resources in the globalization era. A potent manifestation of state weakness is the increasing number of radical Islamic terrorist outfits in India and the increasing incidence of terrorist strikes. In 2007-08 India emerged as the number one country in terms of casualties caused by terrorist attacks.

As for *soft power* resources, strategy and diplomacy are crucial components to compensate for some of the weaknesses in the hard power area. Moreover, effective utilization of national power would require a proper grand strategy. Until recently, the Indian elite avoided this subject due to the fractious nature of its domestic politics.

Grand strategy, in contemporary times, focuses not only on military security, but on economic security as well; it attempts to increase wealth of the country as economic capability is equally important in gaining and retaining a state's power position. A grand strategy is often an intervening variable in translating a state's power capabilities into actual power and influence in the international system. India's lack of a proper grand strategy may be due to the need to accommodate divergent interest groups and political ideologies within India.

Changing Strategic Circumstances

By 2000, India's strategic position had improved appreciably. Many reasons are ascribed for this change. First of all, the US has increasingly perceived India's potential in balancing China. "Economic liberalization, growth, changes in strategic environment, nuclear tests, measured response to Pakistani provocations," all these have earned India the status of a "mature regional power." Through its nuclear tests in 1998, India repositioned itself from a largely marginal player in the international system to a serious candidate or contender for major power status. The test allowed India to get out of the fence-sitter mode on the nuclear weapons issue. Had it remained there, India would have been clubbed with Iran and North Korea by non-proliferation advocates today. It is true though that in the immediate aftermath of the tests, India's relations with Pakistan deteriorated as the so-called stability-instability paradox entered the strategic relationship between these two states. Despite the initial intense opposition by the major powers, all of them in the end entered into a strategic or security dialogue with India.

The reason for India's acceptance as a de facto nuclear power by the international community is the realization among the leading powers that with two nuclear rivals and no membership in any nuclear protection arrangement, India may well have different security dynamics from those other states pursing the nuclear option. Moreover, India has behaved maturely in the nuclear proliferation area by refusing to offer assistance to other states seeking nuclear weapons. While India has thus elevated itself from a middle power to become a candidate major power, as Ayoob (1999) states, this has been achieved without much forethought or strategic preplanning. The strategic dialogue with the US and other major powers also has helped India in clarifying its objectives, but greater levels of cooperation would require concrete policy postures and advancements in capabilities.

Some incremental but crucial changes have taken place in India's foreign policy over the past two decades that reflect the economic and strategic realities that I outlined above. The foreign policy changes are also driven by the conviction of the Indian elite that they ought to make use of the favorable economic and strategic circumstances in order to emerge as a leading world power. These new attitudes are caused by changes in the international system as well as India's internal confidence deriving from newfound economic progress. There are multiple elements to the new foreign policy dynamism that India has exhibited over the recent years. 1. Deepening of the strategic and economic relationship with the United States. 2. Improving relations with all major powers. 3. Increased vigor in pursing the Look East Policy toward its ASEAN neighbors and East Asian states. 4. Engaging with pivotal regional power centers such as Brazil and South Africa in order to form bargaining groups that would strengthen India's position in world trade forums and other issues. 5. A focus on economic diplomacy including vigorous search for new oil sources in Africa and Latin America. 6. Building up of the armed forces, even while pursuing dialogue with neighboring states. 7. Continue peace process with Pakistan and China although major concessions from the Indian side on the border issues are unlikely to come anytime soon. This is largely because of the constraints operating in the fractious democratic polity.

The change in US attitude toward India began in early 1990s, when in response to Soviet collapse, India began to adjust is foreign policy. However, the nuclear issue intervened as a major stumbling bloc. In 1998 India tested its nuclear weapons that caused a major furor in international relations and the US response was harsh with Washington and its allied imposing a series of sanctions on India. However, the US and India initiated a dialogue which eased considerably much of the irritants. The 1999 Kargil conflict was a watershed, when President Bill Clinton sided with India and forced Pakistani Prime Minister Nawaz Shariff to commit to a withdrawal of Pakistani forces from the Kargil Hills on the Indian side that the former had occupied. The Clinton visit to India in March 2000 was a major success, but it was the George W. Bush administration that initiated major changes in the US policy toward India, especially in the nuclear area. The 1995 India-US nuclear deal that the US president signed with Prime Minister Manmohan Singh elevated India to the status of a de facto nuclear weapon state while allowing it to engage in international nuclear trade. A series of steps were undertaken which included India bifurcating its civilian and military facilities, the Hyde Act which exempted non-NPT signatory India from nuclear trade sanctions, the 123 Agreement and the waivers from the IAEA as well as the Nuclear Suppliers Group (NSG), which is expected in September 2008. This deal has major repercussions in both strategic and economic terms for US-India relations. In the post September 11, 2001 world, the Indian perception of the US has changed in a big way. The US was on terror in Afghanistan against Islamic radicals is part of the reasons for the change. It is very plausible that had there been no September 11, attacks, India-US relations would have matured even further. The need for Pakistan's support in the war in Afghanistan somewhat mellowed the level of cooperation that the U.S. could develop with India.

A number of concrete steps have been taken to strengthen this relationship. They include the joint exercise that Indian and US military branches have conducted, several defense deals that made US one of the leading sources of weapons for India, cooperation in the energy field, and bilateral dialogue. The two-way trade also has seen considerable progress over the years. It is not only US companies that invest in India, but the reverse, with more and more Indian companies investing in the US. The US-India economic relations are bound to improve as Washington needs India and

India needs the US for continued economic growth and innovation. Economic, strategic, and demographic reasons call for optimism with the latter emerging as a very important in the coming years. Indian technical students are populating all US graduate schools and Indian technology workers are the largest recipients of H-1 visas.

They will be a key force in linking Indian and American knowledge-based economies in the decades to come. The Indian diaspora is very active as a lobbying group in the U.S. and is emerging as a powerful electoral segment. When economic and security links improve, popular perceptions of Americans and Indians of each other will also change. Today, India is one of the few countries that genuinely sympathize with the US on the war on terrorism (I don't mean Iraq invasion). However, India's foreign policy may diverge on the issue of military action against Iran as well as on global trade issues.

India has also maintained strong ties with Russia, especially as its traditional source of weapons acquisition. It is however, difficult to see the emergence of a deep strategic relationship as happened in the Cold War era even if Russia emerges as a global power once again. This is because India has been diversifying its economic and military sources and Russia has only very limited non-military and non-oil resources for India's fast globalizing economy.

With respect to China, India's foreign policy has maintained an outward cordiality, but there are simmering tensions in relations. Over the past few years, several border incidents have occurred that are not reported by the world media. These incidents reflect the continued rivalry that these states have over territory, influence and policies over Tibet, Pakistan, and the emerging US-India relationship. As China attempts to expand its military bases in Tibet and in the Indian Ocean rim countries such as Myanmar, India is starting to feel the pressure to counter such moves as evident in the increased activism by the two states in Myanmar. The increasing economic links between China and India somewhat cushion the rivalry from escalating to a full-fledged military competition

South Asia and India's Foreign Policy

While India has improved its engagement with the major powers, a notable weakness of the Indian foreign policy approach has been the neglect of its own immediate region, South Asia. This is an inevitable result of India's desire to transcend the region and not to get mired in the quarrels of the smaller neighboring states. The regional states are all weak countries with multiple security, economic and demographic challenges that spill over to India. India is affected by internal and external Islamic terrorist cells that have emerged in the region.

INDIA'S FOREIGN POLICY SEVERELY MAULED BY PAKISTAN

Severely disconnected and in utter disregard of Indian public opinion, it has become the hall-mark of Prime Minister's tenure from 2004 onwards to stubbornly pursue an obsessive peace dialogue with Pakistan. This stubborn obsessiveness generates a "blind spot" in India's foreign policy planning on Pakistan. This "blind spot" induces in the Indian policy establishment a strategic obliviousness to the predominating structural reality of Pakistan, that Pakistan's policy postures are commanded and controlled by Pakistan Army. The latest utterances by Pakistan Army Chief, General Kayani should leave no doubts in any perceptive Indian's mind that Pakistan-India peace is strategically impossible.

India's peace policy approaches towards Pakistan primarily crafted by the Indian Prime Minister Singh and former Foreign Secretary now the Prime Minister's National Security Adviser Shankar Menon, from the ill-advised Havana Accord (2206) to the infamous Sharm-al-Sheikh Declaration (2009) proved to be utter failures. Pakistan is still not strategically inclined towards "sustainable peace" with India despite India's appeasement policies towards Pakistan. The latest Indian policy initiative of resumption of peace dialogue with Pakistan, disregarding that it involves a total "U-Turn" from Prime Minister Singh's declaratory assertions following Mumbai 26/11 of no talks with Pakistan till it makes amends on Mumbai 26/11, also bears the imprint of Prime Minister Singh and the new NSA. As per Indian media reports the outgoing

NSA, MK Narayanan had taken a hard line against resumption of dialogue with Pakistan until India's demands on Mumbai 26/11 were met.

Within days of India's announcement of readiness to resume the peace dialogue with Pakistan, in typical Pakistani official responses, Pakistan's Foreign Minister Qureshi in an arrogant and vituperative public speech in Pakistan on February 10, 2010, covered live on TV for all the world to note, asserted that while Pakistan had stuck to its stands, it was India that had come crawling to Pakistan to seek resumption of peace dialogue.

India's political and strategic analysts have totally missed the point that this was not an isolated act of political demagogy of Pakistan's Foreign Minister. Attendant on this assertion were similar contextual assertions by Pakistan Prime Minister Gilani and Pakistan Army Chief, General Kayani. Pakistan Prime Minister Gilani asserted that Pakistan will not give any guarantees that it can stop terrorism attacks against India, emanating from Pakistan's territories, a key demand made by India following Mumbai 26/11. The Pakistan Army Chief, who controls Pakistan's foreign policy towards India in a Press Conference last week, consistently harping on Pakistan's 'India-centric threat perceptions' gave the impression that peace with India was strategically impossible.

Pakistan's marked re-emergence of intransigence towards India arises from its born-again strategic confidence that in 2009-2010 Pakistan has reinvented its strategic utility to the United States and the West, as the outcome of the London Conference 2010 would indicate.

More importantly, Pakistan has become fully aware that by re-inventing its strategic utility to the United States and the West, Pakistan has been successful not only in severely mauling India's foreign policy towards Pakistan, but also India's foreign policy relationships with the United States and the West. Pakistan is not far wrong in this perception as the infirmities in India's foreign policies in the last few years, enabled Pakistan in one master-stroke to neutralize India's key strategic objectives that it attempted to achieve, banking on the strength of its perceptions that in the ultimate analysis.

Pakistan would count more in relation to India in the current regional security environment.

The perceptional damage on India, regionally and globally by Pakistan's mauling of India's foreign policy objectives is extensive.

Pakistan could do so because the Indian Prime Minister and his former Foreign Secretary and now NSA, perceptional readings on Pakistan and Pakistan's linkages with the United States and the West have been faulty.

This Book intends to focus on the following aspects in this regard:

- India's Key Foreign Policy Objectives Mauled by Pakistan
- Pakistan Army Chief's India-Centric Demands Accepted by United States and NATO
- India's Timid Pakistan Policy Encourages Pakistan for Strategic Diminution of India in Regional and Global Terms
- India's Strategic Imperatives for Strong Policy Postures Against Pakistan.

INDIA'S KEY FOREIGN POLICY OBJECTIVES MAULED BY PAKISTAN

India's key foreign policy objectives in the period 2004-2009 particularly, and earlier too, can be listed in brief as follows (1) Pakistan as the springboard of widespread terrorism attacks against India be neutralized by a policy of peace-engagement with Pakistan and persuasive diplomacy (2) India to establish a substantial presence in Afghanistan both to further her regional power aspirations and also as a strategic pressure point against Pakistan (3) Implicit in the US-India Strategic Partnership was the component hat the United States would facilitate attainment of India's policy objectives as indicated.

India's obsessive peace-engagement with Pakistan by diplomacy, Track II diplomacy, Special Envoys and other back-room channels have not delivered on India's objectives.

Pakistan Prime Minister's latest statement quoted above vividly indicates that Pakistan still views terrorism as an instrument of state policy. India's persuasiveness stands out-matched by Pakistan's continued intransigence. On Afghanistan, the latest developments indicate (1) Pakistan has succeeded in side-lining India in Afghanistan (2) Pakistan outmatched India's utility in Afghanistan to US strategic interests (3) India'soft-power' approaches on Afghanistan have been a dismal failure (4) Pakistan has got ruled out India from any future role in Afghanistan as part of the US regional initiative.

In terms of India's key objectives in the US-India Strategic Partnership in relation to Pakistan and Afghanistan, no success has been forthcoming to India. Pakistan reigns supreme in US military strategy and the United States has given centrality to Pakistan's strategic interests in Afghanistan, over India.

In light of the central pillars of Indian Prime Minister's policy on Pakistan and Afghanistan being knocked down by Pakistan's success in prevailing over the United States, it can be argued that India's Pakistan policy of the existing political dispensation is a failure. It would take a long time for India to retrieve the damage inflicted on India's long term strategic interests by the current Indian weak-kneed policies towards Pakistan.

Centric Demands Accepted by United States

Pakistan Army which double-timed the United States for nearly 10 years on Afghanistan and till date has not handed over Osama bin laden and Mullah Omar to the Americans, and yet got away to emerge again as the central pillar in US strategic calculus in South Asia is a reality which the Indian Prime Minister can ill ignore.

Pakistan Army Chief's demands made on USA and NATO in relation to Afghanistan, India and Pakistan strategic preferences stand accepted in full.

The list of Pak Army Chief's demands accepted by the United States could make any Indian incensed as to how such acceptance has mauled India's misperceived foreign policy. The list is as follows (1) Pakistan Army will not withdraw troops from the borders with India (2) Pakistan would be given a central role in Afghanistan (3) Pakistan Army will not accept any Indian role in training of Afghan National Army or Police (4) Pakistan will be part of any US discussions with the Taliban (5) Pakistan Army demands for US military weapons systems will be met (6) India will not be given any role in a regional solution initiative for Afghanistan. The Indian Government also seems to have forgotten that it was General Kayani on taking over as Pakistan Army Chief who ordered the breach in the four year old ceasefire in 2008 to be broken by firings and escalation of tension along the LOC and the international border. When it comes to impeding the Pakistan – India peace engagement it is the Pakistan Army which does so by firing from the shoulders of the Pakistani President, the Prime Minister and Pakistan Foreign Minister intransigent assertions against India and that too on the verge of resumption of a peace dialogue. The Indian foreign policy establishment needs to get their perceptive readings on Pakistan right.

THE DEBATE IN INDIA: CONVERGENCE OF THE RIGHT AND THE LEFT

A range of opinions was also expressed on the Indo-U.S. nuclear deal in India. The opposition Hindu nationalist Bhartiya Janata Party (BJP) was quick to criticize the pact. Ironically, it was the BJP that had laid the foundations of the emerging Indo-U.S. strategic partnership. The architect of this partnership, former Indian prime minister Atal Bihari Vajpayee, argued that the Indian government had surrendered its right to determine what kind of nuclear deterrent it should have in the future based on its own threat perception.

Vajpayee argued that the new agreement would not only put restrictions on the nuclear research programme, but India would also incur huge costs in separating military and civilian nuclear installations. The Left parties, which are also part of the ruling coalition in India, criticized the government for not consulting them before striking the nuclear deal with the United States.

They also lambasted the government for giving up on India's long-held policy of nuclear disarmament. Other critics of the deal claimed that America's recognition of India as a "responsible state with advanced nuclear technology" that should "acquire the same benefits as other such states" falls short of admitting it into the nuclear club. It was argued that India had committed itself to segregating, in a phased manner, the nation's civilian nuclear facilities; voluntarily placing its civilian nuclear facilities under IAEA safeguards; signing and adhering to an additional protocol with respect to civilian nuclear facilities; continuing the unilateral moratorium on nuclear testing; working with the United States to help conclude a Fissile Material Cut-off Treaty; continuing with stringent non proliferation export controls; and harmonizing with and adhering to the guidelines of the Missile Technology Control Regime and the NSG.

While most of these conditions had long been a part of the Indo-U.S. strategic discourse, for some Indian critics, India had agreed to these conditions without much reciprocity from the United States. Others expressed fears that independent research activities oriented to peaceful purposes, including India's fast breeder programme, might be obstructed or slowed down.

The scientific community in India delivered a mixed verdict. Some, accepting the need for nuclear energy in the coming years, favored the pact, because it would augment India's energy resources.

The deal with the United States was also viewed by many as leading the way for other states in the NSG, such as Canada, France, the United Kingdom, and Russia, to supply India with civil nuclear technology. Others were less than enthusiastic and argued that the separation of civilian and military facilities is an onerous task and might entail serious repercussions for research and development in weapons development and for production facilities needed for the nuclear deterrent.

Incidentally, even the Americans conceded that separating its civilian and military nuclear facilities represented an enormously difficult task for India. Some critics have charged that the very premise of the Indo-U.S. nuclear deal is flawed, because meeting energy needs by importing nuclear reactors will only lead to energy insecurity and exorbitant costs. There were also complaints that the scientific community had been kept completely out of the loop during such an important decision. For a long time it seemed as if the Department of Atomic Energy (DAE) in India was not reconciled to the deal, because it continued to be reluctant in coming up with a credible plan for separating India's civilian and military nuclear facilities.

Several rounds of talks between India and the United States failed primarily because of DAE's strong resistance to the deal, especially its opposition to putting its fast breeder programme on the civilian list. Even as this debate was going on in India, India's decision to vote in favour of the U.S.-sponsored motion in the IAEA that was critical of Iran angered the Left parties in India. They came out strongly against the Indian government for not supporting a fellow member of the Nonaligned Movement against what they viewed as America's hegemonistic ambitions and bullying tactics.

In 2006, much to India's chagrin, Iran's nuclear problem once again emerged as a complicating factor in Indian efforts to finalize the nuclear deal with the United States. Iran decided to remove the seals applied by the IAEA for the purpose of verifying the suspension of Iran's P-1 centrifuge uranium enrichment programme in January 2006 just as the Indian government was engaged in some hard bargaining with the United States on the nuclear pact.

Iran plans to pursue all activities to build, research, develop, and test the P-1 centrifuge. The uranium enrichment activity is part of a process that could be used both to generate electricity and to make nuclear weapons. In response to this, the EU3 (Britain, France, and Germany), along with the United States, called for an emergency meeting of the IAEA in February 2006 to discuss whether to refer Iran to the UN Security Council.

Once again, India came under pressure as the nature of its decision at the meeting of the IAEA Board of Governors could have repercussions for its own nuclear negotiations with the United States. U.S. ambassador to India David Mulford went public with his warning that if India did not vote to send Iran to the UN Security Council, the effect on the deal would be "devastating," because the U.S. Congress would "simply stop considering the matter" and the "initiative will die." In the end, India did vote in support of the U.S.- and EU-sponsored resolution and reasoned that it was done keeping in mind India's own security interests, because a nuclear Iran in a highly unstable Middle East country was not in India's interest. Despite the opposition that the Indo-U.S. deal faced from the right and the left of the political spectrum in India, there were few who were advocating India's withdrawal from the agreement. For most of the Indian strategic community and the media, the Indo-U.S. nuclear deal affirmed the depth and maturity of the India-U.S. partnership. The deal generated a certain sense of euphoria, because it marked an end to India's nuclear isolation and was seen as a tribute to India's growing profile in the global order.

The Indian scientific establishment also started interacting with its U.S. counterpart, giving concrete shape to Indo-U.S. cooperation on areas such as high-energy nuclear physics, nuclear plant design, construction, operation, safety, life extension, and regulatory oversight. Moreover, it was clear to seasoned observers of India's nuclear programme that there was a danger of India's nuclear programme grinding to a halt in a couple of decades if India did not go for international cooperation. India's uranium ore was adequate only for 10,000MW, and India's nuclear weapons programme would have to be accommodated within that. The Indo-U.S. deal, therefore, was seen by most as India's best hope for integrating itself in the global nuclear framework and drawing on its advantages.

THE NUCLEAR BARGAIN

The nuclear agreement ultimately hinged on the ability of the Indian government to come up with a credible plan to separate its tightly entwined civilian and military nuclear facilities that was acceptable to the United States.

After some tough negotiations over a period of seven months—negotiations that were still in progress even as the U.S. president landed in New Delhi on March 1, 2006—the two states managed to arrive at an agreement.

India agreed that fourteen of its twenty-two nuclear reactors would be classified as civilian and would be open to international safeguards. The other reactors, including the fast breeder reactors, would remain as military facilities and would therefore not be subject to international inspections. The accord also allows India to build future breeder reactors and decide whether to keep them in or out of the international inspections regime. India accepted safeguards in perpetuity on its civilian nuclear reactors on the basis of a reciprocal commitment by the United States to guarantee unlimited nuclear fuel supply to India for its civilian programme. Unlike other nuclear weapons states, however, India will not have the right to pull out any of its reactors once they have been put under safeguards.

The IAEA chief, Mohammed ElBaradei, was quick to endorse the deal, claiming that this agreement would not only help satisfy India's growing needs but would also bring India closer as an important partner in the non proliferation regime. He has argued that the deal is not only important because it gives India access to fuel and technology but also because it brings India into the nuclear mainstream, which is very important for the global efforts towards eliminating nuclear weapons.

But developing safeguards specific to India could turn out to be a complicated task. Although India had declared itself a nuclear weapon state after conducting nuclear tests in 1998, it is not recognized as such by the NPT of 1968. This makes India's case unique in a way, and the IAEA safeguards would have to be negotiated accordingly. India might demand that its safeguards regime should be almost equivalent to the level of the inspection regime for the five acknowledged nuclear weapon states.

In fact, the Indian government would like the proposed India-specific safeguards with the IAEA to provide "on the one hand safeguards against the withdrawal of safeguarded nuclear material from civilian use at any time, and on the other, permit India to take corrective measures to ensure uninterrupted operation of its civilian nuclear reactors in the event of disruption of foreign fuel supplies." But this technical nitty-gritty cannot disguise the fact that it is a great deal for India. The nuclear pact allows India access to nuclear fuel that it needs urgently in light of its fuel shortages and burgeoning energy requirements.

It ends three decades of Indian isolation from access to dual use and global high technology flows caused by the restrictions imposed by India's rejection of the global non proliferation order. At the same time, the strategic nuclear weapons programme India has maintained for all these years despite tremendous international pressure remains largely untouched. This is a very sensitive issue for the Indian scientific and strategic community, and the Indian prime minister had to assure the Indian parliament that "India will place under safeguards only those facilities that can be identified as civilian without damaging the nation's deterrence potential."

THE LAST STRETCH

While India celebrated the great "nuclear bargain" extracted from the United States, the real drama shifted to Washington, where there were initial complaints that Bush had given away far too much in the nuclear agreement with India in return for very little. Some, like Democratic representative Edward Markey of Massachusetts, were hyperbolic in claiming that the accord "undermines the security not only of the United States, but of the rest of the world."

While some asked for a detailed briefing from the Bush administration on the implications of the nuclear deal for the nuclear non proliferation regime, others wanted the administration to show Congress how this deal enhanced U.S. security. Even Bush himself admitted that getting the approval of Congress was going to be difficult, because the Bush administration would have to answer a number of questions satisfactorily.

To the administration's credit, that is exactly what it did. Bush sold the deal as part of his energy security plan for the United States and by highlighting the importance of India in the U.S. strategic calculus. It was argued that helping India, whose economy is projected to be one of the five largest by 2020, develop civil nuclear energy will reduce demand for fossil fuels and lower petrol prices for U.S. consumers. As of today, India imports three quarters of its oil, natural gas, and coal and receives only 3 per cent of its power from nuclear energy.

The focus of the U.S. Congress, however, was largely on the consequences of this pact for the nuclear non proliferation regime, especially at a time when U.S. foreign policy was trying to grapple with Iran and North Korea. Some claimed that the deal with India was exactly the wrong message to send when Washington and its European allies were asking the IAEA to refer Iran's case to the UN Security Council for further action.

Iran had attacked the Indo- U.S. nuclear deal when it was signed in July 2005 in an attempt to counter international pressure on its own nuclear programme. Iran's chief nuclear negotiator, Ali Larijani, referred to this deal when he argued that the United States enjoys extensive relations with India in the nuclear field despite India's nuclear weapons programme.

He went on to claim that such a "dual standard" was detrimental to global security. India, however, quickly countered this argument and claimed that India had always been in compliance with its obligations under international treaties and agreements. India, unlike Iran, is not a signatory to the NPT, and having signed the treaty, Iran must fully comply with its international commitments in a transparent manner.

There were also concerns about the implications of this deal for India's nuclear weapons programme. This deal may allow India to ramp up its weapons production, because the supply of nuclear fuel to India would free up India's existing capacity to produce plutonium and highly enriched uranium for its nuclear weapons stockpile.

However, recent research has highlighted the fact that India already has the indigenous reserves of natural uranium necessary to support the largest possible nuclear arsenal it may desire and, consequently, that the U.S.-Indian civilian nuclear cooperation initiative will not materially contribute towards New Delhi's strategic capacities in any consequential way either directly or by freeing up its internal resources.

Nevertheless, the non proliferation community remains unconvinced, considering that India has decided not to accept safeguards on the prototype fast breeder reactor and the fast breeder test reactor, as well as on the reprocessing and enrichment capabilities associated with the fuel cycle for its strategic programme. The idea that India will not focus on nuclear weapons in the future is also unlikely considering the Indian prime minister's categorical assertion that "India will not be constrained in any way in building future nuclear facilities, whether civilian or military, as per [India's] national requirements" and "no constraint has been placed on [India's] right to construct new facilities for strategic purposes."

The nonnuclear states, as identified by the NPT, pledged not to make nuclear weapons and to have their pledge verified through full-scope safeguards applied by the IAEA.

In return, they are entitled to develop nuclear energy for peaceful purposes and to receive assistance in development. Under the U.S.-India nuclear agreement, India will only accept safeguards on its designated peaceful nuclear facilities while the remaining facilities and the breeder programme will continue uninhibited.

Concerns were bound to be raised that this apparent double standard that allowed India to escape fullscope safeguards and still obtain nuclear assistance while other states were held to a tougher standard could create problems for the future of the NPT.

The Bush administration needed to convince the U.S. Congress that the basic bargain of the nuclear non proliferation regime, as exemplified by the NPT, would not come under strain as a result of the agreement with India and that the deal would appreciably strengthen the U.S.-India strategic partnership.

On its part, India decided to shut down the Cirus reactor permanently in 2010 and to shift the Apsara reactor out of the Bhabha Atomic Research Center (BARC) complex.

India was also "prepared to shift the fuel core of the APSARA reactor that was purchased from France outside BARC and make the fuel core available to be placed under safeguards in 2010."

This was done partly to assuage some of the concerns of the non proliferation lobby that has long blamed India for going back on its word by diverting weapons grade plutonium to the Pokhran nuclear test of 1974.

Given the broad-based support that the idea of an Indo-U.S. partnership enjoyed in the U.S. Congress, however, the ratification of the nuclear deal seemed highly likely.

The ratification process received a setback when the Senate failed to pass its version of the nuclear bill before the midterm elections after the House of Representatives had voted overwhelmingly to approve it.

The rout of the Republicans in the midterm elections generated apprehensions in some quarters about the fate of the deal, but the Bush administration insisted on the legislation for the deal being approved by the lame-duck Congress.

In the ultimate analysis, the deal's fate depended on the Bush administration's determination to get the bill signed, sealed, and delivered.

It succeeded in its endeavor when, days after the Republicans lost their majorities in both Houses of the U.S. Congress, the Senate overwhelmingly approved the nuclear deal. After reconciling the House and Senate versions of the bill, the Henry J. Hyde U.S.-India Peaceful Atomic Energy Cooperation Act of 2006 was signed by President Bush, marking a rare foreign policy success for the Bush administration at a time when it was suffering enormous setbacks across the globe.

India's Timid Pakistan Policy Encourages Pakistan

The salient characteristics of PM Singh's Pakistan policy in the last five or six years emerge as one of 'peace at any cost' more reminiscent of Chamberlain' similar obsessions in 1938 encouraging Nazi Germany to Second World War.

The Indian Prime Minister with such a "political romanticism on Pakistan" is reminiscent of another Congress Prime Minister's "romanticism on China" leading to China-India War 1962. Both these syndromes have resulted in India's timid Pakistan policy where Pakistan is encouraged to twiddle India strategically on its thumbs, secure in the belief that India would run to Washington to control Pakistan's disruptive activities against India and Washington would prefer to reward Pakistan strategically to contain its nuisance value.

Ironically, both India and the United States as strong and powerful democracies have failed to control the Pakistan Army's regionally disruptive activities. In case of India's timid foreign policy on Pakistan, it results in strategic diminution of India on two counts.

- In regional terms, India is being perceived as a ponderous giant or stumbling elephant, incapable of protecting its turf
- In global terms, India is being perceived as a potential global power but without the essential pre-requisite of accepting strategic challenges and responsibilities and hence unable to be counted in the global strategic calculus.

On both counts, in the end political game, India's current Pakistan policy leads India to finish up as a "strategic loser nation".

3

India's SAARC Satellite Proposal and Policy

Indian Prime Minister Narendra Modi undertook a two-day official visit to Nepal on August 2–3. Surprisingly, no Indian prime minister had visited Nepal—with whom India shares more than 1,700 kilometers of borders—for 17 years. Modi articulated his vision for Indo-Nepal relationship with four C's: cooperation, connectivity, culture, and constitution. As a part of his vision, he also spoke about developing a satellite to assist India's neighbors. Naturally, Modi is looking at satellite technology as a tool for cooperation and connectivity.

Narendra Modi became India's prime minister on May 27. On June 30, after witnessing the launch of PSLV-C23, carrying the French earth observation satellite SPOT-7, he addressed India's rocket scientists. While congratulating the Indian Space Research Organisation (ISRO) for the successful PSLV launch, he also outlined his vision for India's space program. He argued in favor of changing the perception that India's space program has an elitist agenda. He emphasized that space technologies are being used for socioeconomic development and, over the years, have proved their utility for common people.

During his speech, Prime Minister Modi also argued for the need to share India's space expertise with its neighbors. He proposed to develop a "SAARC satellite" for the region and also to expand the footprint of India's satellite navigation program to South Asia. This indicates that generally New Delhi is keen to use

India's expertise in space as an instrument of foreign policy. It's worth examining and deliberating about the possible design of such a vision in the context of SAARC.

The South Asian Association for Regional Cooperation (SAARC) was established in 1985. This organization has a key focus on economic and developmental issues. SAARC has eight members: Afghanistan, Bangladesh, Bhutan, India, Maldives, Nepal, Pakistan, and Sri Lanka. Additionally, there are some nations with observer status, including the United States, Australia, Japan, and China. Myanmar (Burma) also has the status of an observer, but is keen to become a full member. This country shares more than 1,600 kilometers of borders with India. Owing to geographical and political realities for this discussion, Myanmar is thus considered as a part of SAARC.

Over the years, SAARC has evolved various areas of cooperation, and science and technology is one such area of interest. They have developed a cooperation mechanism that includes areas like environment, energy, education, and media. In the areas of science and technology cooperation, SAARC established a Meteorological Research Centre (SMRC) in 1995. It undertakes collective research in meteorology in the SAARC region. It has a modern and advanced observing system with a reliable and timely communications network. Also, there is a network for regional cooperation on subjects like hydrology, oceanography, seismology, and atmospheric science. Obviously, such networks rely on satellite-derived data.

Amongst the SAARC member states, India is the only spacefaring nation with a number of satellites operating in various orbits. Pakistan is another state with reasonable interest in space field. However, in spite of its early start and its knowledge of "rocket science" (it has a well-developed missile program), Pakistan has not made much progress in space arena. Their space agency, known as Space and Upper Atmosphere Research Commission (SUPARCO), was established during 1961 as a committee and was granted the status of a Commission in 1981. Badr-1 (Badr-A) was Pakistan's first indigenously developed satellite and was launched from China on July 16, 1990. This satellite is no longer operational.

Pakistan's second satellite, BADR-B, an Earth observation spacecraft, was launched on December 10, 2001. Subsequently, Paksat 1, its first geostationary satellite, was acquired in 2002. China launched Paksat-1R, a communication satellite for Pakistan, on August 12, 2011. In November 2013, a CubeSat called iCUBE-1 was launched in a polar orbit to take low-resolution images of the planet.

There are two other SAARC states with satellites in their inventory. One is Sri Lanka. Its first satellite is actually a commercial satellite and was launched by China in 2012. Otherwise, Sri Lanka is likely to launch its first geostationary communications satellite by 2015, in collaboration with a Chinese company. The other nation is Afghanistan, which started using its first satellite in May of this year. This satellite, called Afghansat 1, was acquired to boost the telecommunications sector. This is an orbiting Eutelsat satellite that was launched in December 2008 and with is designed to last until 2020. Afghan's Ministry of Communications and Information Technology is renting this satellite for US$4 million per year.

Apart from these two nations, Bangladesh has shown some interest in research related to space. The Bangladesh Space Research and Remote Sensing Organization (SPARRSO), established in 1980, is a state agency concerned with astronomical research and the application of space technology. They propose to launch their first satellite, called Bangabandhu-1, around 2015. There are some unconfirmed reports that Maldives could be assisted by China to evolve their space agenda in near future.

This is the existing "SAARC space footprint" that is providing assistance to a limited population. By contrast, India's proposed SAARC satellite would be serving the interests of entire SAARC population, almost 1.5 billion people. The SAARC region included many nations plagued by poverty and conflict. In this region, in a relative sense, India is an island of prosperity surrounded by states fighting to win over security and economic challenges. At the same time, within India there are also visible disparities between rich and poor. It's also worth noting that two nuclear weapon states are the part of this grouping and there are some inherent security contradictions amongst some of the states in the region.

The geography of the SAARC region is unique, with coastlines, forests, deserts, and mountains. It has one of the youngest mountain ranges in the world, the Himalayas. They influence the major rain providing system for the region, the monsoon. The major rivers in South Asia are the Ganges, the Indus, and the Brahmaputra. Major deserts include the Thar Desert, which covers large areas of both Pakistan and India, with an approximate area of 175,000 square kilometers. Mainly tropical weather systems influence the Indian peninsula and other island states. Extra-tropical weather systems influence the survival of people staying close to Himalayan region. The region is prone for earthquakes, and a few tsunamis have taken place in the recent past.

These geophysical and geopolitical realities of the region should be taken into account before suggesting any model for the SAARC satellite. India needs to evolve a joint mechanism involving representatives from all member states to decide on the expectations from the proposed SAARC satellite. Before designing such a satellite, it would be important to identify and zero in on the specific and urgent needs of the nations in the region. Broadly, the various socioeconomic challenges of SAARC nations could be at least partially addressed by communications satellites, weather satellites, and remote sensing satellites.

Considering the issues like necessities of member states, cost, time, and expertise required for development and launch of a satellite, the best option for India could be to develop an Earth observation satellite as the first SAARC satellite. Basically, such a satellite could be of much use for land and water resources management for the entire region. India would also be expected to assist member states to develop ground infrastructure and create expertise. Some analysts believe that, at times, SAARC gets held hostage to the divergence of the India-Pakistan relationship. In fact, satellite technology could come very handy to silence such critics. As confidence building measures, such technology could be used to undertake joint surveillance of the border regions and resolve issues related to infiltration, water sharing, and more.

India's Regional Satellite Navigational Network is likely to become operational by the end of 2015. As suggested by Prime

Minister Modi, India could offer these facilities to the SAARC states as well. To assist civilian aircraft for navigation and non-precision approaches over India airspace, ISRO has developed a GPS-Aided Geo Augmented Navigation (GAGAN) system. India could also allow access to this system to aircraft operating within SAARC airspace.

Presently, what is important for India is not to limit itself with the idea of a SAARC satellite but instead to effectively use its existing capabilities in space to assist the various SAARC members. Most of these nations, being novices in the field of satellite technology, may not be in a position to ask India for specific assistance. India needs to become proactive and share with these nations imagery and other relevant data. In 2005, the Asia-Pacific Space Cooperation Organization (APSCO) was established, which is the only multilateral space mechanism presently available for the region. Among the SAARC members, only Bangladesh and Pakistan are members of APSCO and, from the SAARC point of view, such a body is not of much use. India could take a lead to establish a SAARC space cooperation mechanism, which could also bring more transparency into the system. Such agency could play a major role towards coordinating various data sharing and training related activities.

In SAARC, India is the dominant player; in the space arena, it is the only player. It is important for India to guard against developing any form of so-called "big brother attitude." While establishing a relationship with other nations, India should not play only the role of assister. India needs to develop a system where these nations could be made partners in various activities. To reduce rivalry (if any) and promote solidarity among members, India could engage these nations in important space projects to create a sense of belonging. Presently, India is working on a program to develop Astrosat, a dedicated astronomy satellite that is likely to be launched in 2015. India could involve SAARC members in this project and could call this satellite "SAARC Astrosat." Also, with the Sri Lankan government, India could undertake a feasibility study for developing a joint spaceport in that country.

SAARC region is bound together not only by geography but also (in some sense) by culture, ethnicity, traditions, religion, and languages. At the same time, this region has various strategic fault lines with strong differences on issues among some member nations. Any proactive collaboration in the outer space arena is unlikely to resolve all issues of differences. However, in an era of tremendous growth in information technologies, the Internet, mobile telephony, and social media, satellite technology could form the basis to establish a common SAARC identity.

PAKISTAN 2014: A REALITY CHECK FOR INDIA'S FOREIGN POLICY

Prime Minister Designate Narendra Modi's political reachout to SAARC nations to attend his swearing-in ceremony is a bold and imaginative foreign policy initiative especially in relation to Pakistan.

Scheduled interaction between PM Modi is due to take place the day after the swearing-in ceremony. This would enable PM Modi and the SAARC heads to take a measure of each other. In the process of these interactions PM Modi would be able to dispel the negative images of him projected by India's Opposition parties during the 2014 Election Campaign.

It would be a pity therefore that the Pakistan Prime Minister is unable to attend especially when no other external engagements stand scheduled for him. PM Sharif is reputed to have friendly inclinations towards and keen to enhance economic and trade ties with India.

If he is dissuaded in declining PM Modi's invitation when the new Indian Prime Minister is on the threshold of initiating foreign policy changes, Pakistan would have missed a significant opportunity towards moving Pakistani relations to a new footing.

PM Nawaz Sharif is now in office for a year now in what was the first democratic change of regimes in Pakistan. I had written last year and articulated on TV debates that PM Nawaz Sharif would require a year at least to bring about major changes as at that time Pakistani political dynamics were in a flux with impending changes of the Pakistan Army Chief and the Chief Justice of Pakistan. Indian establishment and media were advised not to be euphoric.

It needs to be noted that Pakistan's India and Afghanistan foreign policies are controlled by the Pakistan Army and the new Pakistan Army Chief seems disinclined to let go of this hold to sustain the institutional significance of the Pakistan Army in Pakistani domestic political dynamics and also as leverage with the United States and China.

While all SAARC nations have accepted the invitation, Pakistan is dithering for the last two days indicating the serious institutional divide within Pakistan over its approaches to India.

A reality- check on Pakistan is therefore contextually relevant both for PM Designate Modi and the foreign policy establishment which would need to break-out of the earlier appeasement mode of the last ten years.

Pakistan's reality –check in mid-2014 would indicate the following:

- Pakistan Army continues to maintain a stranglehold on Pakistan's India policy and can never be accepted to change its hostile anti-India mind-sets.
- PM Nawaz Sharif despite all best intentions to move forward in relations with India would be unable to do so.
- Significance of Pakistan Army in United States strategic calculus will enhance as US is in the process of exiting Afghanistan.
- United States in view of above is unlikely to goad Pakistan Army to go along with any friendly approaches made by PM Modi.
- Pakistan Army's notorious ISI intelligence agency has been US cat's-paw in Afghanistan twice over in recent times. US may need it again and those in India who advocate that US assistance should be sought to tame it are being unrealistic of realities.
- China's strategic calculus imperatives also dictate an over-riding importance to the Pakistan Army and its ISI.

In view of the above strategic realities, what are the options available to the new Indian Prime Minister to reorder India's neighbourhood into a more stable and secure region?

While PM Modi should continue to strive and persist in giving windows of opportunity to PM Nawaz Sharif to respond positively to Indian foreign policy initiatives, PM Modi can expectedly be hoped not to repeat the 'mantras' of the previous government in terms 'unending appeasement' and 'peace at any cost'

PM Modi's election slogan modified in the foreign policy context should read as "Friendship for All, Appeasement of None".

Advocated in my earlier Papers on Pakistan that India should adopt the US's China strategy of 'CONGAGEMENT" towards Pakistan would be a worthwhile advocacy at this juncture.

In sum, it implies that Pakistan Army's military adventurist policies towards India in India-proper or in Afghanistan must be met with a strategy of diplomatic and military containment with political and economic engagement in tandem.

In pursuance of India's engagement processes with Pakistan, India-at-large expects PM Modi that the Government under his political leadership would be "sensitive to "India's National Honour" and if India's power leverages have to be used as a last resort then India would display the "Will to Use Power" in a judicious and calibrated manner to ensure India's National Security interests are secured.

SAARC: INDIA NEEDS TO LEAD THE WAY

The upcoming summit of South Asian Association for Regional Cooperation (Saarc) will be held against the backdrop of important global and regional developments. On one hand, it is increasingly clear that the advanced Western economies are unlikely to see off the economic downturn in the short-run. This will have a knock on economic effects on South Asian countries in the form of weakening the demand for their products.

On the other hand, the context in the subcontinent is changing in a manner that augurs well for closer regional economic linkages. Taken together, these trends could provide an opportunity to infuse a muchneeded sense of purpose to Saarc. India should take the lead in re-programming Saarc for the next decade and ahead.

South Asia is one of the least economically integrated regions of the world. Intra-regional trade is just about five per cent of total official trade. The contrast with other sub-regions of Asia – let alone other parts of the world – is sobering. For instance, intra-regional trade in East Asia accounts for over 50 per cent of total trade. The current situation in South Asia seems all the more stark when we set it against its past record as well as its future potential. Before 1947, this region boasted of more or less open borders, allowing for easy movement of goods and services.

Furthermore, the subcontinent also enjoyed close economic ties with other parts of Asia. The regional arc stretching from Kolkata to Singapore was a vibrant network of trade, finance and entrepreneurs that formed the economic heartland of the British empire in Asia. South Asia does not have to rest on its history. It continues to have tremendous potential to grow through trade. The region has the highest population density in the world. It has a large number of cities close to the borders. And there is considerable cultural, ethnic and linguistic overlap of populations across the borders.

What, then, has prevented closer regional and sub-regional economic integration? At one level, the answer can be found in the economic policies and outlook of the countries of South Asia since independence. The experience of colonialism led the newly independent countries – with the notable exception of Sri Lanka – to regard the idea of an open trading system with some suspicion and to pursue more autarkic economic policies and plans.

India and Pakistan also struggled to come to terms not only with the political consequences of Partition but also with its economic implications. The two countries were at odds on economic issues ranging from division of assets to exchange rates – differences that put paid to the idea of free trade between them. The problem was compounded by India's propensity to treat its borders as fences to keep others out rather than using them as gateways for the movement of goods, people and ideas. The under-development of India's own border areas, which were wont to be seen as buffer zones, undermined India's ability to promote regional trade.

These economic issues have been overlaid by political differences. Reconciling the two is not all that simple. Economic affairs tend to have a win-win logic. It is easy to see how cooperative exchange could work to the material benefit of all parties. But in politics moral considerations such as identity and honour can outweigh material interests. This is a problem that India faces with almost every one of its neighbours. What's more, if political differences have a national security angle to them, it becomes all the more difficult for the logic of economic integration to assume primacy. Economic affairs are about absolute advantages accruing from interchange, but security affairs are about relative advantages gained by one side or another.

Here too, India's immense lead in size and power as well as outstanding political disputes have worked to reduce the attraction of closer economic ties in the subcontinent.

The issues will not go away any time soon. But there are some indications that South Asian countries are willing to try according greater importance to economic linkages as opposed to political and security considerations. For one thing, India's economic growth in the last two decades has positioned it to credibly play the role of a regional dynamo. India's neighbours are slowly realising the tremendous opportunity that India presents for their growth prospects. India's free trade agreements with Sri Lanka and Bhutan, and the trade and transit agreement with Nepal have highlighted the potential benefits of regional economic integration.

It is not surprising that Bangladesh wants to greatly enhance trade and connectivity with India, or that Pakistan has at last agreed to confer "Most Favoured Nation" status on India. In the context of the continuing economic downturn in the West, India could become rather more important to its neighbours.

For another, India too has understood the fact that allowing its neighbours to partake of its growth is essential both to draw the sting from political differences and to enable India to play a role on the global stage. Once the largest recipient of foreign aid, India now extends aid and developmental assistance to most of its neighbours. These bilateral programmes are important, but India needs to help institutionalise pan-regional economic cooperation and eventually integration. The South Asian Free Trade Agreement (Safta) needs to be worth more than the piece of paper on which it was written. It's time India took concrete measures to hasten the implementation and expand the provisions of Safta.

THE NEW IDENTITY FOR THE SAARC

With one-fifth of the world's population, the countries of South Asia face formidable challenges resulting from poverty, underdevelopment, and conflict within and among themselves. Their low levels of production, unemployment, and population pressures are not helped by historic exploitation and other adverse legacies. In an historical, cultural, physical and linguistic sense, South Asia is an integrated region, but any commonality across nations has been made impossible by deep-rooted divisions and animosities across the whole region. The latter is hugely polarized, and it has to grapple with gross violations of human rights. Consequently, governments in the region lack the effective initiative and political commitment needed to meet their obligations to respect, protect, and fulfil human rights and fundamental freedoms. Internal conflicts, civil strife, poverty and so-called state anti-terror legislation and measures have resulted in violations of the civil liberties of the people.

The South Asian Association for Regional Cooperation (SAARC) was established in 1985 with the objective of promoting regional cooperation between seven South Asian countries: Bangladesh, Bhutan, India, Nepal, the Maldives, Pakistan and Sri Lanka. Despite the extremely slow pace at which SAARC moves and its very limited achievements, the association did receive an increase in its membership when Afghanistan became the 8th member in 2007. However, the Association has from its very beginning been up against hard politics, mutual fear, and a strong sense of rivalry between its two principle members: India and Pakistan. One reason for SAARC's unimpressive progress is a lack of agreement among the member states on what should be the guiding force towards regionalism. SAARC has consequently been unable in any way to achieve its basic objective of promoting regional cooperation and solidarity. It is a disgrace that after nearly 30 years it has nothing to show and nothing to celebrate.

Even now SAARC is still trying to steady itself. It may not have made any great mark, but at least it has not been disbanded and it continues to function, albeit in a haphazard manner. Sadly, the presence of this regional organization has done nothing to remove historical irritants between members or to lower the levels of suspicion and distrust among neighbors.

Disputes between member states have led to outright wars, low-intensity conflicts, cross-border terrorism, a debilitating arms race and some very hostile propaganda. SAARC has failed to prevent any of these and they in turn have held up SAARC's progress. Belonging to a regional forum for nearly 30 years has led to no shared values or norms and, despite some points of commonality in the past, the member states have been unable to map out a common future.

South Asia today is a black spot for the gross violation of human rights and civil liberties. The people of Bhutan have as yet seen no glimpse of democracy, and they are deprived of all kinds of freedoms under the rule of an assertive kingship.

Pakistan enjoys a pseudo democracy. Nepal has been faced with a serious political crisis from more than a decade: it has no proper government, no constitution, a dead civil society, and a puppet media.

India, a so-called growing economy and the largest democracy on earth, faces political crises and internal instability from Kashmir to Assam. Kashmir is regarded as 'a legal black hole' in terms of human rights violations perpetrated by the armed forces. Most importantly, throughout the SAARC region, the poor are getting poorer and the rich richer: the gap between the two is widening further while the dynastic political elite and business people can enjoy whole states' welfare facilities and opportunities. Why is this happening? Why there is so much that is unjust in this region? Is it not time for a radical rethink? Who is responsible? Is it not high time for the people of SAARC as a whole to seek common answers to common problems?

Despite a serious human rights crisis throughout much of the region, SAARC has not even given thought to adopting a specific, detailed and uniform human rights convention or charter despite the existence of these in all other major regions of the world. Is it not high time then for SAARC states to think seriously about it?

What is required is a widespread formal commitment to human rights across the whole region. This should take the form of bills of rights, the establishment of national human rights institutions, declarations by IGOs, and the establishment of regional human rights regimes. The latter would be relatively independent but coherent human rights sub-regimes operated within the larger framework of international human rights practice. Examples of major regional mechanisms are the European human rights monitoring mechanism, the Inter-American system, and the African system. All these regional mechanisms have created, under their human rights charter, bodies such as a commission and a court of human rights. These have broad mandates to monitor human rights compliance by states parties, to receive reports from states, to receive complaints from individuals and states, to investigate and to order interim measures to prevent any escalation of human rights violations. They also provide appropriate reparations for victims by the violators, and they publish their findings and make recommendations to pressurize the state parties concerned.

Many questions need to be asked today: has SAARC achieved anything in nearly three decades of existence? Why, compared with other regions, are they so backward in terms of everything? In almost every other region there is some kind of regional human rights mechanism: since a fifth of the world's population resides in the SAARC region, why have the SAARC nations never thought having one? Can a region so politically, socially, and economically volatile afford to go on ignoring this issue? Most importantly, can South Asia gear itself for real regional cooperation? Can national and regime interests become sufficiently harmonized in order to promote cooperative trust and mutual confidence among the power elites of the region? The very diversity of South Asia demands the gradual implementation of conceptual steps that build towards a distinct regional identity. One such conceptualization could well be the establishment of a SAARC regional human rights mechanism.

Towards Setting up a South Asian Human Rights Mechanism

Many questions need to be asked: Why is a separate charter for the promotion of human rights so important for the SAARC region? What would it add to existing practices? SAARC countries have signed already several conventions on narcotics, trafficking in women and children for prostitution, promotion of child welfare, and there have been several agreements on food security and various social issues.

However, there has been no regional agreement that specifically focuses on human rights and fundamental freedoms. A regional instrument would be regarded as an appropriate complement to the universal human rights instruments of the United Nations. Such regional human rights mechanisms are already established in the Americas, Europe, Africa and most recently the Arab States: the last major geographic area, therefore, without its own mechanism is the SAARC region. The Council of the League of Arab States adopted its own Arab Charter on Human Rights in 2004, and it has been in force since 2008. The Charter grants a number of human rights and fundamental freedoms to the people, and it provides for the election of a seven-person Committee of Experts on Human Rights to consider states' reports and to monitor states' compliance with the Charter.

Most SAARC countries have common problems concerning torture, trafficking, internal displacement due to conflict, refugees, rights over resources, urban shelter and demolition, domestic violation against women, the practice of the death penalty, and extra-judicial detention and forced disappearances. A few countries of SAARC have national human rights institutions. All SAARC countries have, or in the case of Nepal should soon have, a written constitution under which human rights are recognized as fundamental. Despite these provisions and initiatives, however, there is a deteriorating human rights situation in the region brought about by the anti-terrorism measures adopted in some South Asian countries, by internal political crises and civil strife and by the hostility of governments towards human rights despite their claims to be democratic. The SAARC region has suffered for centuries from the absence of a rule of law and constitutionalism and from a culture of impunity that affects almost all the countries. Is there not then an urgent need to formulate a regional human rights mechanism?

The majority of SAARC member states have still to ratify the optional protocols to the International Convention on Civil and Political Rights (ICCPR) and the Convention on the Elimination of All Forms of Discrimination against Women (CEDAW). Moreover, Bhutan has still to ratify the ICCPR, the International Convention on Economic, Social and Cultural Rights (ICESCR), and the Convention against Torture.

Even where treaties have been ratified, though, implementation has been restricted by the reservations of some countries that follow a narrow interpretation of treaties relating to civil and political rights, and by a limited political commitment to implement economic, social, and cultural rights. An effective regional human rights mechanism would ensure the protection and promotion of human rights in the region especially common issues including the rights of migrant workers, human trafficking, minority rights, the right to development, and, most importantly, it would challenge the existing culture of impunity and lawlessness in the region. Such a mechanism could also provide a less costly, more accessible and effective redress alternative to existing international processes and procedures.

Not all SAARC nations are democratic and those that claim to be on the way to being so easily slide into authoritarianism, as in the case of Bangladesh, Pakistan, and Nepal. The prospect, therefore, of ideological homogeneity across the region would seem to be anything other than bright. With over sixty per cent of its population still forced to survive below the poverty line, how could this region even claim to be democratic? Moreover, how could it claim to have a fully-fledged democracy until human rights are protected and enshrined in the international covenants? The SAARC region faces serious challenges in consolidating democracy and strengthening and promoting human rights and the fundamental freedoms of its people. SAARC should now seriously consider establishing a regional human rights mechanism similar to those of the Inter-American or European Systems. The mechanism would certainly help states to promote and protect rights and freedoms effectively within their jurisdiction. It would ensure that international human rights laws were respected and promoted effectively throughout the SAARC nations. Moreover, such a mechanism could help people in the region to develop a common understanding of universal human rights issues, norms, values and perspectives.

By way of example, the Organization of American States governs human rights protection in the Americas. Both states and individuals can file cases and complaints. Under the American Convention on Human Rights, two bodies protect, promote and monitor human rights: a) The Inter-American Commission whose the primary function is to make a complaint to the Inter-American system whenever an American state is proved to have violated individual human rights; and b) The Inter-American Human Rights Court, which has jurisdiction over contentious cases mostly forwarded by the Commission. In the Inter-American system, both the Commission and the Court have made a major contribution to recognizing human rights, developing human rights jurisprudence and protecting human rights in the Americas. Elsewhere, the Council of Europe drafted a European Convention on Human Rights after Second World War in response to a call issued by Europeans from all walks of life. The Convention was designed to incorporate a traditional civil liberties approach to securing effective political democracy. The Convention created the European Court of Human Rights in Strasbourg, and any person, who feels that a state party has violated his or her rights under the Convention, can take a case to the Court. Judgments confirming violations are binding on all.

To be credible and able to meet both the promotion and protection requirements effectively and practically, a future regional human rights mechanism for SAARC, based on a human rights charter, should have a minimum set of characteristics. These would include an ability to receive and decide upon individual and interstate complaints of human rights violations by the state party. It should have the potential to develop additional mechanisms such as special procedures and subsidiary bodies on thematic issues, working groups, etc. There would be a SAARC Human Rights Commission, with broad powers to investigate, make site visits, receive reports and complaints by states and individuals, and a SAARC Human Rights Court empowered to make binding decisions on human rights issues and grant reparations for victims of human rights violations by states. The human rights mechanism, as with other regional practices, would be able to cooperate with international human rights mechanisms. This would permit reinforcement of the existing human rights framework and the overcoming of procedural and institutional weaknesses in domestic jurisdictions as well as in the international system. It would also help to overcome any lack of expertise or experience in human rights jurisprudence and to ensure effective implementation and enforcement of human rights norms and standards.

National human rights mechanisms are more important and effective in addressing local issues: the regional mechanism would play a complementary role, especially with regard to cross-border matters. The regional mechanism would also be a useful platform for South Asian countries to utilize opportunities under the United Nations's Universal Periodic Review system, which monitors the human rights performance of all UN members. A future SAARC charter on human rights, similar that of the Inter-American system, would be a great breakthrough for the SAARC region.

A Human Rights Culture in the Region

Enough is enough—SAARC must no longer be a hostage of rival powers in the region. The South Asian states have been too reluctant to take forward the regional project in a manner that it deserves. The provisions of the SAARC Charter have been ignored. Regional cooperation remains at a very rudimentary stage, and there is little evidence of any desire to act regionally by building trust and avoiding force. Prominent Nepalese Professor Lok Raj Baral has argued: 'So whatever commonalities and shared values exist in the region, they hardly matter for making SAARC more meaningful for the peoples of the region. Unless the South Asian regimes are reconstructed (and this is perhaps a challenging task for South Asian power elites who come from a variety of backgrounds) for transforming the nature of the region, SAARC cannot make headway.' In the absence of the right political atmosphere no economic, political or social integration is feasible. Establishing a proper regional human rights mechanism could provide an alternative way of establishing a favorable political environment and of reconstructing the region politically, socially and economically.

Of course, there would be enormous challenges in establishing a regional human rights mechanism in South Asia because of the legal and geo-political hurdles. The politics of the South Asia continue to be affected heavily by the continuing tensions in Indo-Pakistan relations. There are contentious issues, too, in South Asia—such as water, migrant workers, trafficking, minority and indigenous communities, refugees, and border disputes—which need to be settled through bilateral and multi-lateral mechanisms. If the SAARC countries fail to address these factors, its very future is bleak. Most importantly, political commitment, sincerity, and establishing a culture of human rights and the rule of law across borders are essential. Now is the time to create a SAARC Charter on Human Rights in treaty form, a consensus document. This must be the primary focus of all SAARC nations. It is essential. It needs to be the departure point for all SAARC agendas; it needs to be the alpha and omega for SAARC's future plans, programs and cooperation. The basic norms and values of human rights guaranteed by the international human rights covenants and national constitutions has to be the guiding force for any economic, social, developmental, and political cooperation among the South Asian countries.

Human rights must also be the guiding force for South Asian politics and for its democratic processes. These values must be above partisan politics and above the narrow interests of one or two nations. It has to be the means to common goals and agendas. Establishing the proposed human rights institution to monitor, promote, and consolidate human rights will bring the SAARC nations together to achieve common aims and ambitions towards peace and prosperity. The new future human rights body must be the common forum and a milestone to bring the South Asian society together as a single body of humanity regardless of religious, political, cultural or ideological differences. The essence of human rights has the power to mend all differences!

NEIGHBOURS FIRST: MODI'S FOREIGN POLICY MANTRA

India's neighbourhood, comprising countries crucially strategic for India's national security, stood grossly neglected in foreign policy formulations of the previous political dispensation for the last 10 years. In the decade, it was internationally being held against India that if India could not re-order its own neighbourhood in the Indian sub-continent, how could she aspire to surge forward as an emerging Asian power and a global player? What this implied was that Indian foreign policy processes stood atrophied by lack of dynamism and proactive approaches to win over confidence, and influence its neighbours.

The Pakistan-centric policy formulations of the last government, under pressure from the US, led to the foreign policy neglect of the rest of the all-important Indian sub-continental neighbourhood. It was being commonly said that during the last 10 years, India's foreign policy stood outsourced to Washington.

Had India diverted equal effort and time to focus on its foreign relations with Nepal, Bhutan, Bangladesh, Myanmar and Sri Lanka, it would not only have gained significant strategic successes, but would also have erased the international criticism that India was found wanting in spreading its influence in its own immediate neighbourhood.

This Indian neglect created a strategic vacuum in which China gleefully entered much to India's discomfiture. The situation was further complicated by inadequate government responses that permitted Indian states like West Bengal and Tamil Nadu to dictate foreign policy responses on the plea that 'political coalition compulsions' fettered India's foreign policy.

Long Overdue Priority

'Neighbours First' was the foreign policy mantra propelled by Prime Minister Modi even before he took oath as India's new prime minister. This was a long overdue foreign policy priority dictated by the previous political dispensation's gross neglect of India's neighbourhood.

Prime Minister Modi's political outreach to the neighbourhood emerged in the form of an invitation to leaders of all SAARC countries to attend his swearing-in ceremony. This was willingly accepted by all leaders, except Pakistan, which took time to accept the invite due to compulsions of the Pakistan Army.

With his political outreach, Prime Minister Modi facilitated a splendid opportunity for first hand interaction with SAARC leaders even before he embarked on a proactive foreign policy. Valuable political discussions with SAARC leaders fostered mutual understanding of both the visiting leaders and Prime Minister Modi.

It also helped the Indian Prime Minister to tailor his initial foreign policy blueprint for the neighbourhood based on his personal perceptions of each SAARC leader. Significantly, Prime Minister Modi selected Bhutan and Nepal for his first visits as part of his 'Neighbours First' foreign policy initiative. He virtually synchronised the visits of Indian Foreign Minister Sushma Swaraj to Bangladesh and Myanmar as part of the political outreach to all neighbours.

Strategic Significance

Prime Minister Modi's priority in selecting Bhutan and Nepal as his first ports of call in India's neighbourhood was systematically missed in Indian media analyses. Strategic determinants, so far absent in Indian foreign policy planning, came into play.

Nepal and Bhutan are strategically crucial for India's national security as they not only share borders with India, but also crucially with an overbearing China in the north. Nepal and Bhutan, therefore, are 'strategic buffer states' which impede China's direct access to Indian boundaries along a wide stretch of our Himalayan borders.

Nepal was virtually gifted away to China's influence by the unimaginative and flawed policies of the previous government. India handed over Nepal to the Nepalese Maoists and facilitated their political legitimacy, something which they could not win in a decade of violent insurgency. Regrettably, no Indian prime minister visited Nepal for the last 17 years.

Bhutan, India's long-standing, steadfast friend, has lately been under Chinese pressure, both diplomatically and militarily. China has indulged in intrusions into Bhutanese territory to enlarge the Chumbi Valley salient pointing at India's Siliguri Corridor.

Prime Minister Modi's visit to Bhutan, therefore, carried rich symbolism both in terms of strategic reassurance and political support appreciative of its India friendship. The visit of the Indian prime minister was well received by Bhutan at all levels and promises to have overcome any minor irritants that may have existed.

Prime Minister Modi's 'Mission Nepal' was more challenging and called for adroit statesmanship. India had to virtually reclaim Nepal to India-friendly postures after decades of anti-India hysteria propagated by both Nepalese domestic politics and Chinese moves.

Prime Minister Modi's visit to the only Hindu nation in the world, including paying obeisance at the historic Pashupatinath Temple in Kathmandu, was particularly welcomed in Nepal. Modi's gesture symbolised the rich common civilisational heritage of both countries.

Imaginative and Visionary Step

Significantly, the 'Modi Magic' seemed to have worked in making his Nepal visit successful. Even top Maoist political leaders were fulsome in praise of Prime Minister Modi and his offerings to Nepal. Significant was his declaration in Nepal that India would never interfere in the country's domestic political dynamics as an overbearing neighbour.

It needs to be noted that Prime Minister Modi took an imaginative and visionary step in selecting Bhutan and Nepal as the first neighbours to be visited. Besides reasons outlined earlier, it was symbolic that even India's small neighbours would henceforth be accorded equitable respect in the Modi government's foreign policy.

Like Bhutan and Nepal, Myanmar also is a strategically located country with long borders with China contiguous to India's

Arunachal Pradesh claimed by China as 'Southern Tibet'. In the 1990s, India's late Prime Minister P V Narasimha Rao, despite Western opposition, initiated the first significant Indian diplomatic outreach to an internationally isolated Myanmar.

The process has somewhat continued thereafter, but without the dynamism that should have been imparted. Prime Minister Modi's initiative in sending the foreign minister to Myanmar in the opening months of his government has injected the necessary dynamism to India's approach to Myanmar. Hopefully, prime minister himself would be able to visit this important neighbour in the near future.

Bangladesh was accorded a similar priority by the visit of Sushma Swaraj. Bangladesh, under the continuing present political dispensation of Sheikh Hasina, has valued friendly and cordial relations with India. It is a pity that the previous Congress government could not come up with matching fast-track initiatives.

In a well-timed, friendly gesture in July 2014, India gracefully accepted the maritime boundaries award given by the Permanent Arbitration Commission of United Nations arbitrating on maritime boundaries disputes. This was a significant confidence building measure extended by the Modi government to Bangladesh. It is an assurance that under his leadership, the river water sharing agreement would also take some positive shape. Interestingly, with this generous gesture, India's international reputation soared even as China has obdurately refused to accept any arbitration on the South China Sea disputes.

With Prime Minister Modi at the helm, India's atrophied foreign policy formulations and processes would acquire imaginative and dynamic contours befitting an emerging Asian Power and a global player.

SOUTH ASIAN ASSOCIATION FOR REGIONAL COOPERATION

The South Asian Association for Regional Cooperation (SAARC) is an economic and political organization of eight countries in Southern Asia. It was established on December 8, 1985 by Bangladesh, Bhutan, Maldives, Nepal, Pakistan, India and Sri

Lanka. In April 2007, at the Association's 14th summit, Afghanistan became its eighth member.

History

In the late 1970s, Bangladeshi President Ziaur Rahman proposed the creation of a trade bloc consisting of South Asian countries. The idea of regional cooperation in South Asia was again mooted in May 1980. The foreign secretaries of the seven countries met for the first time in Colombo in April 1981.

The Committee of the Whole, which met in Colombo in August 1981, identified five broad areas for regional cooperation. New areas of cooperation were added in the following years.

The objectives of the Association as defined in the Charter are:

- to promote the welfare of the people of South Asia and to improve their quality of life;
- to accelerate economic growth, social progress and cultural development in the region and to provide all individuals the opportunity to live in dignity and to realize their full potential;
- to promote and strengthen collective self-reliance among the countries of South Asia;
- to contribute to mutual trust, understanding and appreciation of one another's problems;
- to promote active collaboration and mutual assistance in the economic, social, cultural, technical and scientific fields;
- to strengthen cooperation with other developing countries;
- to strengthen cooperation among themselves in international forums on matters of common interest; and
- to cooperate with international and regional organisations with similar aims and purposes.

The Declaration on South Asian Regional Cooperation was adopted by the Foreign Ministers in 1983 in New Delhi. During the meeting, the Ministers also launched the Integrated Programme of Action (IPA) in nine agreed areas, namely, Agriculture; Rural Development; Telecommunications; Meteorology; Health and Population Activities; Transport; Postal Services; Science and

Technology; and Sports, Arts and Culture. The South Asian Association for Regional Cooperation (SAARC) was established when its Charter was formally adopted on 8 December 1985 by the Heads of State or Government of Bangladesh, Bhutan, India, Maldives, Nepal, Pakistan and Sri Lanka.

Afghanistan was added to the regional grouping at the behest of India on 13 November 2005, and became a member on 3 April 2007. With the addition of Afghanistan, the total number of member states were raised to eight (8). In April 2006, the United States of America and South Korea made formal requests to be granted observer status. The European Union has also indicated interest in being given observer status, and made a formal request for the same to the SAARC Council of Ministers meeting in July 2006. On 2 August 2006 the foreign ministers of the SAARC countries agreed in principle to grant observer status to the US, South Korea and the European Union. On 4 March 2007, Iran requested observer status. Followed shortly by the entrance of Mauritius.

Secretariat

The SAARC Secretariat was established in Kathmandu on 16 January 1987 and was inaugurated by Late King Birendra Bir Bikram Shah of Nepal.

It is headed by a Secretary General appointed by the Council of Ministers from Member Countries in alphabetical order for a three-year term. He is assisted by the Professional and the General Services Staff, and also an appropriate number of functional units called Divisions assigned to Directors on deputation from Member States. The Secretariat coordinates and monitors implementation of activities, prepares for and services meetings, and serves as a channel of communication between the Association and its Member States as well as other regional organizations.

The Memorandum of Understanding on the establishment of the Secretariat which was signed by Foreign Ministers of member countries on 17 November 1986 at Bangalore, India contains various clauses concerning the role, structure and administration of the SAARC Secretariat as well as the powers of the Secretary-General. In several recent meetings the heads of state or government of member states of SAARC have taken some important decisions and bold initiatives to strengthen the organisation and to widen and deepen regional co-operation.

The SAARC Secretariat and Member States observe 8 December as the SAARC Charter Day.

Criticism

Not enough is being done to for rapid economic integration of the region. Apart from the fact that the recently approved South Asian University and the creation of new rail lines linking the region, people to people contacts and connectivity of region needs to be strengthened.

Political Issues

SAARC has intentionally laid more stress on "core issues" mentioned above rather than more decisive political issues like the Kashmir dispute and the Sri Lankan civil war. However, political dialogue is often conducted on the margins of SAARC meetings. SAARC has also refrained itself from interfering in the internal matters of its member states. During the 12th and 13th SAARC summits, extreme emphasis was laid upon greater cooperation between the SAARC members to fight terrorism.

Free Trade Agreement

Over the years, the SAARC members have expressed their unwillingness on signing a free trade agreement. Though India has several trade pacts with Maldives, Nepal, Bhutan and Sri Lanka, similar trade agreements with Pakistan and Bangladesh have been stalled due to political and economic concerns on both sides. India has been constructing a barrier across its borders with Bangladesh and Pakistan. In 1993, SAARC countries signed an agreement to gradually lower tariffs within the region, in Dhaka. Eleven years later, at the 12th SAARC Summit at Islamabad, SAARC countries devised the South Asia Free Trade Agreement which created a framework for the establishment of a free trade area covering 1.4 billion people. This agreement went into force on January 1, 2006. Under this agreement, SAARC members will bring their duties down to 20 per cent by 2007.

DHAKA 2005 SUMMIT

The summit accorded observer status to People's Republic of China, Japan, South Korea and United States of America. The nations also agreed to organize development funds under a single financial institution with a permanent secretariat, that would cover all SAARC programs and also ranging from social, to infrastructure, to economic ones.

Membership

Current members (alphabetically):

- Afghanistan
- Bangladesh
- Bhutan
- India
- Maldives
- Nepal
- Pakistan
- Sri Lanka.

Observers:

- Australia
- China
- European Union
- Iran
- Japan
- Mauritius
- Myanmar (Burma)
- South Korea
- United States.

Future membership:

- The People's Republic of China has shown its interest in joining SAARC. While Pakistan and Bangladesh support China's candidature, India is against the prospect of Chinese membership. China's entry in to SAARC will likely balance India's overbearing presence there. However, during the 2005 Dhaka summit, India agreed on granting observer status to the PRC along with Japan. During the 14th summit, Nepal along with Pakistan and Bangladesh, announced their support for the membership of China. China seeks greater involvement in SAARC, however, finds it too early to apply for full membership.

- Indonesia intends to become an observer as well, and is supported by Sri Lanka.
- Iran, a state with borders to two SAARC members, has traditionally enjoyed strong cultural, economic and political relationships with Afghanistan and Pakistan and has expressed its desire to become a member of the South Asian organization. On 22 February 2005, the Foreign Minister of Iran, Kamal Kharrazi, indicated Iran's interest in joining SAARC by saying that his country could provide the region with "East-West connectivity". On 3 March 2007, Iran asked to join the SAARC as an observer. SAARC Secretary-General Lyonpo Chenkyab Dorji responded by saying that Iran's request for observer status would be taken up during a meeting of ministers of foreign affairs of SAARC member countries in the 3 April summit in New Delhi.
- Russia intends to become an observer as well, and is supported by India.
- Myanmar has expressed an interest in joining as a full member. If done so, Myanmar will become the ninth member in the group. India is currently backing Myanmar. Myanmar's military regime officially applied for full SAARC membership in May 2008. However, the application is still being considered and the government is currently restricted to observer status.
- South Africa has participated in meetings.

SAARC Preferential Trading Arrangement

The Agreement on SAARC Preferential Trading Arrangement (SAPTA) was signed on 11 April 1993 and entered into force on 7 December 1995, with the desire of the Member States of SAARC (India, Pakistan, Nepal, Sri Lanka, Bangladesh, Bhutan and the

Maldives) to promote and sustain mutual trade and economic cooperation within the SAARC region through the exchange of concessions.

The establishment of an Inter-Governmental Group (IGG) to formulate an agreement to establish a SAPTA by 1997 was approved in the *Sixth Summit of SAARC* held in Colombo in December 1991.

The basic principles underlying SAPTA are:

1. overall reciprocity and mutuality of advantages so as to benefit equitably all Contracting States, taking into account their respective level of economic and industrial development, the pattern of their external trade, and trade and tariff policies and systems;
2. negotiation of *tariff reform* step by step, improved and extended in successive stages through periodic reviews;
3. recognition of the special needs of the Least Developed Contracting States and agreement on *concrete preferential measures* in their favour;
4. inclusion of all products, manufactures and commodities in their raw, semi-processed and processed forms.

So far, four rounds of trade negotiations have been concluded under SAPTA covering over 5000 commodities.

SOUTH ASIAN FREE TRADE AREA

The Agreement on the South Asian Free Trade Area is an agreement reached at the 12th SAARC summit at Islamabad, capital of Pakistan on 6 January 2004. It creates a framework for the creation of a free trade area covering 1.4 billion people in India, Pakistan, Nepal, Sri Lanka, Bangladesh, Bhutan and the Maldives. The seven foreign ministers of the region signed a framework agreement on SAFTA with zero customs duty on the trade of practically all products in the region by end 2016. The new agreement i.e. SAFTA, came into being on 1 January 2006 and will be operational following the ratification of the agreement by the seven governments.

SAFTA requires the developing countries in South Asia, that is, India, Pakistan and Sri Lanka, to bring their duties down to 20 percent in the first phase of the two year period ending in 2007. In the final five year phase ending 2012, the 20 percent duty will be reduced to zero in a series of annual cuts. The least developed nations in South Asia consisting of Nepal, Bhutan, Bangladesh and Maldives have an additional three years to reduce tariffs to zero. India and Pakistan have signed but not ratified the treaty.

Bimstec

Bay of Bengal Initiative for Multi Sectoral Technical and Economic Cooperation (BIMSTEC) is an international organisation involving a group of countries in South Asia and South East Asia. The member countries of this group are: Bangladesh, India, Myanmar, Sri Lanka, Thailand, Bhutan and Nepal.

Background

On 6 June 1997, a new sub-regional grouping was formed in Bangkok and given the name BIST-EC (Bangladesh, India, Sri Lanka, and Thailand Economic Cooperation). Myanmar attended the inaugural June Meeting as an observer and joined the organization as a full member at a Special Ministerial Meeting held in Bangkok on 22 December 1997, upon which the name of the grouping was changed to BIMST-EC. Nepal was granted observer status by the second Ministerial Meeting in Dhaka in December 1998. Subsequently, full membership has been granted to Nepal and Bhutan in 2004. In the first Summit on 31 July 2004, leaders of the group agreed that the name of the grouping should be known as BIMSTEC or the Bay of Bengal Initiative for Multi-Sectoral Technical and Economic Cooperation.

Aims and Purposes

According to the Bangkok Declaration on the Establishment of BIST-EC, the aims and purposes of BIST-EC/BIMST-EC are to create an enabling environment for rapid economic development, accelerate social progress in the sub-region, promote active collaboration and mutual assistance on matters of common interest, provide assistance to each other in the form of training and research facilities, cooperate more effectively in joint efforts that are supportive of, and complementary to national development plans of member states, maintain close and beneficial cooperation with existing international and regional organizations, and cooperate in projects that can be dealt with most productively on a sub-regional basis and which make best use of available synergies.

Bimstec was initiated with the goal to combine the 'Look West' policy of Thailand and Asean with the 'Look East' policy of India and South Asia. So it could be explained that Bimstec is a link between Asean and Saarc. Seven members of Bimstec covers 13 Priority Sectors led by member countries in a voluntary manner namely, Trade & Investment, Technology, Energy, Transport & Communication, Tourism, Fisheries, Agriculture, Cultural Cooperation, Environment and Disaster Management, Public Health, People-to-People Contact, Poverty Alleviation and Counter-Terrorism and Transnational Crimes.

What make Bimstec different from other organization would be that Bimstec represent one of the most diverse regions of the world, be it, way of life, religion, language, culture, etc. Bimstec clearly separates issues of development into 13 Priority Sectors besides focusing only on economic cooperation which make Bimstec covers all aspects regarding the word 'developing'. Bimstec provides a unique link between South Asia and Southeast Asia bringing together 1.3 billion people - 21 percent of the world population, a combined GDP of US$750 billion, and a considerable amount of complementarities. A study shows the potential of US$ 43 to 59 billion trade creation under Bimstec FTA.

Regarding economic aspect, Bimstec has Trade Negotiating Committee (Bimtec TNC). The 16th TNC meeting was held during 17-21 March 2008 in India. The 17th TNC meeting was held during 15-17 October 2008 in Colombo, Sri Lanka. TNC Meeting is now working on the List of Goods regarding the Framework Agreement that has been signed in 2004. So far, Bimstec has been working on the FTA and looking forward to finalise our agreement soon.

Membership Criteria

Eligibility: Countries seeking membership should satisfy the conditions of territorial contiguity to, or direct opening into, or primary dependence on the Bay of Bengal for trade and transportation purposes.

Procedure: All applications should be submitted in writing to the Chairman of BIMSTEC. The decision on admitting new members will be taken on the basis of consensus by all the BIMSTEC members. Institutional Structure and Arrangements The BIST-EC Declaration provides for the following institutional mechanisms:

- Annual Ministerial Meetings, which shall be hosted by the Member States on the basis of alphabetical rotation.
- Senior Officials Committee, which shall meet on a regular basis as and when required.
- A Working Group, under the chairmanship of Thailand and having as its members the accredited Ambassadors to Thailand, or their representatives, of the other Member States, to carry on the work in between Annual Ministerial Meetings.
- Specialized task forces and other mechanisms as may be deemed necessary by the senior Officials to be coordinated by Member States as appropriate.

BIMSTEC Priority Sectors

BIMSTEC has thirteen priority sectors cover all areas of cooperation. Six priority sectors of cooperation were identified at the 2nd Ministerial Meeting in Dhaka on 19 November 1998. They include the followings:

1. Trade and Investment, led by Bangladesh
2. Transport and Communication, led by India
3. Energy, led by Myanmar
4. Tourism, led by India
5. Technology, led by Sri Lanka
6. Fisheries, led by Thailand After the 8th Ministerial Meeting in Dhaka on 18-19 December 2005, a number of new areas of cooperation emerged. The number of priority sectors of cooperation increased from 6 to 13. The 7 new sectors were discussed in the 1st BIMSTEC Summit and there has been various activities to enhance those co-operations ever since. The sectors are as follows,
7. Agriculture, led by Myanmar

8. Public Health, led by Thailand
9. Poverty Alleviation, led by Nepal
10. Counter-Terrorism and Transnational Crime, led by India
11. Environment and Natural Disaster Management, led by India
12. Culture, led by Bhutan
13. People to People contact, led by Thailand.

Chairmanship

BIMSTEC uses the alphabetical order for the Chairmanship. The Chairmanship of BIMSTEC has been taken in rotation commencing with Bangladesh (1997 - 1999), India (2000) Myanmar (2001-2002), Sri Lanka (2002 - 2003), Thailand (2003 – 2005), Bangladesh (2005-2006). Bhutan asked for the skip. So it's turned to India (2006-2009).

In November 2009, Myanmar hosted the 12th Ministerial Meeting and assumed BIMSTEC Chairmanship.

Cooperation with ADB

ADB has become BIMSTEC's development partner since 2005, to undertake a study which is designed to help promote and improve transport infrastructure and logistic among the BIMSTEC countries. So far, ADB has already finished the project so called BIMSTEC Transport Infrastructure and Logistic Study (BTILS). The final report of the said study from ADB has already been conveyed to all members and being awaited for the feedback. Other fields of cooperation will be designed later on.

BIMSTEC Centre

At the Sixth BIMSTEC Ministerial Meeting on 8 February 2004 in Phuket, Ministers endorsed the setting up of a Technical Support Facility (TSF). As reflected in the Ministerial Joint Statement, this Technical Support Facility would "serve the BIMSTEC Working Group (BWG) and to coordinate BIMSTEC activities, including those of the BIMSTEC Chamber of Commerce, for a trial period of two years". The decision by the Ministers was based upon the recommendation proposed by BIMSTEC Senior Officials who met in Bangkok during 17-19 September 2003. On this particular item, the SOM had with them a draft report prepared by Mr. David Oldfield, an ESCAP consultant, on "Towards Setting up a BIMSTEC Technical Support Facility and Permanent Secretariat: Considerations and Options". The report recommended that a TSF should be set up in Bangkok and would initially serve just the BWG during the trial period of 2 years.

Since the Establishment of the Permanent Secretariat is awaited to consider in the 2nd Summit, which will be held on 12-13 November 2008 in India, Thailand had already extended the contract of the BIMSTEC Centre for another year from June 2007 - May 2008. So far, the Ministry of Foreign Affairs of Thailand had recently extended the contract for another year from 1 June 2008 – 31 May 2009.

NEWS ANALYSIS OF SAARC SOUTH ASIAN ASSOCIATION FOR REGIONAL COOPERATION

The South Asian Association for Regional Cooperation (SAARC) was established when its Charter was formally adopted on 8 December 1985 by the Heads of State or Government of Bangladesh, Bhutan, India, Maldives, Nepal, Pakistan and SriLanka. The Association provides a platform for the peoples of South Asia to work together in a spirit of friendship, trust and understanding. It aims to promote the welfare of the peoples of South Asia and to improve their quality of life through accelerated economic growth, social progress and cultural development in the region.

Cooperation in the SAARC is based on respect for the principles of sovereign equality, territorial integrity, political independence, noninterference in internal affairs of the Member States and mutual benefit. Regional cooperation is seen as a complement to the bilateral and multilateral relations of SAARC Member States. Decisions are taken on the basis of unanimity. Bilateral and contentious issues are excluded from the deliberations of SAARC. The SAARC Secretariat is based in Kathmandu. It coordinates and monitors implementation of activities, prepares for and services meetings, and serves as a channel of communication between the Association and its Member States as well as other regional organizations. The Secretariat is headed by the Secretary General, who is appointed by the Council of Ministers from Member Countries in alphabetical order for a three-year term. Mr. Q.A.M.A. Rahim from Bangladesh is the current Secretary General. The previous Secretaries General were from Bangladesh, India, Maldives, Nepal, Pakistan and Sri Lanka. The next Secretary General is to be from Bhutan.

The availability of real time maritime intelligence from South and South East Asian countries has been a key factor in the Sri Lankan navy's recent stunning successes against the intrepid and innovative naval wing of the LTTE. (Intelligence Key To Navy's Success: Source, *Hindustan Times*, Correspondent or Reporter, Oct 31, 2007) Pakistan said Monday that it would go ahead with the multi-billion Iran-Pakistan-India (IPI) gas pipeline project.

Pakistan will join hands with India to combat extremism and work with other SAARC countries to develop a mechanism for exchanging information to curb terrorism and drug trafficking, interior minister Aftab Ahmed Khan Sherpao has said. There was solid basis for New Delhi's response to the blasts in Karachi. The two countries are in the process of evolving a mechanism for police cooperation against terrorism and it is in India's interest to make Benazir conform to the....

The SAARC members on Thursday decided to strengthen cooperation in combating terror and crime, with a meeting of home ministers, chaired by Union Home Minister Shivraj Patil, agreeing to a bi-annual meeting of police chiefs.

Saarc countries on Thursday decided to have regular exchange of information to combat terrorism and to work towards establishing a convention for mutual legal assistance in criminal matters. Viewing terrorism as a "serious threat" to South Asia's peace and development, SAARC countries today decided to have regular exchange of information to combat the menace and push efforts for establishing a convention for mutual legal assistance... (SAARC Vows To Combat Terror, *Hindu*, Correspondent or Reporter, Oct 26, 2007)

Home Ministers of SAARC countries on Thursday said terrorism remained a serious threat to peace and development in the region and called upon the member-states to strengthen institutional mechanisms to fight it effectively. (Terrorism A Serious Threat: SAARC, *Hindu*, Correspondent or Reporter, Oct 26, 2007)

Acknowledging that terrorism remains a serious threat to sustainable peace and development of South Asia, SAARC countries underlined the need to give an added push to evolving a treaty on mutual legal assistance with the home or interior ministers... (SAARC Nations For Evolving Treaty On Mutual Legal Aid, *Tribune*, A N Sudarsan Rao, Oct 26, 2007)

After the Karachi bloodbath on October 19 the global condemnation of the terrorists' act and commiseration for Pakistan and Ms Benazir Bhutto was on the expected lines. (Cooperate To End Terrorism, *Tribune*, Gen V.P. Malik (retd), Oct 26, 2007)

Home Secretaries of SAARC countries on Wednesday resolved to move forward in the matter of mutual assistance to check terrorism and trans-border crimes and expressed the need for better cooperation among police organisations of member-countries. (SAARC Ministers On Mutual Assistance To Check Terrorism, *Pioneer*, Correspondent or Reporter, Oct 25, 2007)

Agreeing to share information to check trans-border crimes, police chiefs from SAARC nations on Tuesday suggested a database that could help security agencies combat terrorism, narcotics smuggling and cyber crime. (SAARC Meet: New Database To Combat Terrorism, *Indian Express*, Correspondent or Reporter, Oct 24, 2007). Member countries of the South Asian Association for Regional Cooperation on Tuesday proposed the creation of a database among them for a coordinated action against terrorism, drug trafficking, cyber crimes and financial frauds. (S. Asian Terror Database Proposed, *Dawn*, Jawed Naqvi, Oct 24, 2007)

High-voltage talks are on this week to counter terrorism in the subcontinent, and it may just be coincidental that the move comes in the wake of explosions in Ajmer, Ludhiana and Karachi. (Edits, *Statesman*, Editorial, Statesman, Oct 24, 2007)

India and Pakistan today agreed to work together for identifying measures to beef up the anti-terror mechanism in the light of information shared earlier by the two on terrorist incidents and terror related activities. (India, Pakistan Agree To Work On

Anti-Terror Mechanism, *Statesman,* Correspondent or Reporter, Oct 23, 2007)

The second annual meeting of the SAARC home ministers will begin here tomorrow to hammer out a treaty on mutual legal assistance in criminal matters, forming a regional police forum and evolving a comprehensive mechanism for tackling terror...... (SAARC Home Ministers' Meeting Today, *Tribune,* Correspondent or Reporter, Oct 23, 2007)

India will host the second meeting of SAARC Interior/Home Ministers from Tuesday preceded by second meeting of SAARC Home Secretaries and the sixth SAARC Cooperation on Police Matters. (India To Host SAARC Ministerial Meet, *Pioneer,* Correspondent or Reporter, Oct 23, 2007)

The Pakistani link to the recent terror strikes in Hyderabad, Ajmer and Ludhiana came to the fore on Monday as India sought Pakistan's help in tracking down suspects who are believed to have cross-border links. (At Anti-Terror Meet, India Seeks Pak'S Help In Tracking Bombers, *Indian Express,* Correspondent or Reporter, Oct 23, 2007)

India and Pakistan will hold the second meeting of the Joint Anti-Terrorism Mechanism (JATM) here on Monday, during which Islamabad is expected to raise the issue of Samjhauta Express blast inquiry report. (Second Round Of Indo-Pak Jatm Talks On Monday, *The Economic Times,* Correspondent or Reporter, Oct 22, 2007)

With the British government more or less towing the American line on Iran albeit indirectly and the American pressure on India to clear its stand on the "errant" Iranian President, it looks like from SAARC (South Asian Association for Regional.... (India, Afghan And The Nam, Deccan Herald, Deepali Gaur Singh, Oct 10, 2007)

CLIMATE CHANGE: INDIA TO SIGN TREATY WITH SAARC NATIONS

Marking a shift from its earlier position of staying within the United Nations Framework Convention on Climate Changes, India now appears ready to collaborate with various countries on climate change. On top of the list are the US, China and Japan. In a bid to present itself as a leader on climate change issues in the SAARC region, India is set to sign a treaty on environment with SAARC countries, the draft text of which is ready, *The Indian Express* has learnt. India has also discussed the possibility of a bilateral cooperation with Japan on thermal technology which cuts down on greenhouse gases.

Minister of Environment and Forests Jairam Ramesh met Japanese Environment Minister Sakihito Ozawa on Monday on the issue. SAARC Environment Ministers are at present in New Delhi. On Tuesday, the SAARC delegates are expected to release a joint environmental statement.

Ministry officials said the cooperation will chiefly be in the regions of forestry, biodiversity and wildlife and coastal management. Ramesh, speaking to *The Indian Express*, indicated that India needed to look beyond the Kyoto Protocol. "India has multiple messages to give on climate change, and India cannot be Doctor No," he said. "We are engaging with China, Japan and the US on climate change." This includes, he said, "being open to the discussion of a bilateral with Japan on climate change technologies." The focus is on reducing greenhouse gases through better coal-based thermal power technologies. "We are discussing with Japan coal-based power generation with less greenhouse gases. Japan is helping us with that."

In yet another shift, India seems set to be a donor in the issue of tackling climate change. It will give one-time grants for forestry and coastal management, Ramesh said. "We are looking at assuming a prominent role for climate change and environment in South Asia. The draft for a new environment agreement is also ready from India's side. The crux will be technology and financial transfer. Climate change is becoming a very important issue for SAARC, the theme of the April 2010 SAARC meet at Thimpu will be climate change. We are making one time grants of one million dollars to the SAARC forestry Centre, Thimpu, and one million dollars to SAARC Coastal Management Zone, Maldives.," he said. On a bilateral agreement with the US, Ramesh said: "We are open to it. The PM will discuss this with US President Barack Obama next month. The discussions are likely to be on energy security."

4

India's Foreign Policies in South Asia

INTRODUCTORY BACKGROUND

India's foreign policies in recent years have made commendable progress in terms of relations with major world powers. Relations with the United States are moving towards more strategic cooperation to secure India's national security interests. China despite its traditional rhetoric has seen the wisdom of greater economic cooperation with India and departing from its hostility following the 1998 nuclear tests by India. European Union Countries and Russia have modulated their policies towards India to exploit the vast defence purchase market and economic opportunities that India presents.

However, despite all of the above India's foreign policies in South Asia need a drastic review. If there is a growing recognition worldwide that India is a power to reckon with in South Asia and an emerging key player in global affairs, then India, at the first instance needs to reinforce and press home this reality in the South Asian neighborhood.

India's failure to create this impact in South Asia arises from a combination of the following factors:

- India's lack of political will to use her power to ensure that South Asian nations recognize India's predominance in the Indian sub-continent and the Indian Ocean.

- India's soft handling of Pakistan's "spoiler state" strategies both as a hand-maiden of intrusive external powers and its attempts to provoke other South Asian nations to adopt belittling policies towards India.
- India's inability to spell out firmly to USA and China that while they are free to follow their national interests in Pakistan, their future relationships with India would depend on their demonstrated sensitivity to India's national interests in South Asia and that these cannot be made subservient to theirs.

India therefore has to review and modulate its policies towards South Asian countries by giving predominance to India's strategic imperatives of creating a peaceful South Asian neighbourhood. South Asia as a peaceful region can only emerge by strong and firm Indian policies that brook no playing around with India's national interests. With the above in mind, some view points are expressed below in relation to our foreign policy formulations towards the countries of the region.

PAKISTAN

Pakistan has emerged as a "rogue nuclear state" however much the United States may like to paint it white. It has proliferated uranium enrichment technology to North Korea and Iran too (estimative analysis) and thereby jeopardizing vital United States strategic interests in East Asia and the Middle East. This is taking place with the assistance of and bidding of China. India should not therefore depend on or expect United States and China to restrain Pakistan's disruptive policies in South Asia. In relation to bringing Pakistan to heel in South Asia, India's foreign policies concerning Pakistan must incorporate the following ingredients:

- Pakistan's proxy war against India needs to be carried back into Pakistan. Self-determination movements in Sindh, Baluchistan, Pashtunistan and Northern Areas need to be exploited. India's oft-quoted 'pro-active policies' must be put into effect here.
- Pakistan based terrorist organizations must be struck the way the Israel strikes back at its opponents.

- India's foreign policies and military policies lack the essential ingredient of "Psychological Warfare" and allied operations.
- Pakistan Army's stranglehold over the Pakistani nation-state and thwarting the emergence of democracy and pluralism in Pakistan needs to be vigorously exposed as part of the above operation.
- India must impose an arms-race on Pakistan the pace of which Pakistan can ill-afford economically and nor can its external patrons subsidise.
- In relation to Pakistan, India must make it clear to the other South Asian countries, that they have to choose between India and Pakistan in South Asia. "Either you are with us, or against us" and if their choice is "against us" they should be prepared to face the consequences of their choice.

Some may like to argue that the above are not realistic steps and that India does not have the capabilities to do so. This author would like to maintain, that it is within India's means to do so seeing India's preponderant power attributes. All that India needs is to give a 'shaped-charge' focus to these factors and re-order its priorities in its foreign policies.

As a starter, let India change its stand in relations to the conditions it stipulates for resumption of dialogue with Pakistan. India's strong-man, Deputy PM Advani's constant refrain is that unless Pakistan returns the persons in the "list of 20" no dialogue can take place.

This is not an advisable stand as it reduces India to the level of trading far more important considerations in its approaches towards Pakistan than the extradition of 20 street-side hoodlums.

India's conditions for resumption of dialogue with Pakistan need to rest on far more important considerations, namely that:

- India will enter into dialogue with Pakistan only when a democratically elected government comes into power, through elections supervised by international observers.
- India will not enter into dialogue with Pakistan based on Pakistani imposed pre-conditions of Kashmir and the rest.

- India should maintain that Kashmir is not an issue historically nor is it now. Kashmir's accession to India is non-negotiable as per the unanimous resolution of the Special Session of the Indian Parliament.
- India will enter into a dialogue with Pakistan only when it begins to respect the sanctity of the Line of Actual Control (LAC) in Jammu and Kashmir-a point endorsed by the United States through President Clinton's statement.

Social Relations

Cultural Links

India and Pakistan, to some degree have similar cultures, cuisines and languages which underpin the historical ties between the two. Pakistani singers, musicians, comedians and entertainers have enjoyed widespread popularity in India, with many achieving overnight fame in the Indian filming industry Bollywood.

Likewise, Indian music and films are very popular in Pakistan. Being located in the northernmost region of the South Asia, Pakistan's culture is somewhat similar to that of North India. The Punjab region was split into Punjab, Pakistan and Punjab, India following the independence and partition of the two countries in 1947.

The Punjabi people are today the largest ethnic group in Pakistan and also an important ethnic group of northern India. The founder of the Sikhism religion was born in the modern-day Pakistani Punjab province, in the city of Nankana Sahib. Each year, millions of Indian Sikh pilgrims cross over to visit holy Sikh sites in Nankana Sahib.

The Sindhi people are the native ethnic group of the Pakistani province of Sindh. Many Hindu Sindhis migrated to India in 1947, making the country home to a sizable Sindhi community. In addition, the millions of Muslims who migrated from India to the newly-created Pakistan during independence came to be known as the Muhajir people; they are settled predominantly in Karachi and still maintain family links in India.

Relations between Pakistan and India have also resumed through platforms such as media and communications. Aman ki

Asha is a joint venture and campaign between *The Times of India* and the *Jang Group* calling for mutual peace and development of diplomatic and cultural relations.

Geographic Links

The Indo-Pakistani border is the official international boundary that demarcates the Indian states of Punjab,Rajasthan and Gujarat from the Pakistani provinces of Punjab and Sindh. The Wagah border is the only road crossing between India and Pakistan and lies on the famous Grand Trunk Road, connecting Lahore, Pakistan withAmritsar, India. Each evening, the Wagah border ceremony takes place at the Wagah border in which the flags are lowered and guards on both sides make a pompous military display and exchange handshakes.

Linguistic Ties

Hindustani is the linga franca of North India and Pakistan, as well as the national language of both countries, under the name Hindi and Urdu, respectively. Standard Urdu is mutually intelligible with Standard Hindi. Both languages share the same Indic base and are all but indistinguishable in phonology and grammar. Most linguists consider them to be two standardized forms of a same language; when speaking colloquially, a speaker of Urdu has no trouble understanding a speaker of Hindi.

Apart from Hindustani, India and Pakistan also share a distribution of the Punjabi language (written in the Gurmukhiscript in Indian Punjab, and the Shahmukhi script in Pakistani Punjab), Kashmiri language and Sindhi language.

Matrimonial Ties

Some Indian and Pakistani people marry across the border, particularly with present generation of relatives who had migrated from India at the time of partition.

In April 2010 a high profile Pakistani cricketer, Shoaib Malik married the Indian tennis star Sania Mirza. The wedding received much media attention and was said to transfix both India and Pakistan.

Sporting Ties

Cricket and hockey matches between the two (as well as other sports to a lesser degree such as those of the SAARC games) have often been political in nature. During theSoviet invasion of Afghanistan General Zia-ul Haq traveled to India for a bout of "cricket diplomacy" to keep India from supporting the Soviets by opening another front. Pervez Musharaff also tried to do the same more than a decade later but to no avail.

In tennis, Rohan Bopanna of India and Aisam-ul-Haq Qureshi of Pakistan have formed a successful duo and have been dubbed as the "Indo-Pak Express."

Diasporic Relations

The large size of the Indian diaspora and Pakistani diaspora in many different countries throughout the world has created strong diasporic relations. British Indians and British Pakistanis, the largest and second-largest ethnic minorities living in the United Kingdom respectively, are said to have friendly relations with one another. It is quite common for a "Little India" and a "Little Pakistan" to co-exist in South Asian ethnic enclaves in overseas countries.

There are various cities such as Birmingham, Blackburn andManchester where British Indians and British Pakistanis live alongside each other in peace and harmony. Both Indians and Pakistanis living in the UK fit under the category ofBritish Asian. The UK is also home to the Pakistan & India friendship forum. In the United States, Indians and Pakistanis are classified under the South Asian Americancategory and share many cultural traits. The British MEP Saj Karim is of Pakistani origin. He is a member of the European Parliament Friends of India Group, Karim was also responsible for opening up Europe to free trade with India. He narrowly escaped the Mumbai attacks at Hotel Taj in November 2008. Despite the atrocity, Mr Karim does not wish the remaining killer Ajmal Kasab to be sentenced to death. He said: "I believe he had a fair and transparent trial and I support the guilty verdict. "But I am not a supporter of capital punishment. I believe he should be given a life sentence, but that life should mean life."

Trade Links

Trade across direct routes has been curtailed formally, so the bulk of India-Pakistan trade is routed through Dubai. Re-evaluation

The insurgents who initially started their movement as a pro-Kashmiri independence movement, have gone through a lot of change in their ideology. Most of the insurgents portray their struggle as a religious one. Indian analysts allege that by supporting these insurgents, Pakistan is trying to wage a proxy war against India while Pakistan claims that it regards most of these insurgentgroups as "freedom fighters" rather than terrorists

Internationally known to be the most deadly theatre of conflict, nearly 10 million people, including Muslims, Hindus, and Buddhists, have been fighting a daily battle for survival. The *cross-border firing* between India and Pakistan, and the terrorist attacks combined have taken its toll on the Kashmiris, who have suffered poor living standards and an erosion of human rights.

Indo-Pak Relations: Pragmatism on Kashmir

Though its use in development of WMD is terrible, science has delivered uncountable comforts to mankind. No only that, it is a great social equalizer also. It has helped the humanity to break the millennia old chained social connections. No individual is superior now on the basis of race, religion and region. Whosoever excels in knowledge can enter into the world of his choice. It was not possible earlier because differentiation and its worst forms such as apartheid, caste system and slavery were being practiced puritanically. The science-induced civility has influenced the psyche of nations also. Hence, assimilation or annihilation of small nations is no more possible. Subjugation, however, still continues, and the poverty of knowledge is the only reason behind it. The victims instead of learning and improving their economies are engaged in confrontation from within and without. Who are to be blamed more, literate outsiders or indifferent insiders?

Chances to bring about change inside are always there, and chances to end external confrontation also appear quite often, but they are not availed due to the indecisiveness of leadership. Though the repeated indecisiveness of small nations usually makes them lose more, it does not spare the big nations either? After WW II, the Soviets should have gone for revision of their stagnant system; fifties was the proper time: they wanted to do it, but didn't, and when they did it, they were too late; and eventually the break-up of the Soviet Union was the only remedy left with them.

The situation in the Indian subcontinent is not so grim, so far. But, given the faulty perceptions and indecisiveness of its rulers, it is likely to become so. The concept that militancy in Kashmir is keeping the Kashmir issue alive, and it is bleeding the Indians, is simplistic, cruel, retaliatory, and self-destructive: In this age of enlightenment it is not possible to assimilate or annihilate small nations. So, until Kashmiris are satisfied, their peaceful struggle too will create an impact, which would not be negative as created by the militancy. It would be humane and reconciliatory, and hence positive. As far as Pakistan is concerned, it has become totally dependent economically, as its strategy of bleeding India has backfired. Accordingly India too has failed. Its militarism, even if in retaliation to militancy, has made it lose much; if not technically, on moral front certainly. What is needed is immediate end to confrontation and start of positive engagement. Both activities should start simultaneously. It is a difficult decision but it must be taken.

Leadership of Indian subcontinent took many bold and timely decisions in the past. It arrived at a consensus plan to divide India. Afterwards the Liaqat-Nehru Pact on the question of refugees saved Pakistan from unthinkable miseries. Similarly the most difficult of all the questions, the question of lifeline, the water dispute, was resolved through Indus Basin Treaty. But all the good that happened between India and Pakistan is neither discussed nor appreciated in both the countries. However not everything that happened between the two was good. There were grey areas as well, such as wars of 1948, 1965 and 1971, and warlike clashes in Khem Karn, Siachin and Kargil. Alongside these open examples of extreme confrontation, both countries subtly attempted to increase the intensity of each other's internal and external conflicts. Pakistan supported Sikh and Kashmiri struggles and India attempted to fuel the ethnic tension in Sindh.

Why did the good and bad strategies run side by side in Indo-Pak relationship is a very complicated question. However, if answer is to be summarized in one sentence then it can be said with clarity that the fears created problems, and commonness and commonsense led to solution of some of them and those, which remained unresolved remained so mostly due to indecisiveness of the leadership who had faulty perceptions about the ground realities. Any way the prevailing situation demands complete halt to the confrontation, militancy and militarism, because it has already done a lot of damage, and its continuity would inflict more, and that may eventually lead to irreversibility.

It is widely believed that the source that created tension and ills in the subcontinent is issue of Kashmir. Though it is not even the half-truth, let us take it as such. Again the key to solution of Kashmir issue lies with the leadership of India and Pakistan, and not with the Kashmiris. If India could surrender twenty percent of Kashmir to China in Aksi Chin, if Pakistan could settle Kashmir border issue with China—on Chinese terms, and if India and Pakistan could decide the fate of three rivers of Kashmir, then what does stop them from solving the issue in totality?

However, to find an achievable and acceptable solution is not that easy. The process would first require that the parties involved must turn to acceptance of existing realties and try to know how they were shaped. Kashmir was a part of undivided India, though with a status of princely state. Couple this sub-continental status with enormous confronting diversities that are located and locked in a complex and economically unviable geography of Kashmir, no one can and will take the Kashmiris as a separate nation in totality, no matter what they do, and how they fight; and the earlier this is understood, by the Kashmiris of valley, the better. Allow me to elaborate the argument. Kashmir cannot become independent – though in future it may get a special status under the joint Indo-Pak protection – because of its geography and small resources, and also due to the fact that there is a terrible division among the Kashmiris themselves that has basis in religion, ethnicity, geography and desires. The Gilgatis and Baltis do not count themselves as Kashmiris, and they will prefer that their area should become a province of Pakistan at the earliest. The people of Jammu and Ladakh will be happier if their areas are given separate status of states within the Indian Union. The Azad Kashmiris have socially and economically merged themselves with the Pakistanis and it won't make any difference to them if the status of Azad Kashmir is changed to a province of Pakistan.

Accordingly, whether India is in Kashmir due to inhuman Instrument of Accession (designed jointly by the Muslim League and the Congress; on the insistence of the former) and muscle power, or Pakistan has annexed a part of Kashmir through war and support of Kashmiris, the fact remains that both have attained some kind of legitimacy and fifty-six years of occupation has further entrenched their claims. But Indians' legitimacy is, surely, under constant question in the valley of Kashmir. Though it has roots in the concept that divided India, the politico-economic mismanagement by the Indians played a bigger part. And the rest was done by the Pakistan backed resistance, though at a colossal cost that has brought destruction to everything – to life, to soul, to spirit, to intellect and even to the environment. Probable reconciliation between India and Pakistan would save the Kashmiris of valley from further destruction and recover the paradise lost, we can only hope and pray for that. But what is almost certain is that both countries will again be on the right road that was jointly built by their leadership through Liaqat-Nehru Pact, Indus Basin Treaty, Tashkent Declaration, Shimla Accord and Lahore Declaration. Now, once they are on the road, they should remain on it.

Why is the right road left so often, it looks strange when seen through a broader angle of affinity? That no two nations have as much common between them as Pakistanis and Indians, and this relationship could have been used positively to resolve the remaining contradictions: Instead they are persistently on a warpath. If the reason for that lies within India and Pakistan, then its solution needs to be searched within India and Pakistan, and not in Kashmir. If conflict of Kashmir is the reason, then that certainly has a solution within the premises of Kashmir. Let me elaborate the point. Many analysts present an attractive parallel logic that Kashmir conflict would continue, because it is being used to cover or delay or solve the bigger and terrible conflicts of ethnicity and communalism that exist within Pakistani and Indian societies.

Whatever the reasons and their epicenter, the solution of Kashmir problem must be found. After all for how long innocent Kashmiris, Indian soldiers and Pakistani soldiers would bleed due to it. The solution, however, would not be searched unless we accept many more realities alongside the ones that were debated above. Kashmir of 1947 exists no more and neither Pakistan nor India would surrender a single inch of Kashmir under their control to each other or to create an independent area for Kashmiris. Pakistan cannot afford to do so due to strategic and life (water) related compulsions. India too has strategic compulsions vis-à-vis China: Not only that any unfavorable alteration in area under its control will either create or aggravate immensely societal imbalances between its various ethnic and religious diversities. That is one reality; the other is that neither Pakistan nor India nor the Kashmiri militants can alter the status of the universally recognized Line of Control through force.

These realities and their relationship with the volatile situation in valley, and also with the Indo-Pak societies form the fundamentals, to which leaders of the two countries would certainly pay attention, when they sit to discuss the Kashmir conflict. There are time-bound rational solutions, to be implemented in various phases, which India would like to propose. It could be conditional Independence or greater autonomy or self-rule for Indian Controlled Kashmir (ICK). But differences would surface on whether or not such solution should remain within the parameters of the Indian Constitution. India would insist on keeping its constitutional link and Pakistan would, likely, disagree.

So, if efforts to put the Kashmir issue on front-burner fail, they would fail only due to egoism. Does that mean to remain on the road and to move forward, the issue should be put on backburner? Not necessarily, the Kashmiris of valley can do what elders of India did: Those who are involved in militancy should turn to peaceful struggle. On their part, India and Pakistan should enter into an interdependent economic engagement as early as possible.

It will not only help in finding an ultimate solution of Kashmir problem, but also help resolve the class, communal and ethnic contradictions of Indo-Pak societies. However, due to size and scope of its economy, the responsibility to evolve and nourish a mutually beneficial relationship mostly or perhaps totally lies with the Indians and the actual blueprint for that has to be prepared by them. How superbly it would work is not difficult to visualize. In this regard a simple example of gas pipelines from Iran and Central Asia to India, passing through Pakistan, would suffice. It would earn Pakistan 700 million dollars per annum and India would save billions of dollars through adoption of cheaper land route. Wouldn't it be an extraordinary achievement for both? Imagine how many doors Pakistan knocks at for assistance of a few hundred million dollars. Imagine also the after-affects of conditionalities attached to such assistance. Similarly look at the costly attempts and agreements that India is making or would make with various countries of the Gulf to secure its growing energy needs. Can't they adopt a wise route?

Besides gas pipelines, even oil lines are a possibility, and extending the interaction further would do magic for the economies of the two countries as the trade route, via land, from India to Europe would be opened. Here it must be understood that Pakistan would not act as an excise collecting state only. It would also gain in the fields where it is lagging far behind, and it is lagging in almost all the fields. Knowledge based manufacturing, which it couldn't attain through fifty years of its friendship with the others, China and America, would surely be achieved by acquiring this new relationship; and that is what the economic blueprint would also mean, and that would require India to invest a lot financially in gas lines and also in other areas.

The economic engagement would eventually lead to opening of Indo-Pak borders including that of Kashmir, and to defend them would also become a collective responsibility. Similarly with that magnitude of economic inter-activity the subjects of communication and the foreign policy would mostly become a mutual affair. Moreover the relationship in itself and social goodwill and the economic uplift connected to it would also help in solving the internal problems of ethnicity and communalism that have gripped the Indo-Pak societies. And a day would certainly come when Kashmir would be given a special status jointly by a prosperous Pakistan and a super power India, though that may happen after many decades.

The great nations have no ego problems. America withdrew from Vietnam and Russia from Afghanistan and it didn't reduce their honor and authority. West Germany recognized East Germany, and Egypt recognized Israel and that were the jobs no one would ever think of. And can there be a better example in entire history of mankind than the one that the Indian subcontinent provided. Division of a subcontinent was not a small thing. That it was attained peacefully through a consensus decision, taken by the Congress and the Muslim League, made the whole exercise unique and exemplary. If we were wiser fifty-five years ago, why cannot we act wisely now? And the time demands that the direction of wisdom should now be steered towards evolving a relationship on the pattern of European Union. Given the encouraging environment of today, and the political will of the present Indo-Pak leadership, it can be done. It must be done.

What if the newly appeared chance is not availed, which according to Prime Minister Vajpayee is the last attempt from his side? If cruelties continue, the Kashmiris would obviously continue to suffer. The Pakistanis would continue to live with the unaffordable conflicts, and that would certainly add to their poverty.

The Indians may not suffer as much immediately, but ultimately they too would repent. If the westward land route remains closed on them, they would lose a lot. Contained as they are now, they would remain so, for a long time to come; and that would surely stop them from becoming a major player in the world, and internally too their economic and social development would be curtailed drastically. Would Pakistan or India go for a war to change the status quo? No, they will not; at least not during the current decade.

Yet, the continuity of tension for a longer period would amount to the same, because the losses that a war brings in a short period would also be brought, though gradually, by the confrontation.

But, whether it is slow or sudden, poisoning remains poisoning. The times ahead would see the developed world preparing itself for a journey to a planet outside our solar system. Meanwhile where would the nations carrying the unbearable load of conflicts go: may be back to the mud houses: may be into the black holes of history: Who knows?

NEPAL

Nepal has been wracked by a Maoist insurgency for the last five or six years. India has remained a passive bystander witnessing the growing erosion of Nepal's state power.

Other than giving some military materiel for counter insurgency operations, no weighty measures have been taken.

India has not recognized the gravity of a Maoist take-over of Nepal as American analysts have done in depth. As per American analysts, the strategic implications of a Maoist take-over of Nepal are:

- Nepal becomes a total client state of China. A Maoist Nepal under Chinese tutelage would be a serious disruptive factor for US global strategies in the region.
- Maoist-insurgents ruled Nepal would inextricably get dragged into Islamic terrorist organizations linkages, besides China's policies towards the Islamic world.

India needs to realise the gravity of the strategic implications, specific to India, namely:

- A China-aligned Nepal, removes an important buffer state between India and China. India would have to militarily man the India-Nepal border in strength, which may eat up two to three infantry divisions.
- A China-aligned Nepal adds to the existing China-client states in South Asia i.e. Pakistan and Bangladesh. It would be a very unholy trinity with not only the Western and Eastern flanks of India under China's influence, but the Northern flank too added.
- For the majority peoples of India, the only Hindu kingdom in the world would slide down ignobly into a Chinese-Islamic coalition in South Asia.

India must therefore, immediately, cast away its existing reluctance and inhibitions to act firmly, even militarily, to prevent a Maoist take-over of Nepal. Fortunately in Nepal's current Maoist-threatened environment, convergence of security interests exist between the United States and India. India must therefore jointly work with the United States to protect the sovereignty of the Nepalese state against a Maoist takeover.

It was so stated by US Assistant Secretary of State, Christiana Rocca during her recent visit to New Delhi: " Working in tandem, our governments can help Nepal defeat the Maoists threat and re-establish democratic institutions responsive to the needs of the people".

India must therefore act forcefully and unapologetically in Nepal forthwith to secure her national interests. It would be a convincing demonstration of what this paper espouses: " India will intervene forcefully to secure her national interests in the region".

Independent Political History

1950-1970

In the 1950s, Nepal welcomed close relations with India, but as the number of Nepalese living and working in India increased and the involvement of India in Nepal's economy deepened in the 1960s and after, so too did Nepalese discomfort with the special relationship.

Tensions came to a head in the mid-1970s, when Nepal pressed for substantial amendments in its favour in the trade and transit treaty and openly criticized India's 1975 annexation of Sikkim which was considered as part of Greater Nepal. In 1975 King Birendra Bir Bikram Shah Dev proposed that Nepal be recognized internationally as a zone of peace; he received support from China and Pakistan.

In New Delhi's view, if the king's proposal did not contradict the 1950 treaty and was merely an extension of nonalignment, it was unnecessary; if it was a repudiation of the special relationship, it represented a possible threat to India's security and could not be endorsed. In 1984 Nepal repeated the proposal, but there was no reaction from India. Nepal continually promoted the proposal in international forums, with Chinese support; by 1990 it had won the support of 112 countries.

1970-1980

In 1978 India agreed to separate trade and transit treaties, satisfying a long-term Nepalese demand. In 1988, when the two treaties were up for renewal, Nepal's refusal to accommodate India's wishes on the transit treaty caused India to call for a single trade and transit treaty. Thereafter, Nepal took a hard-line position that led to a serious crisis in India-Nepal relations. After two extensions, the two treaties expired on March 23, 1989, resulting in a virtual Indian economic blockade of Nepal that lasted until late April 1990. Although economic issues were a major factor in the two countries' confrontation, Indian dissatisfaction with Nepal's 1988 acquisition of Chinese weaponry played an important role. treaty and letters exchanged in 1959 and 1965, which included Nepal in India's security zone and precluded arms purchases without India's approval. India linked security with economic relations and insisted on reviewing India-Nepal relations as a whole. Nepal had to back down after worsening economic conditions led to a change in Nepal's political system, in which the king was forced to institute a parliamentary democracy. The new government sought quick restoration of amicable relations with India.

1990s

The special security relationship between New Delhi and Kathmandu was reestablished during the June 1990 New Delhi meeting of Nepal's prime minister Krishna Prasad Bhattarai and Indian prime minister V.P. Singh. During the December 1991 visit to India by Nepalese prime minister Girija Prasad Koirala, the two countries signed new, separate trade and transit treaties and other economic agreements designed to accord Nepal additional economic benefits.

Indian-Nepali relations appeared to be undergoing still more reassessment when Nepal's prime minister Man Mohan Adhikary visited New Delhi in April 1995 and insisted on a major review of the 1950 peace and friendship treaty. In the face of benign statements by his Indian hosts relating to the treaty, Adhikary sought greater economic independence for his landlocked nation while simultaneously striving to improve ties with China.

21st Century

In 2005, after King Gyanendra took over, Nepalese relations with India soured. However, after the restoration of democracy, in 2008, Prachanda, the Prime Minister of Nepal, visited India, in September 2008. He spoke about a new dawn, in the bilateral relations, between the two countries. He said, "I am going back to Nepal as a satisfied person. I will tell Nepali citizens back home that a new era has dawned. Time has come to effect a revolutionary change in bilateral relations. On behalf of the new government, I assure you that we are committed to make a fresh start." He met Indian Prime minister, Manmohan Singh, and Foreign Minister, Pranab Mukherjee. He asked India to help Nepal frame a new constitution, and to invest in Nepal's infrastructure, and its tourism industry.

In 2008, Indo-Nepali ties got a further boost with an agreement to resume water talks after a 4 year hiatus. The Nepalese Water Resources Secretary Shanker Prasad Koirala said the Nepal-India Joint Committee on Water Resources meet decided to start the reconstruction of breached Kosi embankment after the water level goes down. During the Nepal PM's visit to New Delhi in September the two Prime Ministers expressed satisfaction at the age-old close, cordial and extensive relationships between their states and expressed their support and cooperation to further consolidate the relationship. The two issued a 22-point statement highlighting the need to review, adjust and update the 1950 Treaty of Peace and Friendship, amongst other agreements. India would also provide a credit line of up to 150 crore rupees to Nepal to ensure uninterrupted supplies of petroleum products, as well as lift bans on the export of rice, wheat, maize, sugar and sucrose for quantities agreed to with Nepal. India would also provide 20 crore as immediate flood relief.

In return, Nepal will take measures for the "promotion of investor friendly, enabling business environment to encourage

Indian...investments in Nepal." Furthermore, a three-tier mechanism at the level of ministerial, secretary and technical levels will be built to push forward discussions on the development of water resources between the two sides. Politically, India acknowledged a willingness to promote efforts towards peace in Nepal. Indian External affairs minister Pranab Mukherjee promised the Nepali Prime Minister Prachanda that he would "extend all possible help for peace and development."

In 2008, the Bollywood film *Chandni Chowk to China* was banned in Nepal, because of a scene suggesting the Gautama Buddha was born in India. Some protesters called for commercial boycott of all Indian films.

INDIA-NEPAL RELATIONS

India-Nepal relationship is shaped by the centuries old social-cultural, historical and geographic linkages. Extensive people-to-people contacts permeate all aspects of the lives of the people of India and Nepal and transcend borders and governments. Welfare of the people of the two countries is interlinked and developments in one country invariably have an impact on the other. Few other sovereign states in the world can take pride in a relationship as wide-ranging and multi-faceted as that shared between India and Nepal.

Beginning with the 12-Point Understanding reached between the Seven Party Alliance (SPA) and the Maoists in Delhi in November 2005. Government of India welcomed the roadmap laid down by the historic Comprehensive Peace Agreement of November 2006 towards political stabilization in Nepal through peaceful reconciliation and inclusive democratic processes, India has consistently responded with a sense of urgency to the needs of the people and Government of Nepal in ensuring the success of the peace process and institutionalization of multi-party democracy through the framing of a new Constitution by a duly elected Constituent Assembly. India was the first country to welcome the restoration of democracy in Nepal. India has also provided material assistance to strengthen the government machinery in Nepal and for successful CA elections. Overall, over

Rs.170 crores of assistance in the form of supply and equipment has been extended as part of India's support to the peace process in Nepal in response to requests from the Government of Nepal.

The visit of Prime Minister Hon'ble Mr. G.P. Koirala to India one month after the restoration of multi-party democracy in Nepal saw India extend a comprehensive package of assistance to help Nepal tide over immediate financial needs and support peace, democracy and stability. A comprehensive economic package worth Rs.1000 crores was announced during the visit. A soft credit line of USD 100 million for infrastructure development projects was extended, and outstanding dues on defence purchases worth NRs. 1.6 billion waived. Government of India also agreed to doubling the number of GOI scholarships for Nepalese students and to supply of 25,000 metric tons of fertilizers to Nepal at subsidized prices.

Prime Minister Hon'ble Pushpa Kamal Dahal 'Prachanda' paid an official visit to India from 14-17 September 2008, and met President, Vice President, Prime Minister, and External Affairs Minister as well as Chairperson of UPA and the Leader of Opposition. A Joint Press Statement was issued at the conclusion of the visit, reiterating the special features of the bilateral relationship and committing both sides to work towards further improving relations. India agreed to implement the Naumure hydro-electric project on Rapti river besides the Rs. 20 crores assistance for Kosi breach relief. Credit of up to Rs 150 crores was also provided to GON to ensure uninterrupted supplies of petroleum products. We have also permitted export of 10,000 tonnes of wheat and 15,000 tonnes of rice to Nepal, along with lifting of ban on other food items. PM Prachanda visited India again from November 12-14, 2008 to attend the BIMSTEC Summit.

The Foreign Minister of Nepal Hon'ble Mrs. Sujata Koirala visited India from 5-10 August 2009 where she held fruitful discussions with their counterparts. Foreign Secretary of India visited Nepal on 14-15 September 2009 to exchange views on the future course of cooperation between the two countries.

Prime Minister Hon'ble Mr. Madhav Kumar Nepal paid an official visit to India from August 18 – 22, 2009 at the invitation of the Prime Minister of India. The two leaders had also met earlier on the sidelines of the XVth NAM Summit in Sherm-el-Sheikh, Egypt.

The two Prime Ministers expressed their satisfaction on the age-old, close, cordial and multifaceted relations between Nepal and India and agreed to expand them further. India expressed full support for the ongoing peace process and the efforts to bring about economic transformation in Nepal. The two Governments decided to reinvigorate bilateral relations by ensuring effectiveness of all established institutional mechanisms.

The two sides also agreed to enhance bilateral trade on a sustainable basis. To facilitate Nepalese foreign trade, India agreed to utilization of Vishakhapatanam port for movement of transit traffic to and from Nepal. A MoU was signed for continuation of Indian grant assistant for "Goiter Control Programme" in Nepal.

Nepal assured India that it will not allow its territory to be used for any activity against India and India also gave the same assurance to Nepal. A number of projects with Government of India assistance with a total outlay of over Rs. 1600 Crores were agreed upon including, construction of National Police Academy in Nepal, construction of poly-technique at Hetauda, construction of two integrated check-posts, construction of 660 kilometres of roads in the Terai region, construction of two cross-border rail-lines and continuing provision of Indian faculty to B.P. Koirala Institute of Health Sciences, Dharan.

The two Governments also agreed to take up preventive measures and consultations to address the problem of inundation to border areas between Nepal and India. The Government of India also agreed, in principle, to double the number of scholarships offered to Nepalese students and to increase the number of slots offered for training of Nepalese Government officials.

The two sides also agreed to facilitate increased Indian public and private sector involvement to harness Nepalese hydro-power potential. It was also decided to cooperate bilaterally in areas such as culture, science and technology, tourism and sports and to facilitate contact and cooperation among the parliamentarians of the two countries.

The Minister of External Affairs of India (EAM), H.E. Mr. S.M. Krishna paid an official visit to Nepal from January 15 – 17, 2010 at the invitation of Hon'ble Deputy Prime Minister and Minister of Foreign Affairs of Nepal Ms. Sujata Koirala. During his visit, EAM called on Rt. Hon. Dr. Ram Baran Yadav, President of Nepal and Rt. Hon'ble Mr. Madhav Kumar Nepal, Prime Minister of Nepal. He conveyed to them the greetings of the Indian leadership and reiterated that India attaches the highest priority to its relations with Nepal.

EAM also called on Rt. Hon'ble Mr. Subas Chandra Nembang, Chairman of the Constituent Assembly and held an interactive discussion with Parliamentarians representing the different political parties in the Constituent Assembly.

He also met senior political leaders representing various political parties of Nepal. During his visit, EAM held official talks with the Deputy Prime Minister and Minister for Foreign Affairs of Nepal on all aspects of bilateral relations and issues of mutual interest. The two Ministers expressed their satisfaction regarding the age-old, multifaceted relations that exist between Nepal and India and agreed to expand these further.

They also reviewed the implementation of the decisions taken during the official visit of the Prime Minister of Nepal, Rt. Hon. Madhav Kumar Nepal to India from 18 – 22 August 2009. A total of four MoUs for various projects to be conducted with Government of India's assistance were signed that included (i) MoU for construction of Terai roads with an estimated cost of IRs. 805 Crores; (ii) MoU for construction of a Science Learning Centre at an estimated cost of IRs 16.6 Crores; (iii) MoU between Nepal Stock Exchange Limited (NEPSE) and Central Depository Services (India) Ltd. (CDSIL), India at an estimated cost of IRs. 9.2 Crores; and (iv) MoUs for electrification of five different VDCs in Nepal at a total cost of IRs. 6.3 Crores.

In keeping with the tradition of regular high-level exchange of visits between India and Nepal, President, Hon'ble Dr. Ram Baran Yadav, first President of Nepal, paid a state visit to India from 15-18 February 2010 at the invitation of our President. He was accompanied by Mr. Sharat Singh Bhandari, Minister for

Tourism and Civil Aviation and a high-level official delegation. During the visit he met the President. The Vice President, the Prime Minister, Minister of Finance, External Affairs Minister, Minister for Home Affairs, the Chairperson of UPA and the Leader of Opposition and the Foreign Secretary called upon the visiting President. He also visited Haridwar and met a cross section of political leaders in India. During the visit of President of Nepal to India (15-18 February 2010) four MoUs/agreements were signed in the presence of the President of Nepal and our Prime Minister. These included (i) Air Services Agreement between India and Nepal; (ii) MoU for extension of railway lines to five cross border points along the India Nepal border; (iii) MoU on establishment of Nepal-Bharat Maitree Polytechnique at Hetauda and (iv) MoU on establishment of Nepal Bharat Maitri Sabhagraha in Birgunj. In response to Nepal's request for supply of food items, our Prime Minister announced that India will supply 50,000 metric tones of wheat, 25,000 metric tones of rice and 10,000 metric tones of pulses to Nepal. Our willingness to supply an additional 200 thousand metric tones of wheat, if required, was also conveyed. To facilitate economic and infrastructure development in Nepal, Prime Minister also announced the extension of a new concessional Line of Credit for US $ 250 million.

India remains steadfast in its commitment to extend assistance for Nepal's economic development and political stabilization. India's support continues to be in accordance with the wishes and priorities of the people and Government of Nepal. India Nepal Economic Cooperation stands to be further strengthened with the ushering in of a new era of hope and peace in Nepal.

CHANGING PARADIGMS IN INDIA-NEPAL RELATIONS

Today Nepal stands at the crossroads amidst the swiftly changing political tracts and it becomes a scarce to found a closer understanding over the core issues among all the political parties. Such political opportunism truly missing the plight of democracy besides pulling down the national priorities in crucial matters; indeed it's an outcome of internal political strife instead from an imposed international pressure. Stability is very crucial for India in the case of Nepal where India hasn't any option except to see a sovereign Nepal; concerned authority in India's External Affairs Ministry has been consistently showing similar concern and landed all possible support to assist in Nepal's integration. Through an honest introspection it's easily revealed that India never resolute any action in past against the national interest of Nepal, further India never obstruct the formation of any democratic government even including the Maoist government and send their foreign secretary just three days before the government formation.

India-Nepal relations are so strong that it's very hard to shape in mere words because these two neighbouring nation has a history of deep ties and shared concern from ancient times. Quality of relationship between these two countries shouldn't be seen in terms of treaty; having faith in each other's role any dispute can be solved and consensus could be formed between these two friendly nations. Indeed there are no reasons among the peoples of the both side of border to involved in any sort of hate campaign against each other; any development in this regard would be ended with an impractical and unviable consequences. So, it must realized that that interest of India wouldn't affect the any move of peace process in Nepal; it's need of hour to end the causes of political insecurity among the diasporas on the both side of borders.

State of Nepal's internal security possessed as much concern as her own existential safety for India, so any anti Indian move will jeopardize the friendly terms and left alarming ramifications for both the country. India's concern over the presence of ISI's agents inside the territory of Nepal must be seen in genuine light by the Nepalese government since it could be highly disturbing in long term for Nepal's own sake as well. Indian government is very serious towards tackling the terrorist network with wrenched resoluteness and would keep affirming on Nepalese government to check their activities from their sovereign territory.

With more meticulous action some unfortunate developments may be easily avoided; that would required a consensus based approach in top notch Nepalese political circle and within their civil society towards the India's plight for security. India never felt any sort of discontents with the democratic proceedings in Nepal; of course Maoist should stay and play active role within their national political framework. Indian government would remains very keen for strengthening of democracy in Nepal and issues like human rights would be a key priority for them with putting finest efforts to see it in universal way beyond the geographical boundaries. In recent past Gorkha's role in Indian Arm Forces has gained some critical applauds from a reactionary section in Nepal which is quite unfortunate and is an effort to dampen the historic and marvelous symbolic ties between these two friendly nation.

The word consensus has been largely misused in Nepal consequently ultra nationalism in Nepal largely seen in the context of anti-Indian sentiment; a very lucid approach would be needed from Nepalese side over such relentless unfortunate developments. In international affairs domain Nepal needs to play more matured role and must develop a sense of its own best interest; mutual integrated relationship with India paves way for safe passages of trust between them which is quite symmetric to the actual requirements and should remain a foremost concern for both the countries to keep intact these flame of spirits; any constructive solution of joint interest would be emerged from mutual effort instead through isolatory stances.

In changing circumstances it's quite essential for both the countries to make immediate revisions in bilateral treaties and shaping them as per the suitability of present time. Infrastructures are major issues that needs to look on in such active manner since perennial floods is a major impediment for socio-economic structure of Terain region in Nepal and entire north Bihar. A radical shift in policy towards the existing infrastructure of water management is the first step that required to be taken by the governments of both countries. Water management possessed very crucial and strategic place in the sphere of India-Nepal relations as their catchments are very productive for the vast agricultural areas as well an alternative source of energy; projects like Pancheswar, Saptakosi, Naumure etc. needs rational handling as they are immensely crucial for the sake of both countries energy requirements. Border management is another issue that needs more regulated treatment though it should remain open as even before because prevalence of open border is the biggest asset of India-Nepal relation and it has potential to be framed as an ideal border of south Asia. Indeed open border plays utmost significance in the lives of population adjacent to border; since time immemorial they have been sharing the ties of Roti (Bread) and Beti (Matrimonial ties) which even creates complexities of identity.

In present state Nepal is coping with the difficulties of constitution making besides having to win the trust of peoples in democratic institution which shown severe fluctuation in immediate past. In this situation grooming of an idea of ethnic federalism and other major issues wouldn't be less than a fatal as handling of such major issues depends upon the state of stability which is completely out of seen in present circumstances. Terain's plight and refugee's problems are some other rudimentary issues that need proper concern and action from the governments of both the side as law and order situation is a matter that requires the co-operation of other side due to geographical nature and open borders. In decade long civil war like situation, the Terai region faced adverse setbacks and witnessed the losses of human lives, infrastructure, ecology, law and order etc. Even in last few months toll of losses in Terai is quite frightening, almost 1200 peoples has been killed and more than 3600 were abducted; situation is still very grim inside the Terai region and peoples have some distraught feeling as they used to feel during the bloody strife phase. Glorifications of Terain Armed groups are caused by the political affiliations and patronage that's making situation worse in any effort to contain and disband their growing role; catchments areas of North Bihar or Mithilanchal region becomes a hideout place for these groups in the absence of a specified and clear set of mechanism on joint level; a strategic move in this regard is immediately required.

Till today Nepal is missing the actual taste of democracy and whatever has been represented on the name of democracy that never touched the ground of actual aspiration of its citizen. Maoists short stint in government couldn't materialized their own professed goals instead they turn up to attack on religious identities, authoritarianism, non-pluralism, against right of property besides showing very immature stand on Nepalese Armed Force chief Rukmangad Kotwal; such bad conflict management with Arm force deciphered the feeble understanding of realpolitik in Maoist camp.

Before that incident Nepali Army has history of passive presence and following the civil supremacy which was very conducive with the expectation of Nepalese intelligentsias. But now stands humiliated, Nepalese Army becomes more powerful and strategic which may played crucial roles in further phage of development. India too witnessed some implications after this incident as the role of India felt prominent by a section of reactionaries in Nepalese politics; former Prime Minister Prachanda's remarks as "Promped by Prabhu" to present Prime Minister Madhav Kumar Nepal was clearly referred towards the India which was completely unjustifiable. India maintains silence over such rambling propositions even the Indian side never downbeat with the growing Chinese influence in Maoists rule and regarded it just as lacking immune system. India has utmost concern with Nepalese state of affairs in similar manner; Nepal too has immense benefits from a stronger India, so despite some ups and down in events it would be compatible to remains in same strong bond of sharing forever' Brotherhood always remains a great idea as in such set of relationship every member has some specific roles to play irrespective of identities like big brother and small brother; being sanguine for same must in case of India-Nepal relations.

MAOISTS RHETORIC ON INDIA-NEPAL RELATIONS

India's External Affairs Minister SM Krishna will undertake a three-day official visit to Kathmandu from January 15, 2010. According to the Indian Embassy in Kathmandu, at least five memorandums of understanding will be signed during Krishna's visit. The possible MoUs include construction of a National Police Academy at Panauti in Kavre district, Indian assistance for the Nepal Stock Exchange, construction of roads in the Terai, establishment of a science learning centre and a solar electrification project. Krishna will also take up issues related to Indian security and counterfeit currency issues.

Though the visit is timely and significant, uncertainties over the future of the peace process continue due to differences between the political parties on contentious issues like federalism, rehabilitation of Maoist combatants, and the nature of Constitution.

The UCPN-Maoist leader Prachanda has accused the ruling parties of being puppets of the Indian ruling class, accused the Indian establishment of intervening in Nepal's internal affairs and trying to derail the peace process. He also said that the UCPN-Maoist should hold direct talks with New Delhi since the ruling parties are guided by remote control and talks with them to establish civilian supremacy have been failing.

The Maoists have made elaborate arrangements to express displeasure during Krishna's visit. Recently, they declared the fourth phase of their nationwide agitation demanding restoration of civilian supremacy and formation of a Maoist-led national government. As part of the fourth round of protest programmes, senior party leaders will visit those locations along the open border with India where India has reportedly occupied Nepal's territories. The Maoists will organise mass rallies at several bordering regions 'encroached' by India and torch the copies of the various treaties with India. They will hold demonstrations outside the Indian Embassy and Singha Durbar on January 19.

Krishna's visit is taking place at a time when the Maoist sponsored anti-India feeling is at an all time high in Nepal. Maoists have been consistently branding the 1950 treaty as unequal, raising issues such as illegal encroachment and the recruitment of Nepalse Gurkhas into the Indian Army. But none of these demands are genuine and valid. The Maoists, in fact, do not want to resolve these issues since these give them huge political dividends to retain public support. Pushpa Kamal Dahal alias Prachanda, during his nine month tenure as prime minister, did not take any steps to withdraw from the 1950 treaty though clause 10 of the agreement cleanly mentions that the "Treaty shall remain in force until it is terminated by either party by giving one year's notice." The issue figured prominently during his visit to New Delhi in September

2008. On this occasion, Prachanda had agreed with India's Prime Minister to "review, adjust and update" the 1950 Treaty of Peace and Friendship and other agreements, while giving due recognition to the special features of the bilateral relationship. Why did Prachanda not use clause 10 of the treaty and agreed to review the same during his visit?

Regarding the Gurkha recruitment issue, Pracahnda preferred to remain tightlipped during his visit to India. On the eve of the visit, Deepak Bahadur Gurung, chairman of the Nepal Ex-Servicemen's Association, warned that his organisation would start a new 'People's War' if the Maoist government stopped the recruitment. Most importantly, Maoists' argument about Gurkaha recruitment being colonial is illogical because Gurkha Nepalese have been joining the Indian Army purely on a voluntary basis. This is not forced recruitment or conscription by the Indian Army.

Given the geographical dynamics in the border region, "encroachment" is more a natural phenomenon than man-made. Rivers flowing from Nepal to India frequently shift their course during the monsoons. As a result, certain portions of the border region either come to Nepal or to India depending on the shifting of the river course. Since farmers from both countries find that part of the land fertile, they encroach upon it for agricultural purposes. In fact, Prachanda during his last visit to India acknowledged the problem of inundation in the border areas and agreed to take up necessary work for its effective prevention on the basis of bilateral consultation. Both countries have already (unofficially) agreed that 98 per cent of the border is demarcated except two disputed areas in Kalapani and Susta. India's former external affairs minister Pranab Mukhrjee during his official visit to Kathmandu in November 2008 talked about it before the media. Interestingly, then the Maoist-led government in Kathmandu did not contradict his view on border demarcation. The issue rose to prominence again only after Prachanda's resignation. The Maoists have accused encroachment of Nepalese territory by Indian security forces in the Dang district.

The problem is not only with the Maoists. India has consistently given space to the Maoists to take advantage of the faultlines in

India-Nepal relations. Till date, India has hardly clarified its stand on these controversial bilateral issues in a public forum. All discussions have taken place only at the official level, which have been tampered with and then highlighted by the pro-Maoist or Royalist Nepalese media. One such faultline is the absence of high-level political engagements from the Indian side while Nepal is passing through political turbulence.

In the last 13 years, seven Prime Ministers of Nepal have visited India in return for one Prime Ministerial visit from India to Nepal. Prime Minister I. K. Gujaral visited Kathmandu in June 1997. The political imbalance in the relationship has been gradually eroding India's traditional leverages in Nepal. If the vacuum continues, other countries including China may consolidate in near future. Another major faultline is unnecessary statements from various agencies of India about internal developments in Nepal. Third, India has a very good relationship with many leaders of Nepal cutting across party lines. But it is yet to introduce a comprehensive policy towards Nepal.

INDIA'S OPTIONS IN NEPAL

1. Stability in Nepal is extremely important for India. It has to acknowledge that the present political stalemate is an internal matter of Nepal and encourage the stakeholders to hammer out their differences. India should strike a neutral stance and play the role of an honest negotiator to bring the various factions together.
2. Existing controversial treaties, border disputes, encroachment issues and the Indian Embassy's alleged support to certain groups in the Terai region and personal level support to Nepali Congress leaders are major irritants in India-Nepal relations. These issues have been generating huge anti-India feelings and thus need immediate attention. This will help prevent the growing Chinese role in Nepal. India needs to come out with a clear policy on these issues and express positive views to resolve them.
3. India should focus more on socio-economic and development programmes. India's assistance to Nepal

should be enhanced and directed towards projects which benefit the Nepalese people directly.

4. Hydro-projects and dams situated on the Indo-Nepal border should be maintained and managed by the Union Government under the Ministry of External affairs.
5. Border crossing should be mechanized. People crossing the border should be treated with dignity.
6. India should realize that the monarchy is gone for ever although the pro-monarchy sentiment remains. India needs to acknowledge the emergence of new forces in Nepal and learn to deal with them.
7. India should enhance and upgrade co-operation with Nepalese agencies to patrol and manage the border.

Anti-India feeling is a permanent phenomenon in India's neighbourhood including in Nepal. India should not deterred by these activities. This visit is a golden opportunity for India to reactivate its relationship and reassure both the ruling and opposition parties about India's positive contribution to the peace process. During the visit, India should come out with some official statements that India is interested more in people to people relations and the prosperity of Nepal. If possible, India should seriously engage and talk to the Maoists. They may have their own ideology which may not be comfortable to India. But there is no harm in talking to them and learn about their concerns. Similarly, India should make its concerns in Nepal clear to the Maoists. It should clarify through actions and declare that India has no intention to interfere in Nepal, that it respects Nepal's sovereignty and that it is ready to work with any dispensation in Nepal for furthering mutual security and economic concerns.

INVESTMENT POLICIES IN NEPAL AND INDIA

The Constitution of the Kingdom of Nepal 1990 refers to that " The State shall, for the purposes of national development, pursue a policy of taking measures necessary for the attraction of foreign capital and technology, while at the same time promoting indigenous investment Constitution of the Kingdom of Nepal, 1990: 19)". The Tenth Plan, 2002-07 has the objective to develop

Nepal as an attractive and reliable investment center at international perspective. The Plan states that procedures to attract foreign investment will be made simple, comprehensive and transparent through administrative and legal reforms. Also the Plan will review Foreign Investment and Transfer of Technology Act 1992; Industrial Enterprises Act 1992; existing labour policy and Labour Act 1992 and make investment-friendly.

The Tenth Plan has the policy to provide facilities and infrastructure services to investors from one window; procedures will be simplified to repatriate investment made by the investors; in no case facilities and incentives provided to attract FDI in Nepal will be less than what is available in the neighbouring countries; Labour Act will be made more flexible; on the basis of feasibility studies and identification of areas of comparative advantages information will be provided to investors to promote investment in Nepal; and the Royal Nepalese Embassies abroad will be urged to promote foreign investment in Nepal through mobilizing investors in respective countries (Tenth Plan, 2002: 79-80). Since 1990 Nepal has adhered to the policy of liberalization in trade and investment regime.

Statutory Provisions

The Foreign Investment and Technology Transfer Act (FITTA) 1992 govern the entry of FDI in Nepal. FDI is permitted in all industries in Nepal except for those reserved exclusively for national investors and statutory state monopolies. Foreign individuals are not permitted to own land but resident companies may do so even if foreign owned.

Foreign ownership of commercial banks is limited to 66 percent. Foreign investment is allowed in the areas except specified in the "negative list". These include: (a) sensitive industries related to national security; cottage industries; personal services of a kind that would normally be performed by self employed people; and real estate business. In these areas amendments would be possible only through parliament, and (b) retail business; travel agency; cigarette, tobacco and alcohol production other than for export; a range of small tourist related activities, including tourist lodging but not hotels; some small scale farming; and consultancy services.

In these areas government has the authority for amendments, if it is necessary.

Inclusion of consultancy services in the negative list is strange, which explicitly includes management, accounting, engineering and legal services. International accounting and law firms, and other professionals are not allowed to practice for an establishment in Nepal. In case of business in Nepal wishes to engage such services from an offshore provider, which falls within the jurisdiction of "transfer of technology", requires government approval. These features add up to a protectionist regime wherein it would be difficult for foreign investors to access "brand" international services or head office services (UNCTAD, 2003). The other items included in the negative list are not so unusual. However, FDI in Nepal is restrained to 32 public enterprises due to existing negative list.

Privatization is one of the cornerstones of liberal economic policy followed by Nepal after 1990. As per Privatization Act 1994 the Government has either privatized or liquidated a total of 23 public enterprises by the end of FY 2002/03 (Economic Survey, FY 2002/03). Of the total public enterprises, four are of statutory monopolies. These are: (a) Nepal Oil Corporation (monopoly on the import of refined petroleum fuels), (b) Nepal Drinking Water Corporation, (c) Nepal Telecommunication Corporation, and (d) Nepal Electricity Authority. The Government has recently announced to privatize, dissolve or liquidate 9 public enterprises during FY 2003/04. The Budget for current FY refers to that "the companies wholly owned by Nepalese entrepreneurs or with 50 percent foreign equity participation and registered in Nepal will be allowed to import and deal in petroleum products" (Budget Speech, 2003). This is the manifestation of flexibility over the existing provisions that would help attract FDI to Nepal.

"Within the ambit of these corporations some private investment, including FDI potentially, is possible. Private investors may operate value-added network services in telecommunications and the industry regulator is separate from the Nepal Telecommunications Corporation. Private investment is encouraged in electricity generation, whilst the Nepal Electricity

Authority retains a monopoly of domestic transmission and distribution. Also water reticulation and sanitation are municipal services but it may be possible to contract out these services to private operators" (UNCTAD, 2003).

Existence of large number of SOEs would minimize FDI potential. However, a majority of SOEs incurred huge loss attributing to over-manning, political entrenchment and corruption. Given the condition, foreign investors may consider the proposal for investing in privatized enterprises as compared to diversify investment in nascent sector that involves relatively higher level of risks and uncertainty at this critical juncture of recession and political impasse. Privatization ensures competition that would be instrumental in promoting FDI. This could be applicable to even the worst cases of sick cement factories and Royal Nepal Airlines Corporation.

Thus, it is essential to privatize SOEs as per the regulatory framework provided by FITTA, which would foster competition-ensuring security to investment through higher profit and growth. However, in some cases foreign investors have gone into competition with SOEs such as the herbs production and processing company. A further source of risk to private investors is the inadequate separation of the regulatory function of a line ministry and its links with an SOE in the sector concerned.

All FDI including reinvestment and matters relating to loan from abroad requires a prior approval in Nepal. All applications are processed by Department of Industries that approves FDI for projects with an investment cost of about US $ 12.5 million. The Industrial Promotion Board (IPB) decides applications for large-scale investments. The IPB is a high level Committee headed by the Minister for Industry consisting of Heads of various Ministries, Nepal Rastra Bank (Central Bank of Nepal) and representatives of the private sector. FDI procedures are implemented through "One window" system. Application for work permit, visa and investment-related foreign exchange control approval need prior sanction of the Department of Industry. The applicant is required to submit extensive information on inputs and output, financing, sources and uses of foreign exchange and commercial agreements entered into.

However, explanation is not required to a rejection and there is no right of appeal. Foreign policy is silent on why government approval is required for every proposed foreign investment. Sensitive industries are covered by the negative list. This approval requirement in a market economy appears to be an unnecessary and intrusive hurdle for foreign investors".

"Foreign investors wish to conclude agreements for the transfer of technology as an integral part of their operations, which includes agreements for the use of intellectual property for management, marketing and other services from abroad. All such agreements require approval under similar procedures as for FDI applications through the Ministry of Industries. It is not explicit what objectives the requirement for government approval is meant to serve" (UNCTAD, 2003). Modern international practice does not require prior approval of such agreements.

INDIA-CHINA RELATIONS

Sino-Indian relations, also called Indo-China relations, refers to the bilateral relationship between the People's Republic of China (PRC) and the Republic of India. Relations began in 1950 when India was among the first countries to break relations with the Republic of China on Taiwan and recognize the PRC. China and India are the world's most populous countries and alsofastest growing major economies. The resultant growth in China and India's global diplomatic and economic influence has also increased the significance of their bilateral relationship.

China and India are two of the world's oldest civilizations and have coexisted in peace for millennia. Cultural and economic relations between China and India date back to ancient times. The Silk Road not only served as a major trade route between India and China, but is also credited for facilitating the spread of Buddhism from India to East Asia. During the 19th century, China's growing opium trade with the British Raj triggered the Opium Wars. During World War II, India and China played a crucial role in halting the progress of Imperial Japan.

Relations between contemporary China and India have been characterized by border disputes, resulting in three major military conflicts — the Sino-Indian War of 1962, the Chola incident in 1967, and the 1987 Sino-Indian skirmish. However, since late 1980s, both countries have successfully attempted to reignite diplomatic and economic ties. In 2008, China emerged as the largest trading partner of India and the two countries have also attempted to extend their strategic and military relations. Despite growing economic and strategic ties, several issues continue to strain Sino-Indian relations.

Though bilateral trade has continuously grown, India faces massive trade imbalance heavily in favor of China. The two countries have failed to resolve their long-standing border dispute and Indian media outlets repeatedly report Chinese military incursions into Indian territory.

Both nations have steadily built-up military infrastructure along border areas. Additionally, India harbors suspicions about China's strong strategic relations with its arch-rival Pakistan while China has expressed concerns about Indian military and economic activities in disputed South China Sea.

Recently, China has said that "Sino-Indian ties" would be the most "important bilateral partnership of the century". On June 21, 2012, Wen Jiabao, the Premier of China and Manmohan Singh, the Prime Minister of India set a goal to increase bilateral trade between the two countries to 100 billion dollars by 2015

Geographical Overview

China and India are separated by the formidable geographical obstacles of the Himalayan mountain chain. China and India today share a border along the Himalayas and Nepal and Bhutan, two states lying along the Himalaya range, and acting as buffer states.

In addition, the disputed Kashmir province of India (claimed by Pakistan) borders both the PRC and India. As Pakistan has tense relations with India, Kashmir's state of unrest serves as a natural ally to the PRC.

Two territories are currently disputed between the People's Republic of China and India: Aksai Chin and Arunachal Pradesh. Arunachal Pradesh is located near the far east of India, while Aksai Chin is located near the northwest corner of India, at the junction of India, Pakistan, and the PRC. However, all sides in the dispute have agreed to respect the Line of Actual Control and this border dispute is not widely seen as a major flashpoint.

Early history

Antiquity

India and China had relatively little modern political contact before the 1950s. However, both countries have had extensive and close historical cultural contact since the 1st century, especially with the transmission of Buddhism from India to China. Trade relations via the Silk Road acted as economic contact between the two regions.

China and India have also had some contact before the transmission of Buddhism. References to a people called the *Chinas*, now believed to be the Chinese, are found in ancient Indian literature.

The Indian epic *Mahabharata* (c. 5th century BC) contains references to "China", which may have been referring to the Qin state which later became the Qin Dynasty. Chanakya (c. 350-283 BC), the prime minister of the Maurya Empire and a professor at Takshashila University, refers to Chinese silk as "cinamsuka" (Chinese silk dress) and "cinapatta" (Chinese silk bundle) in his *Arthashastra*.

In the *Records of the Grand Historian*, Zhang Qian (d. 113 BC) and Sima Qian (145-90 BC) make references to "Shendu", which may have been referring to the Indus Valley (the Sindh province in modern Pakistan), originally known as "Sindhu" in Sanskrit. When Yunnan was annexed by the Han Dynasty in the 1st century, Chinese authorities reported an Indian "Shendu" community living there.

Middle Ages

After the transmission of Buddhism from India to China from the 1st century onwards, many Indian scholars and monks travelled to China, such as Batuo (fl. 464-495 AD)—founder of the Shaolin Monastery—and Bodhidharma—founder of Chan/Zen Buddhism—while many Chinese scholars and monks also travelled to India, such as Xuanzang (b. 604) and I Ching (635-713), both of whom were students at Nalanda University in Bihar. Xuanzang wrote the *Great Tang Records on the Western Regions*, an account of his journey to India, which later inspired Wu Cheng'en's Ming Dynasty novel *Journey to the West*, one of the Four Great Classical Novels of Chinese literature.

Tang and Harsha dynasties

During the 7th century, Tang Dynasty China gained control over large portions of the Silk Road and Central Asia. Wang Xuancehad sent a diplomatic mission to northern India, which was embroiled by civil war just following the death of Emperor Harsha (590–647). After the murder of 30 members of this mission by usurper claiments to the throne, Wang fled, and returned with allied Nepaliand Tibetan troops to back the opposing claimant. With his forces, Wang besieged and captured the capital, while his deputy Jiang Shiren captured the usurper and sent him back to Emperor Tang Taizong (599-649) in Chang'an as a prisoner.

During the 8th century, the astronomical table of sines by the Indian astronomer and mathematician, Aryabhata (476-550), were translated into the Chinese astronomical andmathematical book of the *Treatise on Astrology of the Kaiyuan Era* (*Kaiyuan Zhanjing*), compiled in 718 AD during the Tang Dynasty. The *Kaiyuan Zhanjing* was compiled by Gautama Siddha, an astronomer and astrologer born in Chang'an, and whose family was originally from India. He was also notable for his translation of the Navagrahacalendar into Chinese.

Ming Dynasty

Between 1405 and 1433, the Ming Dynasty China sponsored a series of seven naval expeditions. Emperor Yongle designed them to establish a Chinese presence, impose imperial control over trade, and impress foreign people in the Indian Ocean basin. He also might have wanted to extend the tributary system, by which Chinese dynasties traditionally recognized foreign peoples.

Admiral Zheng He was dispatched to lead a series of huge naval expeditions to explore these regions. The largest of his voyages included over 317 ships and 28,000 men, and the largest of his treasure ships were over 126.73 m in length. During his voyages, he visited numerous Indian kingdoms and ports. On the first three voyages, Zheng He visited southeast Asia, India, Bengal, andCeylon. The fourth expedition went to the Persian Gulf and Arabia, and later expeditions ventured down the east African coast, as far as Malindi in what is now Kenya. Throughout his travels, Zheng He liberally dispensed Chinese gifts of silk, porcelain, and other goods. In return, he received rich and unusual presents from his hosts, including African zebras and giraffes that ended their days in the Ming imperial zoo. Zheng He and his company paid respects to local deities and customs, and in Ceylon they erected a monument (Galle Trilingual Inscription) honouring Buddha, Allah, and Vishnu.

Sino-Sikh War

In the 18th to 19th centuries, the Sikh Confederacy of the Punjab region in India was expanding into neighbouring lands. It had annexed Ladakh into the state of Jammu in 1834. In 1841, they invaded Tibet with an army and overran parts of western Tibet. Chinese forces defeated the Sikh army in December 1841, forcing the Sikh army to withdraw from Tibet, and in turn entered Ladakh and besieged Leh, where they were in turn defeated by the Sikh Army. At this point, neither side wished to continue the conflict, as the Sikhs were embroiled in tensions with the British that would lead up to the First Anglo-Sikh War, while the Chinese was in the midst of the First Opium War with the British East India Company. The Chinese and the Sikhs signed a treaty in September 1842, which stipulated no transgressions or interference in the other country's frontiers.

After Independence

Jawaharlal Nehru based his vision of "resurgent Asia" on friendship between the two largest states of Asia; his vision of an internationalist foreign policy governed by the ethics of the Panchsheel, which he initially believed was shared by China, came to grief when it became clear that the two countries had a conflict of interest in Tibet, which had traditionally served as a geographical and political buffer zone, and where India believed it had inherited special privileges from the British Raj. However, the initial focus of the leaders of both the nations was not the foreign policy, but the internal development of their respective states. When they did concentrate on the foreign policies, their concern wasn't one another, but rather the United States of America and the Union of Soviet Socialist Republics and the alliance systems which were dominated by the two superpowers.

1950s

On October 1, 1949 the People's Liberation Army defeated the Kuomintang (Nationalist Party) of China in a civil war and established the People's Republic of China. On August 15, 1947, India became an independent dominion under British Commonwealth and became a federal, democratic republic after its constitution came into effect on January 26, 1950. Mao Zedong, the Commander of the Liberation Army and the Chairman of the Communist Party of China viewed Tibet as an integral part of the Chinese State. Mao was determined to bring Tibet under direct administrative and military control of People's Republic of China and saw Indian concern over Tibet as a manifestation of the Indian Government's interference in the internal affairs of the People's Republic of China. The PRC sought to reassert control over Tibet and to end Lamaism (Tibetan Buddhism) and feudalism, which it did by force of arms in 1950. To avoid antagonizing the People's Republic of China, Nehru informed Chinese leaders that India had neither political nor territorial ambitions, nor did it seek special privileges in Tibet, but that traditional trading rights must continue. With Indian support, Tibetan delegates signed an agreement in May 1951 recognizing PRC sovereignty but guaranteeing that the existing political and social system of Tibet would continue. Direct negotiations between India and the PRC commenced in an atmosphere improved by India's mediation efforts in bringing about a ceasefire to the Korean War (1950–1953).

Meanwhile, India was the 16th state to establish diplomatic relations with the People's Republic of China, and did so on April 1, 1950. In April 1954, India and the PRC signed an eight-year agreement on Tibet that set forth the basis of their relationship in the form of the Five Principles of Peaceful Coexistence(or *Panch*

Shila). Although critics called the Panch Shila naive, Nehru calculated that in the absence of either the wherewithal or a policy for defense of the Himalayan region, India's best guarantee of security was to establish a psychological buffer zone in place of the lost physical buffer of Tibet.

It is the popular perception that the catch phrase of India's diplomacy with China in the 1950s was *Hindi-Chini bhai-bhai*, which means, in Hindi, "Indians and Chinese are brothers" but there is evidence to suggest that Nehru did not trust the Chinese at all. Therefore, in unison with diplomacy, Nehru sought to initiate a more direct dialogues between the peoples of China and India in various ways, including culture and literature.

Around that time, the famous Indian artist (painter) Beohar Rammanohar Sinha from Visva-BharatiSantiniketan, who had earlier decorated the pages of the original Constitution of India, was sent to China in 1957 on a Government of India fellowship to establish a direct cross-cultural and inter-civilization bridge. Noted Indian scholar Rahul Sankrityayan and diplomat Natwar Singh were also there, and Sarvapalli Radhakrishnan paid a visit to PRC.

Between 1957 and 1959, Beohar Rammanohar Sinha not only disseminated Indian art in PRC but also became skilled in Chinese painting and lacquer-work. He also spent time with great masters Qi Baishi, Li Keran, Li Kuchan as well as some moments with Mao Zedong and Zhou Enlai. Consequently, up until 1959, despite border skirmishes and discrepancies between Indian and Chinese maps, Chinese leaders amicably had assured India that there was no territorial controversy on the border though there is some evidence that India avoided bringing up the border issue in high level meetings.

In 1954, India published new maps that included the Aksai Chin region within the boundaries of India (maps published at the time of India's independence did not clearly indicate whether the region was in India or Tibet). When an Indian reconnaissance party discovered a completed Chinese road running through the Aksai Chin region of theLadakh District of Jammu and Kashmir, border clashes and Indian protests became more frequent and serious. In January 1959, PRC premier Zhou Enlai wrote to Nehru, rejecting Nehru's contention that the border was based on treaty and custom and pointing out that no government in China had accepted as legal the McMahon Line, which in the 1914 Simla Convention defined the eastern section of the border between India and Tibet.

The Dalai Lama, spiritual and temporal head of the Tibetan people, sought sanctuary in Dharmsala, Himachal Pradesh, in March 1959, and thousands of Tibetan refugees settled in northwestern India, particularly in Himachal Pradesh. The People's Republic of China accused India of expansionism and imperialism in Tibet and throughout the Himalayan region. China claimed 104,000 km^2 of territory over which India's maps showed clear sovereignty, and demanded "rectification" of the entire border.

Zhou proposed that China relinquish its claim to most of India's northeast in exchange for India's abandonment of its claim to Aksai Chin. The Indian government, constrained by domestic public opinion, rejected the idea of a settlement based on uncompensated loss of territory as being humiliating and unequal.

1960s

Sino-Indian War

1962 Border disputes resulted in a short border war between the People's Republic of China and India in 20 October 1962. The PRC pushed the unprepared and inadequately led Indian forces to within forty-eight kilometres of the Assam plains in the northeast and occupied strategic points in Ladakh, until the PRC declared a unilateral cease-fire on 21 November and withdrew twenty kilometers behind its contended line of control.

At the time of Sino-Indian border conflict, a severe political split was taking place in the Communist Party of India. One section was accused by the Indian government as being pro-PRC, and a large number of political leaders were jailed. Subsequently, CPI split with the leftist section forming the Communist Party of India (Marxist) in 1964. CPI(M) held some contacts with the Communist Party of China in the initial period after the split, but did not fully embrace the political line of Mao Zedong.

Relations between the PRC and India deteriorated during the rest of the 1960s and the early 1970s as Sino-Pakistani relations improved and Sino-Soviet relations worsened. The PRC backed Pakistan in its 1965 war with India. Between 1967 and 1971, an all-weather road was built across territory claimed by India, linking PRC's Xinjiang Uyghur Autonomous Region with Pakistan; India could do no more than protest, however 1971 war with Pakistan, India won a landslide victory. The PRC continued an active propaganda campaign against India and supplied ideological, financial, and other assistance to dissident groups, especially to tribes in northeastern India. The PRC accused India of assisting the Khampa rebels in Tibet. Diplomatic contact between the two governments was minimal although not formally severed. The flow of cultural and other exchanges that had marked the 1950s ceased entirely. The flourishing wool, fur and spice trade between Lhasa and India through the Nathula Pass, an offshoot of the ancientSilk Road in the then Indian protectorate of Sikkim was also severed. However, the biweekly postal network through this pass was kept alive, which exists till today.

Sri Lanka played the role of chief negotiater to withdraw the Chinese troops from the Indian territory. It is the Colombo proposals which both countries agreed to adopt and settle this dispute.<The Foreign Policy of Sirimavo Bandaranaike - THE COLOMBO POWERS AND THE SINO-INDIAN WAR OF 1962></ref>

Later Skirmishes

In late 1967, there were two skirmishes between Indian and Chinese forces in Sikkim. The first one was dubbed the "Nathu La incident", and the other the "Chola incident". Prior to these incidents had been the Naxalbari uprising in India by the Communist Naxalites and Maoists. In 1967, a peasant uprising broke out in Naxalbari, led by pro-Maoist elements. A pronunciation by Mao titled "Spring Thunder over India" gave full moral support for the uprising. The support for the revolt marked the end for the relations between CPC and CPI(M). Naxalbari-inspired communists organized armed revolts in several parts of India, and in 1969 they formed the Communist Party of India (Marxist-Leninist). However, as the naxalite movement disintegrated in various splits, the PRC withdrew its political support and turned non-committal towards the various Indian groups.

On 11 September 1967, troops of the Indian Army's 2nd Grenadiers were protecting an Engineering Company that was fencing the North Shoulder of Nathu La, when Chinese troops opened fire on them. This escalated over the next five days to an exchange of heavy artillery and mortar fire between the Indians and the Chinese. 62 Indian soldiers, from the 2nd Grenadiers and the Artillery regiments were killed. Brigadier Rai Singh Yadav, the Commanding Officer, was awarded the MVC and Capt PS Dager was awarded a Vir Chakra (posthumous) for their gallant actions. The extent of Chinese casualties in this incident is not known.

In the second incident, on 1 October 1967, a group of Indian Gurkha Rifles soldiers (from the 7th Battalion of the 11th Regiment) noticed Chinese troops surrounding a sentry post near a boulder at the Chola outpost in Sikkim. After a heated argument over the control of the boulder, a Chinese soldier bayoneted a Gurkha rifleman, triggering the start of a close-quarters knife and fire-fight, which then escalated to a mortar and HMG duel. The Chinese troops had to signal a ceasefire just after three hours of fighting, but later scaled Point 15450 to establish themselves there. The Gurkhas outflanked them the next day to regain Point 15450, and the Chinese retreated across the LAC. 21 Indian soldiers were killed in this action. The Indian government awarded Vir Chakras to Rifleman Limbu (posthumous) and battalion commander Major K.B. Joshi for their gallant actions. The extent of Chinese casualties in this skirmish is also not known.

1970s

In August 1971, India signed its Treaty of Peace, Friendship, and Cooperation with the Soviet Union, and the United States and the PRC sided with Pakistan in its December 1971 war with India. Although China strongly condemned India, it did not carry out its veiled threat to intervene on Pakistan's behalf. By this time, the PRC had just replaced the Republic of China in the UN where its representatives denounced India as being a "tool of Soviet expansionism."

India and the PRC renewed efforts to improve relations after Indian Prime Minister Indira Gandhi's Congress party lost the 1977 elections to Morarji Desai's Janata Party. The new Desai government sought to improve long-strained relations with India and the PRC. In 1978, the Indian Minister of External Affairs Atal Bihari Vajpayee made a landmark visit to Beijing, and both nations officially re-established diplomatic relations in 1979. The PRC modified its pro-Pakistan stand on Kashmir and appeared willing to remain silent on India's absorption of Sikkim and its special advisory relationship with Bhutan. The PRC's leaders agreed to discuss the boundary issue, India's priority, as the first step to a broadening of relations. The two countries hosted each other's news agencies, and Mount Kailash and Mansarowar Lake in Tibet, the mythological home of the Hindu pantheon, were opened to annual pilgrimages

1980s

In 1981 PRC minister of foreign affairs Huang Hua was invited to India, where he made complimentary remarks about India's role in South Asia. PRC premier Zhao Ziyang concurrently toured Pakistan, Nepal, and Bangladesh.

In 1980, Indian Prime Minister Indira Gandhi approved a plan to upgrade the deployment of forces around the Line of Actual Control to avoid unilateral redefinitions of the line. India also increased funds for infrastructural development in these areas.

In 1984, squads of Indian soldiers began actively patrolling the Sumdorong Chu Valley in Arunachal Pradesh (formerly NEFA), which is north of the McMahon Line as drawn on the Simla Treaty map but south of the ridge which Indian claims is meant to delineate the McMahon Line. The Sumdorong Chu valley "seemed to lie to the north of the McMahon line; but is south of the highest ridge in the area, and the McMahon line is meant to follow the highest points" according to the Indian claims, while the Chinese did not recognize the McMahon Line as legitimate and were not prepared to accept an Indian claim line even further north than that. The Indian team left the area before the winter. In the winter of 1986, the Chinese deployed their troops to the Sumdorong Chu before the Indian team could arrive in the summer and built a Helipad at Wandung. Surprised by the Chinese occupation, India's then Chief of Army Staff, General K.Sundarji, airlifted a brigade to the region.

Chinese troops could not move any further into the valley and were forced to move sideways along the Thag La ridge, away from the valley. By 1987, Beijing's reaction was similar to that in 1962 and this prompted many Western diplomats to predict war. However, Indian foreign minister N.D. Tiwari and Prime Minister Rajiv Gandhi travelled to Beijing over the following months to negotiate a mutual de-escalation.

After the Huang visit, India and the PRC held eight rounds of border negotiations between December 1981 and November 1987. These talks initially raised hopes that progress could be made on the border issue. However, in 1985 the PRC stiffened its position on the border and insisted on mutual concessions without defining the exact terms of its "package proposal" or where the actual line of control lay. In 1986 and 1987, the negotiations achieved nothing, given the charges exchanged between the two countries of military encroachment in the Sumdorung Chu Valley of the Tawang tract on the eastern sector of the border. China's construction of a military post and helicopter pad in the area in 1986 and India's grant of statehood to Arunachal Pradesh (formerly the North-East Frontier Agency) in February 1987 caused both sides to deploy new troops to the area, raising tensions and fears of a new border war. The PRC relayed warnings that it would "teach India a lesson" if it did not cease "nibbling" at Chinese territory. By the summer of 1987, however, both sides had backed away from conflict and denied that military clashes had taken place.

A warming trend in relations was facilitated by Rajiv Gandhi's visit to China in December 1988. The two sides issued a joint communiqué that stressed the need to restore friendly relations on the basis of the Panch Shila and noted the importance of the first visit by an Indian prime minister to China since Nehru's 1954 visit. India and the People's Republic of China agreed to broaden bilateral ties in various areas, working to achieve a "fair and reasonable settlement while seeking a mutually acceptable solution" to the border dispute. The communiqué also expressed

China's concern about agitation by Tibetan separatists in India and reiterated China's position that Tibet was an integral part of China and that anti-China political activities by expatriate Tibetans was not to be tolerated. Rajiv Gandhi signed bilateral agreements on science and technology cooperation, on civil aviation to establish direct air links, and on cultural exchanges. The two sides also agreed to hold annual diplomatic consultations between foreign ministers, and to set up a joint ministerial committee on economic and scientific cooperation and a joint working group on the boundary issue. The latter group was to be led by the Indian foreign secretary and the Chinese vice minister of foreign affairs.

1990s

As the mid-1990s approached, slow but steady improvement in relations with China was visible. Top-level dialogue continued with the December 1991 visit of PRC premier Li Peng to India and the May 1992 visit to China of Indian president R. Venkataraman. Six rounds of talks of the Indian-Chinese Joint Working Group on the Border Issue were held between December 1988 and June 1993. Progress was also made in reducing tensions on the border via confidence-building measures, including mutual troop reductions, regular meetings of local military commanders, and advance notification of military exercises. Border trade resumed in July 1992 after a hiatus of more than thirty years, consulates reopened in Bombay (Mumbai) and Shanghai in December 1992, and, in June 1993, the two sides agreed to open an additional border trading post. DuringSharad Pawar's July 1992 visit to Beijing, the first ever by an Indian minister of defence, the two defense establishments agreed to develop academic, military, scientific, and technological exchanges and to schedule an Indian port call by a Chinese naval vessel.

Substantial movement in relations continued in 1993. The sixth-round joint working group talks were held in June in New Delhi but resulted in only minor developments. However, as the year progressed the long-standing border dispute was eased as a result of bilateral pledges to reduce troop levels and to respect the cease-fire line along the India-China border. Prime Minister Narasimha Rao and Premier Li Peng signed the border agreement and three other agreements (on cross-border trade, and on increased cooperation on the environment and in radio and television broadcasting) during the former's visit to Beijing in September. A senior-level Chinese military delegation made a six-day goodwill visit to India in December 1993 aimed at "fostering confidence-building measures between the defense forces of the two countries." The visit, however, came at a time when press reports revealed that; as a result of improved relations between the PRC and Burma, China was exporting greater amounts of military matériel to Burma's army, navy, and air force and sending an increasing number of technicians to Burma. Of concern to Indian security officials was the presence of Chinese radar technicians in Burma's Coco Islands, which border India's Union Territory of the Andaman and Nicobar Islands. Nevertheless, movement continued in 1994 on troop reductions along theHimalayan frontier. Moreover, in January 1994 Beijing announced that it not only favored a negotiated solution on Kashmir, but also opposed any form of independence for the region.

Talks were held in New Delhi in February 1994 aimed at confirming established "confidence-building measures" and discussing clarification of the "line of actual control", reduction of armed forces along the line, and prior information about forthcoming military exercises. China's hope for settlement of the boundary issue was reiterated.

The 1993 Chinese military visit to India was reciprocated by Indian army chief of staff General B. C. Joshi. During talks in Beijing in July 1994, the two sides agreed that border problems should be resolved peacefully through "mutual understanding and concessions." The border issue was raised in September 1994 when PRC minister of national defense Chi Haotian visited New Delhi for extensive talks with high-level Indian trade and defense officials. Further talks in New Delhi in March 1995 by the India-China Expert Group led to an agreement to set up two additional points of contact along the 4,000 km border to facilitate meetings between military personnel. The two sides also were reported as "seriously engaged" in defining the McMahon Line and the line of actual control vis-à-vis military exercises and prevention of air intrusion. Talks in Beijing in July 1995 aimed at better border security and combating cross-border crimes and in New Delhi in August 1995 on additional troop withdrawals from the border made further progress in reducing tensions.

Possibly indicative of the further relaxation of India-China relations, at least there was little notice taken in Beijing, was the April 1995 announcement, after a year of consultation, of the opening of the Taipei Economic and Cultural Center in New Delhi. The center serves as the representative office of the Republic of China (Taiwan) and is the counterpart of the India-Taipei Association in Taiwan; both institutions have the goal of improving relations between the two sides, which have been strained since New Delhi's recognition of Beijing in 1950.

Sino-Indian relations hit a low point in 1998 following India's nuclear tests in May. Indian Defense Minister George Fernandes declared that "China is India's number one threat", hinting that India developed nuclear weapons in defense against China's nuclear arsenal. In 1998, China was one of the strongest international critics of India's nuclear tests and entry into the nuclear club. During the 1999 Kargil War China voiced support for Pakistan, but also counseled Pakistan to withdraw its forces.

2000s

With Indian President K. R. Narayanan's visit to China, 2000 marked a gradual re-engagement of Indian and Chinese diplomacy. In a major embarrassment for China, the 17th Karmapa, Urgyen Trinley Dorje, who was proclaimed by China, made a dramatic escape from Tibet to the Rumtek Monastery in Sikkim.

Chinese officials were in a quandary on this issue as any protest to India on the issue would mean an explicit endorsement on India's governance of Sikkim, which the Chinese still hadn't recognised. In 2002, Chinese Premier Zhu Rongji reciprocated by visiting India, with a focus on economic issues. 2003 ushered in a marked improvement in Sino-Indian relations following Indian Prime Minister Atal Bihari Vajpayee's landmark June 2003 visit to China. China officially recognized Indian sovereignty over Sikkim as the two nations moved toward resolving their border disputes.

2004 also witnessed a gradual improvement in the international area when the two countries proposed opening up the Nathula andJelepla Passes in Sikkim which would be mutually beneficial to both countries. 2004 was a milestone in Sino-Indian bilateral trade, surpassing the $10 billion mark for the first time. In April 2005, Chinese Premier Wen Jiabao visited Bangalore to push for increased Sino-Indian cooperation in high-tech industries.

In a speech, Wen stated "Cooperation is just like two pagodas (temples), one hardware and one software. Combined, we can take the leadership position in the world." Wen stated that the 21st century will be "the Asian century of the IT industry." The high-level visit was also expected to produce several agreements to deepen political, cultural and economic ties between the two nations. Regarding the issue of India gaining a permanent seat on the UN Security Council, on his visit, Wen Jiabao initially seemed to support the idea, but had returned to a neutral position on the subject by the time he returned to China. In the South Asian Association for Regional Cooperation (SAARC) Summit (2005) China was granted an observer status. While other countries in the region are ready to consider China for permanent membership in the SAARC, India seems reluctant.

A very important dimension of the evolving Sino-Indian relationship is based on the energy requirements of their industrial expansion and their readiness to proactively secure them by investing in the oilfields abroad - in Africa, the Middle East and Central Asia.

On the one hand, these ventures entail competition (which has been evident in oil biddings for various international projects recently). But on the other hand, a degree of cooperation too is visible, as they are increasingly confronting bigger players in the global oil market. This cooperation was sealed in Beijing on January 12, 2006 during the visit of Petroleum and Natural Gas Minister Mani Shankar Aiyar, who signed an agreement which envisages ONGC Videsh Ltd (OVL) and the China National Petroleum Corporation (CNPC) placing joint bids for promising projects elsewhere. This may have important consequences for their international relations.

On July 6, 2006, China and India re-opened Nathula, an ancient trade route which was part of the Silk Road. Nathula is a pass through the Himalayas and it was closed 44 years prior to 2006 when the Sino-Indian War broke out in 1962. The initial agreement for the re-opening of the trade route was reached in 2003, and a final agreement was formalized on June 18, 2006. Officials say that the re-opening of border trade will help ease the economic isolation of the region.

In November 2006, China and India had a verbal spat over claim of the north-east Indian state of Arunachal Pradesh. India claimed that China was occupying 38,000 square kilometres of its territory in Kashmir, while China claimed the whole of Arunachal Pradesh as its own. In May 2007, China denied the application for visa from an Indian Administrative Service officer in Arunachal Pradesh. According to China, since Arunachal Pradesh is a territory of China, he would not need a visa to visit his own country. Later in December 2007, China appeared to have reversed its policy by granting a visa to Marpe Sora, an Arunachal born professor in computer science. In January 2008, Prime Minister Manmohan Singh visited China and met with President Hu Jintao and Premier Wen Jiabao and had bilateral discussions related to trade, commerce, defense, military, and various other issues.

Until 2008 the British Government's position remained the same as had been since the Simla Accord of 1913: that China held suzerainty over Tibet but not sovereignty. Britain revised this view on 29 October 2008, when it recognised Chinese sovereignty over Tibet by issuing a statement on its website. The Economist stated that although the British Foreign Office's website does not use the word sovereignty, officials at the Foreign Office said "it means that, as far as Britain is concerned, 'Tibet is part of China. Full stop.'" This change in Britain's position affects India's claim to its North Eastern territories which rely on the same Simla Accord that Britain's prior position on Tibet's sovereignty was based upon.

In October 2009, Asian Development Bank formally acknowledging Arunachal Pradesh as part of India, approved a loan to India for a development project there. Earlier China had exercised pressure on the bank to cease the loan, however India succeeded in securing the loan with the help of the United States and Japan. China expressed displeasure at ADB for the same.

2010s

Chinese Premier Wen Jiabao paid an official visit to India from Dec.15-17,2010 at the invitation of Prime Minister Manmohan Singh. He was accompanied by 400 Chinese business leaders, who wished to sign business deals with Indian companies.

"India and China are two very populous countries with ancient civilizations, friendship between the two countries has a time-honoured history, which can be dated back 2,000 years, and since the establishment of diplomatic ties between our two countries, in particular the last ten years, friendship and cooperation has made significant progress. Premier Wen Jiabao at the Tagore International School, Dec 15 2010" In April 2011, the first BRICS summit was held in Sanya, Hainan, China. During the event, the two countries agreed to restore defence co-operation, and China had hinted that it may reverse its policy of administering stapled visas to residents of Jammu and Kashmir. This practice was later stopped, and as a result, defence ties were resumed between the two nations and joint military drills were expected.

It was reported in February 2012 that India will reach US$100 billion dollar trade with China by 2015. The second BRICS summit was held in New Delhi, India. It was agreed during the summit that China's government would encourage domestic companies to import more products from India in order to balance the trade deficit. Also during the summit, Chinese President Hu Jintao told Indian Prime Minister Manmohan Singh that "it is China's unswerving policy to develop Sino-Indian friendship, deepen strategic cooperation and seek common development" and "China hopes to see a peaceful, prosperous and continually developing India and is committed to building more dynamic China-India relationship". Other topics were discussed, including border dispute problems and a unified BRICS central bank.

In response to India's test of a missile capable of carrying a nuclear warhead to Beijing, the PRC called for the two countries to "cherish the hard-earned momentum of co-operation".

A three-week standoff between Indian and Chinese troops in close proximity to each other and the Line of Actual Control between Jammu and Kashmir's Ladakh region andAksai Chin was defused on May 5, 2013, days before a trip by Indian Foreign Minister Salman Khurshid to China; Khurshid said that both countries had a shared interest in not having the border issue exacerbate or "destroy" long-term progress in relations. It was also reported by the Indian Foreign Ministry that Chinese Premier Li Keqiang would visit India at the end of the May 2013. The Chinese eventually agreed to withdraw their troops in exchange for an Indian agreement to demolish several "live-in bunkers" in the Chumar sector, south of the disputed border. India and China: As China Rises, India Stirs

Sino-Indian relations, also called India-China relations, refer to the ties and relations between the People's Republic of China and the Republic of India. The economic and diplomatic importance of China and India, which are the two most populous states and the world's fastest growing major economies, has in recent years increased the significance of their bilateral relationship.

Relations between China and India date back to ancient times. China and India are two of the world's oldest civilizations and have coexisted in peace for millennia. Trade relations via the Silk Road acted as economic contact between the two regions. However, since the early 1950s, their relationship has been characterized by border disputes, resulting in military conflict (the Sino-Indian War of 1962, the Chola incident in 1967, and the 1987 Sino-Indian skirmish). Both countries have in recent years successfully attempted to reignite diplomatic and economic ties, and consequently, the two countries' relations have become closer. Today, China is India's largest trading partner, and has recently reverted its stance on India's bid for a UNSC seat, after Chinese assistant Foreign Minister Kong Quan formally declared that China will back India's UNSC bid.

AFGHANISTAN

Bilateral relations between India and Afghanistan have been traditionally strong and friendly. While India was the only South

Asian country to recognize the Soviet-backed Democratic Republic of Afghanistan in the 1980s, its relations were diminished during the Afghan civil wars and the rule of the Islamist Taliban in the 1990s. India aided the overthrow of the Taliban and became the largest regional provider of humanitarian and reconstruction aid.

The new democratically-elected Afghan government strengthened its ties with India in wake of persisting tensions and problems with Pakistan, which was suspected of continuing to shelter and support the Taliban. India pursues a policy of close cooperation to bolster its standing as a regional power and contain its rival Pakistan, which it maintains is supporting Islamic militants in Kashmir and other parts of India. India is the largest regional investor in Afghanistan, having committed more than US$2.2 billion for reconstruction purposes.

BANGLADESH

For far too long has India been oblivious to the playing of the 'Indian-Card' (for or against) in Bangladesh's domestic politics. For far too long has India tolerated the use of Bangladesh as a springboard for Pakistan's strategic de-estabilisation of India's North-Eastern states. India could borrow a leaf from Myanmar's dealing with the Rohinggya problem emanating from Saudi based organizations in Bangladesh. Al Qaeda's tentacles exist in Bangladesh.

Bangladesh too is a fit case where Indian foreign policy objectives could gain a convergence with United States national interests. The China-Bangladesh Defence Cooperation Agreement adds an additional dimension to the other threats as analysed in an earlier Paper of this author.

India needs to draw red-lines in terms of India's national interests which Bangladesh must not overstep with impunity. In tandem, India through its big business houses should integrate Bangladesh into more commercial linkages. Increased Indian economic investments in Bangladesh could generates thousands of job and remove the root cause of Bangladesh's instability and move towards Islamic fundamentalism.

Historical Background

During the Partition of India after independence in 1947, the Bengal region was divided into two: East Bengal (present-day Bangladesh) and West Bengal. East Bengal was made a part of the Islamic Republic of Pakistan due to the fact that both regions had an overwhelmingly large Muslim population, more than 86%. In 1955, the government of Pakistan changed its name from East Bengal to East Pakistan.

There were some confrontations between the two regions though. Firstly, in 1948, Muhammad Ali Jinnah declared that only Urdu would the sole official language of the entire nation, though more than 95% of the East Bengali population spoke Bengali. And when protests broke out in Bangladesh on February 21, 1952, Pakistani police fired on the protesters, killing hundreds. Secondly, East Bengal/East Pakistan was allotted only a small amount of revenue for its development out of the Pakistani national budget. Therefore, a separatist movement started to grow in the isolated province. When the main separatist party the Awami League, headed by Sheikh Mujibur Rahman, won 167 of 169 seats up for grabs in the 1970 elections and got the right to form the government, the Pakistan president under Yahya Khan refused to recognize the election results and arrested Sheikh Mujibur Rahman.

This led to widespread protests in East Pakistan and in 1971, the Liberation War, followed by the declaration (by Sheikh Mujibur Rahman on 7 March 1971) of the independent state of Bangladesh.

India under Indira Gandhi fully supported the cause of the Bangladeshis and its troops and equipment were used to fight the Pakistani forces. The Indian Army also gave full support to the main Bangladeshi guerrilla force, the Mukti Bahini. Finally, on 26 March 1971, Bangladesh emerged as an independent state. Since then, there have been several issues of agreement as well as of dispute.

Areas of Agreement

1. India played a central role in the independence of Bangladesh. About 250,000 Indian soldiers fought for, and 20,000 losing their lives for the cause of an independent

Bangladesh. India sheltered over 10 million refugees who were fleeing the atrocities of the occupying West Pakistan Army. India and its ally Bhutan were the first countries to recognize Bangladesh as an independent nation. Bangladeshis have some awareness of their obligation and gratitude towards India.

2. Sheikh Mujibur Rahman's first foreign visit as Prime Minister and the Founding Father of the newly born nation was to India and it was then decided Indo-Bangladesh relations would be guided by principles of democracy, socialism, nonalignment and opposition to colonialism and racism. Indira Gandhi too visited Bangladesh in 1972 and assured that India would never interfere in the internal affairs of the country.
3. In 1972, both the countries signed a 'Treaty of Friendship and Peace'. An Indo-Bangladesh Trade Pact was also signed.
4. The mainstream party Awami League is generally considered to be friendly towards India.

Areas of Contention

1. A major area of contention has been the construction and operation of the Farakka Barrage by India to increase water supply in the river Hoogly. Bangladesh insists that it does not receive a fair share of the Ganga waters during the drier seasons, and gets flooded during the monsoons when India releases excess waters.
2. There have also been disputes regarding the transfer of Teen Bigha Corridor to Bangladesh. Part of Bangladesh is surrounded by the Indian state of West Bengal. On 26 June 1992, India leased three bigha land to Bangladesh to connect this enclave with mainland Bangladesh. There is dispute regarding the indefinite nature of the lease.
3. Terrorist activities carried out by outfits based in both countries, like Banga Sena and Harkat-ul-Jihad-al-Islami. Recently India and Bangladesh had agreed to jointly fight terrorism.
4. The Sharing of Ganges Waters was also a matter of dispute.

INDIA-MALDIVES RELATIONS

Bilateral relations between the Republic of India and the Republic of Maldives have been friendly and close in strategic, economic and military cooperation. India contributed to maintaining security on the island nation and has forged an alliance with respect to its strategic interests in the Indian Ocean.

The Maldives is located south of India's Lakshadweep Islands in the Indian Ocean and approximately 700 kilometres from Sri Lanka. Both nations established diplomatic relations after the independence of Maldives from British rule in 1966.

Since then, India and Maldives have developed close strategic, military, economic and cultural relations.

India has supported Maldives' policy of keeping regional issues and struggles away from itself, and the latter has seen friendship with India as a source of aid as well as a counter-balance to Sri Lanka, which is in proximity to the island nation and its largest trading partner.

Development of Bilateral Relations

India and Maldives officially and amicably decided their maritime boundary in 1976, although a minor diplomatic incident occurred in 1982 when the brother of the President of Maldives Maumoon Abdul Gayoom declared that the neighbouring Minicoy Island that belonged to India were a part of Maldives; Maldivies quickly and officially denied that it was laying claim to the island. India and Maldives signed a comprehensive trade agreement in 1981.

Both nations are founding members of the South Asian Association for Regional Cooperation (SAARC), the South Asian Economic Union and signatories to the South Asia Free Trade Agreement. Indian and Maldivian leaders have maintained high-level contacts and consultations on regional issues.

Operation Cactus

In November 1988 speedboats carrying 80 armed militants of the People's Liberation Organisation of Tamil Eelam landed in Maldives and along with allies who had infiltrated the country, began taking over the government. The plot, planned in Sri Lanka by the Tamil nationalist group was believed to be an attempt by a Maldivian businessman and politician opposed to the regime of the President of Maldives Maumoon Abdul Gayoom to gain control while the PLOTE sought a safe haven and base for its activities.

The militants took control of the airport in Male, the national capital, but failed to capture the President of Maldives Maumoon Abdul Gayoom, who had fled and asked for military aid from India on November 3. The then-Indian Prime Minister Rajiv Gandhi ordered 1,600 troops to aid the Maldivian government. In a military operation codenamed "Operation Cactus," Indian forces arrived within 12 hours of the request for aid being made, squashed the coup attempt and achieved full control of the country within hours. 19 PLOTE militants were killed and 1 Indian soldier wounded.

India's intervention was endorsed by other nations such as the United States, Soviet Union, Great Britain and its neighbours Nepal and Bangladesh. Its speedy and decisive victory and the restoration of the Maldivian government brought both nations even closer in friendship and cooperation. In wake of internal security crises and tensions with Sri Lanka, Maldives saw its relationship with India as a source of future security.

Commercial Relations

Since the success of Operation Cactus, the relations between India and Maldives have expanded significantly. India has provided extensive economic aid and has participated in bilateral programs for the development of infrastructure, health, civil aviation, telecommunications and labour resources. It established the Indira Gandhi Memorial Hospital in Male, the capital of Maldives, expanded telecommunications and air links and increased scholarships for Maldivian students. While India's exports to Maldives during 2006 were worth Rs. 384 crores, imports were worth less than Rs. 6 crores. The State Bank of India has contributed more than USD 500 million to aid the economic expansion of Maldives. India and Maldives have announced plans to jointly work to expand fisheries and tuna processing.

Military Relations

On 7 March 2005 Defence Attaché's Office (DAO) was established in the High commission of the Republic of Maldives in India by making Lt.Colonel Abdulla Shamaal as first defence attaché. This was the first Defence Attaché's office set up abroad. Given, that defence relations is a major component of the Indo-Maldives bilateral relations and both counties have a long record of strengthening their defence ties through a wide range of activities, such as Military Joint Exercises, exchange of visits of senior officers of the Armed forces, training of large number of defence services personnel from the Maldives at Indian defence establishments, provision of military aid, and intelligence and information sharing, the necessity for a DAO was felt.

Hence, the DAO was instituted to further strengthen and consolidate the already existing bilateral defence relations in a mutually beneficial manner. As a result, the DAO functions as the primary mechanism integrated in the resident Mission of the Republic of Maldives in New Delhi, India to guide direct and coordinate defence ties between the two countries.

On April 2006 Indian Navy gifted a Trinkat Class Fast Attack Craft of 46m length to Maldives National Defence Force's Coast Guard. India start the process to bring the island country into India's security grid. The move comes after the moderate Islamic nation approached New Delhi earlier this year over fears that one of its island resorts could be taken over by terrorists given its lack of military assets and surveillance capabilities. India is also signing an agreement later this year which includes following things.

- India will permanently base two helicopters in the country to enhance its surveillance capabilities and ability to respond swiftly to threats. One helicopter from the Coast Guard is likely to be handed over during Antony's visit while another from the Navy will be cleared for transfer shortly.
- Maldives has coastal radars on only two of its 26 atolls. India will help set up radars on all 26 for seamless coverage of approaching vessels and aircraft.

- The coastal radar chain in Maldives will be networked with the Indian coastal radar system. India has already undertaken a project to install radars along its entire coastline. The radar chains of the two countries will be interlinked and a central control room in India's Coastal Command will get a seamless radar picture.
- The Indian Coast Guard (ICG) will carry out regular Dornier sorties over the island nation to look out for suspicious movements or vessels. The Southern Naval Command will overlook the inclusion of Maldives into the Indian security grid.
- Military teams from Maldives will visit the tri-services Andaman Nicobar Command (ANC) to observe how India manages security and surveillance of the critical island chain.

SRI LANKA

India's national interests demand maintaining the unity and sovereignty of the Sri Lanka nation state. India's domestic Tamil politics should not become the touch stone of India's policies towards Sri Lanka. India needs to react forcefully to ensure that Sri Lanka remains a unified state with a set up that would meet the just aspirations of a majority of Tamils.

The above proposition entails once again the forging of mutual national interests convergence of India and the United States Sri Lanka is an important component of United States India Ocean strategy and it is felt that United States-India convergences exist already. Joint USA-India strategies and foreign policies towards Sri Lanka would be helpful in counter-acting Chinese and Pakistani overtures to wean away Sri Lanka from India's influence.

Development of Bilateral Relations

India and Sri Lanka established diplomatic relations when the latter gained its independence in 1948. Both nations proceeded to establish extensive cultural, commercial, strategic and defence ties to establish a common sphere of influence in the region, adopting nonalignment to control Western and Soviet influence. The close relationship between the then-Indian Prime Minister Indira Gandhi and then-Sri Lankan Prime Minister Sirimavo Bandaranaike led to the development of strong bilateral relations. In 1971, Indian armed forces helped squash a Communist rebellion against the Sri Lankan government.

Indian Intervention in the Sri Lankan Civil War

In the 1980s, private entities and elements in the state government of Tamil Nadu were believed to be encouraging the funding and training for the Liberation Tigers of Tamil Eelam, a separatist insurgent force..In 1987, faced with growing anger amongst its own Tamils, and a flood of refugees, India intervened directly in the conflict for the first time after the Sri Lankan government attempted to regain control of the northern Jaffna region by means of an economic blockade and military assaults, India supplied food and medicine by air and sea. After subsequent negotiations, India and Sri Lanka entered into an agreement. The peace accord assigned a certain degree of regional autonomy in the Tamil areas with Eelam People's Revolutionary Liberation Front (EPRLF) controlling the regional council and called for the Tamil militant groups to lay down their arms. Further India was to send a peacekeeping force, named the IPKF to Sri Lanka to enforce the disarmament and to watch over the regional council.

Even though the accord was signed between the governments of Sri Lanka and India, with the Tamil Tigers and other Tamil militant groups not having a role in the signing of the accord, most Tamil militant groups accepted this agreement, the LTTE rejected the accord because they opposed the candidate, who belonged to another militant group named Eelam Peoples Revolutionary Liberation Front (EPRLF), for chief administrative officer of the merged Northern and Eastern provinces. Instead the LTTE named three other candidates for the position. The candidates proposed by the LTTE were rejected by India. The LTTE subsequently refused to hand over their weapons to the IPKF.

The result was that the LTTE now found itself engaged in military conflict with the Indian Army, and launched their first attack on an Indian army rations truck on October 8, killing five Indian para-commandos who were on board by strapping burning tires around their necks. The government of India then decided that the IPKF should disarm the LTTE by force, and the Indian Army launched number of assaults on the LTTE, including a month-long campaign dubbed *Operation Pawan* to win control of the Jaffna peninsula from the LTTE. When the IPKF engaged the LTTE, the then president of Sri Lanka, Ranasinghe Premadasa, began supporting LTTE and funded LTTE with arms. During the warfare with the ltte IPKF was also alleged for human rights violation against the civilians. Notably, IPKF was alleged to have perpetrated Jaffna teaching hospital massacre which was the killing of over 70 civilians including patients, doctors and nurses. The ruthlessness of this campaign, and the Indian army's subsequent anti-LTTE operations made it extremely unpopular amongst many Tamils in Sri Lanka. The conflict between the LTTE and the Indian Army left over 1,000 Indian soldiers dead.

The Indo-Sri Lankan Accord, which had been unpopular amongst Sri Lankans for giving India a major influence, now became a source of nationalist anger and resentment as the IPKF was drawn fully into the conflict. Sri Lankans protested the presence of the IPKF, and the newly-elected Sri Lankan president Ranasinghe Premadasa demanded its withdrawal, which was completed by March 1990. On May 21, 1992, Rajiv Gandhi was assassinated and the LTTE was alleged to be the perpetrator. As a result India declared the LTTE to be a terrorist outfit in 1992. Bilateral relations improved in the 1990s and India supported the peace process but has resisted calls to get involved again. India has also been wary of and criticised the extensive military involvement of Pakistan in the conflict, accusing the latter of supplying lethal weaponry and encouraging Sri Lanka to pursue military action rather than peaceful negotiations to end the civil war.

Commercial Ties

India and Sri Lanka are member nations of several regional and multilateral organisations such as the South Asian Association for Regional Cooperation (SAARC), South Asia Co-operative Environment Programme, South Asian Economic Union and BIMSTEC, working to enhance cultural and commercial ties. Since a bilateral free trade agreement was signed and came into effect in 2000, Indo-Sri Lankan trade rose 128% by 2004 and quadrupled by 2006, reaching USD 2.6 billion. Between 2000 and 2004, India's exports to Sri Lanka in the last four years increased by 113%, from USD 618 million to $1,319 million while Sri Lankan exports to India increased by 342%, from $44 million to USD $194 million. Indian exports account for 14% of Sri Lanka's global imports. India is also the fifth largest export destination for Sri Lankan goods, accounting for 3.6% of its exports. Both nations are also signatories of the South Asia Free Trade Agreement (SAFTA). Negotiations are also underway to expand the free trade agreement to forge stronger commercial relations and increase corporate investment and ventures in various industries.

India's National Thermal Power Corp (NTPC) is also scheduled to build a 500 MW thermal power plant in Sampoor (Sampur). The NTPC claims that the this plan will take the Indo-Srilankan relationship to new level.

Fishermen Issue

There have been several incidents of firing on Indian fishermen fishing in Palk Bay.Indian Government has always taken up the issue of safety of Indian fishermen on a priority basis with the Government of Sri Lanka. Presently there is no bona fide Indian fisherman in the Sri Lankan custody. A Joint Working Group (JWG) has been constituted to deal with the issues related to Indian fishermen straying in Sri Lankan territorial waters, work out modalities for prevention of use of force against them and the early release of confiscated boats and explore possibilities of working towards bilateral arrangements for licensed fishing. The JWG last met in Jan 2006.

Development Cooperation

India is active in a number of areas of development activity in Sri Lanka. About one-sixth of the total development credit granted by GOI is made available to Sri Lanka.

Lines of credit: In the recent past three lines of credit were extended to Sri Lanka: US$ 100 million for capital goods, consumer durables, consultancy services and food items, US$ 31 million for supply of 300,000 MT of wheat and US$ 150 million for purchase of petroleum products. All of these lines of credit have been fully utilized. Another line of credit of US$ 100 million is now being made available for rehabilitation of the Colombo-Matara railway. A number of development projects are implemented under 'Aid to Sri Lanka' funds. In 2006-07, the budget for 'Aid to Sri Lanka' was Rs 28.2 Crs.

Small Development Projects: A MoU on Cooperation in Small Development Projects has been signed. Projects for providing fishing equipments to the fishermen in the East of Sri Lanka and solar energy aided computer education in 25 rural schools in Eastern Sri Lanka are under consideration.

Health Projects: We have supplied medical equipments to hospitals at Hambantota and Point Pedro, supplied 4 state of the art ambulances to the Central Province, implemented a cataract eye surgery programme for 1500 people in the Central Province and implemented a project of renovation of OT at Dickoya hospital and supplying equipment to it. The projects under consideration are: Construction of a 150-bed hospital at Dickoya, upgradation of the hospital at Trincomalee and a US$ 7.5 million grant for setting up a Cancer Hospital in Colombo.

Education Projects: Upgradation of the educational infrastructure of the schools in the Central province including teachers' training, setting up of 10 computer labs, setting up of 20 e-libraries (Nenasalas), Mahatma Gandhi scholarship scheme for +2 students and setting up of a vocational training centre in Puttalam. India also contributes to the Ceylon Workers Education Trust that gives scholarships to the children of estate workers.

Training: A training programme for 465 Sri Lankan Police officers has been commenced in Dec 2005. Another 400 Sri Lankan Police personnel are being trained for the course of 'Maintenance of Public Order'.

Concluding Observations: India's emergence as a regional power and a key global player depends largely on her image and standing in the South Asian neighbourhood. If India cannot effectively generate and ensure her key status in South Asia, how can the world be convinced that it can carve influence farther afield.

India's nuclear weapons, space programmes, missiles development and her overwhelming superiority in military strength are of no use, if the South Asian neighbourhood takes India for granted and merrily tramples on India's national interests and her image. India needs to introduce an element of 'unilateralism' in her state-craft in South Asia.

Fortunately for India, with the exception of Pakistan, joint convergences of national interests exist between United States and India. This could greatly facilitate India's forceful assertion in South Asian affairs for greater regional good. Once this is achieved, a marginalised Pakistan in South Asia, may see the dawn of South Asia's strategic realities.

5

India's Relationship with Her Neighbors!

India has a long land frontier and coastline. It shares boundaries with Pakistan, Nepal, Bhutan, China, Bangladesh, Myanmar (Burma) and Sri Lanka. India has adopted a foreign policy of neutrality and non-involvement.

MINISTRY OF EXTERNAL AFFAIRS

The Ministry of External Affairs is the governmental body most concerned with foreign affairs, with responsibility for some aspects of foreign policy making, actual implementation of policy, and daily conduct of international relations. The ministry's duties include providing timely information and analysis to the prime minister and minister of external affairs, recommending specific measures when necessary, planning policy for the future, and maintaining communications with foreign missions in New Delhi. In 1994 the ministry administered 149 diplomatic missions abroad, which were staffed largely by members of the Indian Foreign Service. The ministry is headed by the minister of external affairs, who holds cabinet rank and is assisted by a deputy minister and a foreign secretary, and secretaries of state from the Indian Foreign Service.

In 1994 the total cadre strength of the Indian Foreign Service numbered 3,490, of which some 1,890 held posts abroad and 1,600 served at the Ministry of External Affairs headquarters in New Delhi. Members of the Indian Foreign Service are recruited through annual written and oral competitive examinations and come from a great variety of regional, economic, and social backgrounds. The Foreign Service Training Institute provides a wide range of courses for foreign service officers, including a basic professional course, a comprehensive course in diplomacy and international relations for foreign service recruits, a refresher course for commercial representatives, and foreign language training.

The Ministry of External Affairs has thirteen territorial divisions, each covering a large area of the world, such as Eastern Europe and the post-Soviet states, or smaller areas on India's periphery, such as Afghanistan, Iran, and Pakistan. The ministry also has functional divisions dealing with external publicity, protocol, consular affairs, Indians abroad, the United Nations (UN) and other international organizations, and international conferences.

Two of the eighteen specialized divisions and units of the ministry are of special note. The Policy Planning and Research Division conducts research and prepares briefs and background papers for top policy makers and ministry officials. The briefs cover wide-ranging issues relating to India's foreign policy and role in the changing international environment, and background papers provide information on issues concerning international developments.

The Economic Division has the important task of handling foreign economic relations. This division augments its activities to reflect changes in the government's economic policy and the international economic environment. In 1990 the division established the Economic Coordination Unit to assess the impact on India of the Persian Gulf crisis arising from Iraq's invasion of Kuwait, changes in Eastern Europe and the Soviet Union, and formation of a single market in the European Economic Community (after 1993 the European Union), as well as to promote foreign investment.

The Economic Division also runs India's foreign aid programmes, including the Indian Technical and Economic Cooperation Programme, the Special Commonwealth African Assistance Programme, and aid to individual developing countries in South Asia and elsewhere. The ministry runs the Indian Council for Cultural Relations, which arranges exhibits, visits, and cultural exchanges with other countries and oversees the activities of foreign cultural centers in India.

The Ministry of External Affairs had a budget of Rs8.8 billion for fiscal year 1994. The largest single expense was the maintenance of missions abroad: Rs3.8 billion, or close to 44 percent of the ministry's expenditures. Foreign aid totaled Rs1.3 billion, or 15.1 percent of the ministry's expenditures. The single largest recipient—as in most previous years—was Bhutan (Rs690 million), whose government operations and development are heavily subsidized by India.

OTHER GOVERNMENT ORGANIZATIONS

Besides the Office of the Prime Minister and the Ministry of External Affairs, there are other government agencies that have foreign policy-making roles. In theory, the ministers of defence, commerce, and finance provide input to foreign policy decisions discussed in cabinet meetings, but their influence in practical terms is overshadowed by the predominant position of the prime minister and his advisers. The armed forces are removed from policy making and have influence only through the minister of defence, to whom they are subordinate. Only a limited role in foreign policy making is provided for India's bicameral Parliament. Negotiated treaties and international agreements become legally binding on the state but are not part of domestic law unless passed by an act of Parliament, which also has no say in the appointment of diplomats and other government representatives dealing with foreign affairs. For the most part, because of the widespread domestic support for India's foreign policy, Parliament has endorsed government actions or sought information. The most important official link between Parliament and the executive in the mid-1990s is the Committee on External Affairs of the Lok Sabha (House of the People), the lower chamber of Parliament. The committee meets regularly and draws its membership from many parties. Usually it has served either as a forum for government briefings or as a deliberative body.

INDIA AS A RISING POWER

India has a number of power capabilities that are necessary ingredients for claiming a rising power status. Elsewhere, Baldev Raj Nayar and I (2003) have argued that India is perhaps the leading contender for major power status from the developing world in the 21st century due to its comprehensive national capabilities, defined in both hard and soft power resources. The hard power resources include: extant military capabilities, economic resources, and technological and demographic assets. The soft power assets include: leadership in international institutions; cultural appeal, democracy, secularism, and a federal polity. Moreover, India is geographically situated at a major strategic location with the Indian Ocean being the crucial waters for the world's oil transportation. In addition, among most of the emerging powers, India has shown the highest inclination, in terms of its elite and public positioning, and in terms of its invocation of its grand civilizational history, for the position of major power. More concretely, what are the sources of India's aspirations in this regard?

Hard Power Indicators: Military Power

In terms of military power India has always been pivotal for the regional security order. In recent years, it has made some major strides. In manpower, with 1.485 million regular troops India holds the third largest armed forces after China and the U.S. In terms of conventional capabilities, it has the air, naval and land assets that it can now extend beyond the immediate South Asian region to a shorter periphery, such as Southeast Asia and the Persian Gulf. It has acquired nuclear weapons and delivery systems, including IRBMs that can reach major cities of China. The shorter range Prithvi, Agni I and II missiles are meant for deterrence against Pakistan, while the Agni III has the reach of 5000 km that can potentially offer a key deterrent towards China. It is likely to have ICBM capacity (using its PSLV) long range launching capability, but is unlikely to deploy or develop it in the near term, due to concerns about potential implications for relations with the US. It is also acquiring capabilities in the naval area and air power that would extend its power projection capabilities. Moreover, if the planned deployments of missile defense systems materialize, India may have defensive capacities as well. In recent years India has been on a major arms buying spree, in its efforts to replace its ageing fighter jets, aircraft carriers, battlefield tanks, and other systems that will give it an edge in technological capabilities vis-à-vis major regional rivals.

Economic Power

In terms of economic power, India will become a leading economy by the middle of the 21st century, if its growth rate continues at the present level. This outcome is possible because at a growth rate of 6-7 per cent per annum, India's GNP will double every 10 years or so. A quadrupling of the economy in the space of 30 years could dramatically alter India's power position, especially given the prospect that many developed countries are unlikely to grow at that rate. In dollar terms the Indian economy can become number three in the next decade and number two by 2050. This economic change has foreign policy as well as strategic implications. Since the mid-1980s, India's growth has been incremental, but accelerated during the past 17 years. Barring unforeseen turbulence, India's economic growth will continue and it might even reach 8-10 per cent annually. In India, a domestically growing capitalist class is emerging which is making use of economic globalization fairly effectively.

Although China has done better than India in attracting foreign direct investment (FDI), the interesting fact is that the Indian economy is growing closer to the Chinese rate. Notably, India registers 28 per cent savings rate compared to China's 40 per cent. In 2007 China received an FDI of $758.9 billion while India $95.28 billion. The foreign trade statistics of China versus India is also stark. In 2007 China's exports were to the tune of $1.127 trillion while India's $150.8 billion. India has made some major strides in increasing its foreign trade (with a recent annual growth rate of 20 per cent or more), but it still suffers from infrastructure constraints and bureaucratic bottlenecks. India has established several special economic zones that are beginning to attract foreign investment. It is planning to reach a target of $200 billion in exports by 2009. A dramatic opening of the economy like China is politically difficult for India. The fractious political system and the requirements of coalition governments at the Center constrain India in adopting a blitzkrieg economic strategy. But India's development seems more stable and locally-generated, relying on knowledge based industries which are likely to stay pivotal for growth in the 21st century. If India can increase FDI flows and foreign trade, it may exceed China's growth rate. India's concentration on services is a smart strategy given the working population available, but manufacturing is also an area where India has great potential.

Technology assets are linked to both economic and military power and in India's case these are most noticeable in information and space arenas. India's space program has succeeded in placing different categories of satellites in space, and in developing and deploying different types of launch vehicles. With the Polar Satellite Launch Vehicle (PSLV) launch, India has been able to place heavier remote-sensing satellites at higher altitudes. On April 18, 2001 India used the GSLV (Geosynchronized Satellite Launch Vehicle) to place a 1.53 ton communications satellite in orbit at 36,000 km in space. In April 2008, India launched 10 satellites using a single launch vehicle. Currently, India has 11 national satellites including 7 remote sensing satellites in orbit (BBC News). It is also planning a mission to Moon in the near future which it will use the PSLV launch vehicle. India's emerging space capabilities will likely give it a key role in the future international system, especially if space becomes militarized and there is competition among the major powers for control of the outer space.

Demographic asset also provide India certain advantages (and disadvantages). India will have the largest number of working age population in the world during the next three decades or so. Between 2000 and 2020 India will add 310 million people to its population. The median age of the Indian population in 2007 was 25.1 to China's 33.6. Although 25 per cent of the Indian population still lives under abject poverty, the low age of the working population brings certain advantages. However, clear policy initiatives, especially in education and poverty alleviation are needed to bring this population to productive use. Considerable social and economic disparities exist in the Indian society along caste, class and gender bases, making it difficult to use the population asset optimally.

Soft Power

In terms of *soft power* indicators, India's position is significantly high in some areas while it has considerable potential in others. India has played a leading role in world trade talks at the Doha rounds along with China and Brazil and will emerge as crucial in the conclusion of any such deals in the future as well. At the UN, India has been very active provider of peacekeeping forces. It is not a permanent member of the Security Council yet, but this might be a continuing issue for India's peaceful integration into the world order. India has been assiduously cultivating its relationship with EU, ASEAN and other regional forums in an effort to embolden its institutional credentials.

India has unique cultural assets that not many other countries possess: cuisine, art, music, film and dance. It offers an alternative to the Western dominant cultural systems. Bollywood is second only to Hollywood in terms of movie industry and viewership worldwide. Over the years, Indian themes also have become prominent in English literature. And the wide use of English by Indians gives them an advantage as English has emerged as the key language of the information revolution. At the domestic level, India's democracy, federalism and secularism (although imperfect) offer a model for reasonable accommodation of minority rights, and adjustments of diversity in terms of ethnicity and language. The three language policy of India (Hindi, English and native language) has brought linguistic peace.

INDIA'S LINGERING CONSTRAINTS

India faces several constraints at the international/regional, domestic and perceptual levels in achieving a global leadership role in the near term. At the international level, India's late arrival as an independent state in 1947 (two years after the post-World War II order was finalized in San Francisco), precluded a leading role in the UN system. The UN Security Council was set up then with five permanent members who were allies in the winning coalition of the War. That set up still continues because the leading powers in the Security Council are unwilling to alter the composition of the Council. No systemic event has yet to upset the post-WW II order in terms of the structure of international institutional governance. The Cold War rivalry caused India to avoid joining alliances, and led it to pursue a non-aligned policy which also allowed it to somewhat compensate for the immediate dearth of hard power resources. However, India's quasi-alliance with the Soviet Union during 1970s and 80s precluded Western support for it to gain a leading role.

Regionally, India has been constrained by the conflict with Pakistan and China and the need to bifurcate its military forces into two fronts. The off and on alliance that the US and Pakistan have formed and China's continuing balancing coalition with Pakistan have constrained India's power in the region. The conflict in Kashmir also took considerable amount of Indian attention, and it is still simmering. In recent years, India has been affected by the weak states populating its neighborhood, especially Afghanistan, Pakistan, Bangladesh, Nepal and Sri Lanka. All these states have internal conflicts that have affected India. Nepal has emerged as major source of security challenge to India, through the Maoists (Naxalites) who now form a corridor in India's tribal belts from North to the South. Large scale migration form Bangladesh has caused internal conflict in Assam and Tripura.

The external pressures have been accentuated by the weak state syndrome of India itself. The Indian state has strength in some areas, but it is often called a 'soft state' in dealing with pressing national problems. Many parts of India, especially in states such as Bihar, UP and Jharkhand are similar to Sub-Saharan Africa in terms of state control and governance. The ability of the state to provide public goods, and services, especially in the security area, has been in decline or stagnant, despite the fact that the State has acquired considerable resources in the globalization era. A potent manifestation of state weakness is the increasing number of radical Islamic terrorist outfits in India and the increasing incidence of terrorist strikes. In 2007-08 India emerged as the number one country in terms of casualties caused by terrorist attacks.

As for *soft power* resources, strategy and diplomacy are crucial components to compensate for some of the weaknesses in the hard power area. Moreover, effective utilization of national power would require a proper grand strategy. Until recently, the Indian elite avoided this subject due to the fractious nature of its domestic politics.

Grand strategy, in contemporary times, focuses not only on military security, but on economic security as well; it attempts to increase wealth of the country as economic capability is equally important in gaining and retaining a state's power position. A grand strategy is often an intervening variable in translating a state's power capabilities into actual power and influence in the international system. India's lack of a proper grand strategy may be due to the need to accommodate divergent interest groups and political ideologies within India.

Changing Strategic Circumstances

By 2000, India's strategic position had improved appreciably. Many reasons are ascribed for this change. First of all, the US has increasingly perceived India's potential in balancing China. "Economic liberalization, growth, changes in strategic environment, nuclear tests, measured response to Pakistani provocations," all these have earned India the status of a "mature regional power." Through its nuclear tests in 1998, India repositioned itself from a largely marginal player in the international system to a serious candidate or contender for major power status. The test allowed India to get out of the fence-sitter mode on the nuclear weapons issue. Had it remained there, India would have been clubbed with Iran and North Korea by non-proliferation advocates today. It is true though that in the immediate aftermath of the tests, India's relations with Pakistan deteriorated as the so-called stability-instability paradox entered the strategic relationship between these two states. Despite the initial intense opposition by the major powers, all of them in the end entered into a strategic or security dialogue with India.

The reason for India's acceptance as a de facto nuclear power by the international community is the realization among the leading powers that with two nuclear rivals and no membership in any nuclear protection arrangement, India may well have different security dynamics from those other states pursing the nuclear option. Moreover, India has behaved maturely in the nuclear proliferation area by refusing to offer assistance to other states seeking nuclear weapons. While India has thus elevated itself from a middle power to become a candidate major power, as Ayoob (1999) states, this has been achieved without much forethought or strategic preplanning. The strategic dialogue with the US and other major powers also has helped India in clarifying its objectives, but greater levels of cooperation would require concrete policy postures and advancements in capabilities.

Some incremental but crucial changes have taken place in India's foreign policy over the past two decades that reflect the economic and strategic realities that I outlined above. The foreign policy changes are also driven by the conviction of the Indian elite that they ought to make use of the favorable economic and strategic circumstances in order to emerge as a leading world power. These new attitudes are caused by changes in the international system as well as India's internal confidence deriving from newfound economic progress.

There are multiple elements to the new foreign policy dynamism that India has exhibited over the recent years.

1. Deepening of the strategic and economic relationship with the United States.
2. Improving relations with all major powers.
3. Increased vigor in pursing the Look East Policy toward its ASEAN neighbors and East Asian states.
4. Engaging with pivotal regional power centers such as Brazil and South Africa in order to form bargaining groups that would strengthen India's position in world trade forums and other issues.
5. A focus on economic diplomacy including vigorous search for new oil sources in Africa and Latin America.

6. Building up of the armed forces, even while pursuing dialogue with neighboring states.
7. Continue peace process with Pakistan and China although major concessions from the Indian side on the border issues are unlikely to come anytime soon.

This is largely because of the constraints operating in the fractious democratic polity.

The change in US attitude toward India began in early 1990s, when in response to Soviet collapse, India began to adjust is foreign policy. However, the nuclear issue intervened as a major stumbling bloc. In 1998 India tested its nuclear weapons that caused a major furor in international relations and the US response was harsh with Washington and its allied imposing a series of sanctions on India. However, the US and India initiated a dialogue which eased considerably much of the irritants.

The 1999 Kargil conflict was a watershed, when President Bill Clinton sided with India and forced Pakistani Prime Minister Nawaz Shariff to commit to a withdrawal of Pakistani forces from the Kargil Hills on the Indian side that the former had occupied. The Clinton visit to India in March 2000 was a major success, but it was the George W. Bush administration that initiated major changes in the US policy toward India, especially in the nuclear area. The 1995 India-US nuclear deal that the US president signed with Prime Minister Manmohan Singh elevated India to the status of a de facto nuclear weapon state while allowing it to engage in international nuclear trade.

A series of steps were undertaken which included India bifurcating its civilian and military facilities, the Hyde Act which exempted non-NPT signatory India from nuclear trade sanctions, the 123 Agreement and the waivers from the IAEA as well as the Nuclear Suppliers Group (NSG), which is expected in September 2008. This deal has major repercussions in both strategic and economic terms for US-India relations. In the post September 11, 2001 world, the Indian perception of the US has changed in a big way. The US was on terror in Afghanistan against Islamic radicals is part of the reasons for the change. It is very plausible that had there been no September 11, attacks, India-US relations would have matured even further. The need for Pakistan's support in the war in Afghanistan somewhat mellowed the level of cooperation that the U.S. could develop with India.

A number of concrete steps have been taken to strengthen this relationship. They include the joint exercise that Indian and US military branches have conducted, several defense deals that made US one of the leading sources of weapons for India, cooperation in the energy field, and bilateral dialogue. The two-way trade also has seen considerable progress over the years. It is not only US companies that invest in India, but the reverse, with more and more Indian companies investing in the US. The US-India economic relations are bound to improve as Washington needs India and India needs the US for continued economic growth and innovation. Economic, strategic, and demographic reasons call for optimism with the latter emerging as a very important in the coming years. Indian technical students are populating all US graduate schools and Indian technology workers are the largest recipients of H-1 visas. They will be a key force in linking Indian and American knowledge-based economies in the decades to come. The Indian diaspora is very active as a lobbying group in the U.S. and is emerging as a powerful electoral segment. When economic and security links improve, popular perceptions of Americans and Indians of each other will also change. Today, India is one of the few countries that genuinely sympathize with the US on the war on terrorism (I don't mean Iraq invasion). However, India's foreign policy may diverge on the issue of military action against Iran as well as on global trade issues.

India has also maintained strong ties with Russia, especially as its traditional source of weapons acquisition. It is however, difficult to see the emergence of a deep strategic relationship as happened in the Cold War era even if Russia emerges as a global power once again. This is because India has been diversifying its economic and military sources and Russia has only very limited non-military and non-oil resources for India's fast globalizing economy.

With respect to China, India's foreign policy has maintained an outward cordiality, but there are simmering tensions in relations.

Over the past few years, several border incidents have occurred that are not reported by the world media. These incidents reflect the continued rivalry that these states have over territory, influence and policies over Tibet, Pakistan, and the emerging US-India relationship. As China attempts to expand its military bases in Tibet and in the Indian Ocean rim countries such as Myanmar, India is starting to feel the pressure to counter such moves as evident in the increased activism by the two states in Myanmar. The increasing economic links between China and India somewhat cushion the rivalry from escalating to a full-fledged military competition

South Asia and India's Foreign Policy

While India has improved its engagement with the major powers, a notable weakness of the Indian foreign policy approach has been the neglect of its own immediate region, South Asia. This is an inevitable result of India's desire to transcend the region and not to get mired in the quarrels of the smaller neighboring states. The regional states are all weak countries with multiple security, economic and demographic challenges that spill over to India. India is affected by internal and external Islamic terrorist cells that have emerged in the region.

INDIA AND CHINA

When the Communists came to power in China, India had welcomed the change and was one of the first countries to recognise her. She also advocated China's admission to the UN.

In 1954, Indian Prime Minister Jawaharlal Nehru and the Chinese Prime Minister, Chou- en-lai, had signed the "Panchsheel" agreement.

They adopted five principles:

1. Mutual respect for each other's territorial integrity and sovereignty.
2. Mutual non-aggression.
3. Mutual non-interference in each other's internal affairs.
4. Equality and mutual benefit.
5. Peaceful coexistence.

In spite of this, in 1962, China attacked India in the North-East and occupied a part of Indian Territory. The war ended soon but relations between India and China remained strained for a long time to come.

The visits of the Indian Prime Ministers Rajiv Gandhi (in 1988) and Narasimha Rao (in 1993) to China have improved the situation to some extent. Several trade agreements have also been signed. But it is not an easy task to restore peace and mutual trust between the two countries.

INDIA AND SOUTH ASIA

South Asia comprises the countries lying to the south of the Himalayas and the Hindukush mountains. India, Pakistan, Nepal, Bhutan, Bangladesh, Maldives and Sri Lanka are the countries belonging to the region. Most of these countries were previously ruled by the British. They have similar cultures, social habits and economic problems.

All these countries face problems arising out of overpopulation, poverty, malnutrition, illiteracy etc. It is believed that these countries of South Asia could progress fast only through cooperation with each other and by devising common plans for development. This concept led to the formation of the South Asian Association for Regional Cooperation (SAARC) with the objective of mutual economic and social development.

THE SOUTH ASIAN ASSOCIATION

The late President Zia-ur-Rehman of Bangladesh first proposed the setting up of a regional body, countries, held discussions on the need for cooperation among them and identified several areas where cooperation was urgently needed.

The Foreign Ministers of these seven South Asian countries studied these proposals. The first South the SAARC Asian summit held in Dhaka in 1985 marked the formation of the SAARC.

It's Objectives

The Dhaka Declaration states its objective as the making of "the full use of all the human and natural resources and accelerate the economic and social development of the region". Broadly speaking, the objectives are:

1. Strengthening economic cooperation so as to improve the quality of life of the people of South Asia;
2. Increasing the pace of economic growth;
3. Giving mutual assistance and cooperation in areas like agriculture, scientific development, etc.; and
4. Promoting social progress and cultural development.

It was made clear from the very beginning that no member state would interfere in the internal affairs of another. Only those matters would be discussed which concerned all the member states.

After the formation of the SAARC, a number of summits were held. Each summit undertook several specific programmes. The South Asian Preferable Trade Agreement (SAPTA) was signed to inaugurate a new era of economic cooperation in South Asia. India hosted the first festival of the SAARC countries in 1992. Artists, musicians and dancers from all the SAARC countries participated in the festival. The first SAARC Trade Fair was held in New Delhi in 1996. Bangladesh, Pakistan, Nepal, Bhutan, Sri Lanka and India participated in the fair.

Achievements

The progress of regional cooperation among the SAARC countries was slow. Yet a few noteworthy developments took place.

1. It established a cultural link among the SAARC countries. The SAVE (SAARC Audio-Visual Exchange programme) was launched in 1987 to make people aware of one another's cultures and make them conscious of the need for cultural exchange. Regular monthly programmes on radio and television are contributed by each member country.
2. The SAARC Regional Convention on the Suppression of Terrorism came into force in August 1988. The members also signed a SAARC Convention on Narcotic Drugs in 1990 to combat the problem of drug trafficking and drug abuse.

3. A SAARC Trade Fair with the theme "Cooperation for Growth" was organized in New Delhi.
4. The South Asian Federation (SAF) Games are held by turn in each of the member countries.

It is difficult for the SAARC to achieve its objectives because of internal dissent. There are differences between India and Pakistan on the Kashmir issue and cross-border terrorism. India also has a dispute with Bangladesh over the sharing of river waters and strained relations with Sri Lanka on Tamil militancy.

THE ASSOCIATION OF SOUTH-EAST ASIAN NATIONS (ASEAN)

The South-East Asian countries of Malaysia, Myanmar (Burma), Thailand and Vietnam are economically important countries. While Myanmar, Thailand and Vietnam are rice- producing countries, Malaysia produces rubber.

Possibly for fear of communist domination, the governments of Indonesia, Malaysia, Thailand, Philippines and Singapore formed the Association of South-East Asian Nations (ASEAN) in 1967. It was decided to make the region a "Zone of Peace, Freedom and Neutrality". Later on Brunei, Vietnam, Myanmar and Laos joined the ASEAN.

The ASEAN was founded with the objective of accelerating economic growth, social progress and cultural development in the region. It sought dialogue with the powerful nations of the world in order to attract investment. These nations were called "Dialogue Partners".

INDIA AND THE ASEAN

India has cordial relations with the ASEAN countries. She was made a full-fledged Dialogue Partner in 1995. Her relations with the ASEAN countries improved. India was also represented at the ASEAN Regional Forum Conference in Manila (1998).

India and Nepal

Being a small landlocked country, Nepal depends on India for economic support and transit facilities. Almost all of her imports pass through Indian ports. India has made a significant contribution to economic and social developments of Nepal. She built the 204 km long Mahendra Raj Marg to link Kathmandu and India. Agreements have been signed for greater cooperation in trade, education, industrial development and cultural exchange programmes.

There are very few travel restrictions between India and Nepal. Nepalese workers are employed in India and Nepalese students study in Indian universities.

India and Bhutan

Bhutan, a small Himalayan kingdom, is one of the poorest countries of the world. India has helped Bhutan in her telecommunication and hydroelectric projects and in the construction of hospitals, roads and bridges.

India and Myanmar

Myanmar (Burma), which was a part of British India, became independent in 1948. Since India and Myanmar share common boundaries, they have to face problems of smuggling and illegal migration. Rajiv Gandhi visited Myanmar in 1987 and the two countries agreed to solve these problems through greater vigilance.

India supports Aung-San Suu Kyi, the Nobel peace prize winner who is the leader of the democratic movement in Myanmar.

India and Pakistan

In 1947, India was partitioned and the country of Pakistan was born. The two countries share the same historical, linguistic and cultural heritage. Yet, ever since independence, relations between the two countries are marked by hostilities.

The Kashmir Issue

The Kashmir problem had begun from 1947, the year of our independence. The Mountbatten Plan had given the Indians States the option of joining either India or Pakistan or remaining independent. When the British left India, Pakistan attacked Kashmir and occupied a part of the Kashmir Valley. The Maharaja of Kashmir decided to join India and signed the instrument of accession.The

Indian army moved into Kashmir and pushed back the invaders. After UN intervention, North-West Kashmir was controlled by Pakistan and the rest of the state was placed under Indian control.

The Indo-Pak War (1965)

In August 1965, Pakistan made another attempt to seize Kashmir. A war started. After UN intervention, a truce was declared and an agreement (the Tashkent Agreement) was signed in 1966. But cordiality and friendship were not established.

The Indo-Pak War (1971)

Hostilities between India and Pakistan again started in 1971 when India helped Bangladesh to become independent. By the Simla Agreement (1972), Prime Minister Indira Gandhi of India and Z.A. Bhutto of Pakistan agreed to settle all problems peacefully. However, relations between India and Pakistan continue to remain strained.

Kargil War (1999)

War again broke out between the two countries when Pakistan occupied portions of Indian Territory in the Kargil area. India defeated Pakistan. Relations between India and Pakistan further worsened because of Pakistan's involvement in terrorist activities in various parts of India, especially in the Punjab and Kashmir. This cross- border terrorism instigated by Pakistan is a grave threat to India's security.Restraint, understanding and cooperation are needed for the establishment of lasting peace in this region.

India and Bangladesh

In 1971, a civil war broke out between the people of East Pakistan and West Pakistan. India helped East Pakistan in her war of independence against West Pakistan. In 1971, East Pakistan became independent with India's support. A new nation, Bangladesh, was born under Mujibur Rehman.

Subsequently, India helped Bangladesh to set her economy on a sound footing by giving her loans and technical assistance. She also sent relief to Bangladesh during natural calamities like flood and drought. Relations with Bangladesh deteriorated over the sharing of the water of the River Ganges and the refugee problem. In 1990 the two countries entered into an arrangement covering various aspects of trade and sharing of water. A 30-year treaty has been signed between the two countries over the sharing of the water of the Ganges (1996).

India and Sri Lanka

India has cultural, historical and religious ties with Sri Lanka. Sri Lanka is facing a civil war in her northern provinces. A predominantly Tamil Hindu population of northern Sri Lanka started a movement demanding an independent state. This powerful separatist movement is led by the Liberation Tigers of Tamil Eelam (LTTE).

India, on the request of the Government of Sri Lanka sent a peace-keeping force there to restore normalcy. The Indian forces were withdrawn after three years (1990) without restoring peace.

India wants Sri Lanka to find a solution to her conflict with the Tamils who are fighting for independence. Rajiv Gandhi himself became a victim of this unresolved crisis when he was assassinated in 1991. Cordial relations have been restored between the two countries. As member states of the SAARC, both countries are working together on developmental issues.

India and the Maldives

The republic of Maldives is a group of islands in the Indian Ocean. India shares a close and cordial relationship with Maldives. Trade and tourism are being developed between the two countries.

ASIA-PACIFIC

Australia

The strongest ties between these two states is the commonwealth connection. Cricketing and Bollywood ties also help foster relations as in the frequent travel for games, and, more importantly, the presence of Australian cricketers in India for commercial gain.

This was further enhanced with the IPL, and, to a lesser degree, the ICL. Bollywood has also improved ties as with John Howard's visit to Mumbai to increase tourism to Australia. Furthermore, there is a going strategic connection to forming an "Asian NATO" with India, Japan, the US and Australia. The bilateral agreements have worked out for all but the Indo-Australian angle, though this has been hurt by India's refusal to sign the NPT and Australia's consequent refusal to provide India with uranium until the latter do so. The Australian and Indian militaries have already worked well together. Of late the relations between the two countries were jolted, with attacks on Indian Community students in Melbourne, Australia. Indian Government lodged strong protests with the Australian Government. Australian Prime Minister Mr. Kevin Rudd said that "Australia valued its education system and International Students are valued more here in Australia. " Mr. Rudd though said that his Govt. has ordered a thorough probe into the attacks and also condemned it in strongest possible terms no significant break through has been achieved.

Fiji

Fijis relationship with the Republic of India is often seen by observers against the backdrop of the sometimes tense relations between its indigenous people and the 44 percent of the population who are of Indian descent. India has used its influence in international forums such as the Commonwealth of Nations and United Nations on behalf of ethnic Indians in Fiji, lobbying for sanctions against Fiji in the wake of the 1987 coups and the 2000 coup, both of which removed governments, one dominated and one led, by Indo-Fijians.

Japan

India-Japan relations have always been strong. India has culturally influenced Japan through Buddhism. During the Indian Independence Movement, the Japanese Imperial Army helped Netaji Subhash Chandra Bose's Indian National Army. Relations have remained warm since India's independence.

Japanese companies, like Sony, Toyota, and Honda, have manufacturing facilities in India, and with the growth of the Indian economy, India is a big market for Japanese firms. The most prominent Japanese company to have a big investment in India is automobiles giant Suzuki which is in partnership with Indian automobiles company Maruti Suzuki, the largest car manufacturer in India. Honda is also a partner in "Hero Honda", one of the largest motor cycle sellers in the world. In December 2006, Prime Minister Manmohan Singh's visit to Japan culminated in the signing of the "Joint Statement Towards Japan-India Strategic and Global Partnership". Japan has funded some major infrastructure projects in India, most notably the Delhi Metro subway system. Indian applicants were welcomed in 2006 to the JET Program, starting with just one slot available in 2006 and 41 in 2007. Also, in the year 2007, the Japanese Self Defence Forces took part in a naval exercise in the Indian Ocean, known as Malabar 2007, which also involved the naval forces of India, Australia, Singapore and the United States.

In October 2008, Japan signed an agreement with India under which it would grant the latter a low-interest loan worth US$4. 5 billion to construct a high-speed rail line between Delhi and Mumbai. This is the single largest overseas project being financed by Japan and reflects growing economic partnership between the two. India is also one of three countries with whom Japan has security pact, the other being Australia and the United States.

Laos

In recent years, India has endeavoured to build relations, with this small Southeast Asian nation. They have strong military relations, and India shall be building an Airforce Academy in Laos.

Indonesia

In 1950, the first President of Indonesia-Sukarno called upon the peoples of Indonesia and India to "intensify the cordial relations" that had existed between the two countries "for more than 1000 years" before they had been "disrupted" by colonial powers. Fifteen years later in Djakarta, government-inspired mobs were shouting: "Down with India, the servant of imperialists" and "Crush India, our enemy. " Yet in the spring of 1966, the foreign ministers of both countries began speaking again of an era of friendly relations. India had supported Indonesian independence and Nehru had raised the Indonesian question in the United Nations Security Council. Today, India has an embassy in Jakarta and Indonesia operates an embassy in Delhi.

Malaysia

India has a high commission in Kuala Lumpur, and Malaysia has a high commission in New Delhi. Both countries are full members of the Commonwealth of Nations, and the Asian Union. India and Malaysia are also connected by various cultural and historical ties that date back to antiquity. The two countries are on excellently friendly terms with each other seeing as Malaysia is home to a strong concentration of Indian immigrants. Mahathir bin Mohamad the fourth and longest serving Prime Minister of Malayasia is of Indian origin, his father Mohamad Iskandar, was a Malayalee Muslim (who migrated from Kerala) and his mother Wan Tampawan, was Malay.

Singapore

India and Singapore share long-standing cultural, commercial and strategic relations, with Singapore being a part of the "Greater India" cultural and commercial region. More than 300, 000 people of Indian origin live in Singapore. Following its independence in 1965, Singapore was concerned with China-backed communist threats as well as domination from Malaysia and Indonesia and sought a close strategic relationship with India, which it saw as a counter-balance to Chinese influence and a partner in achieving regional security. Singapore had always been an important strategic trading post, giving India trade access to Maritime Southeast Asia and the Far East. Although the rival positions of both nations over the Vietnam War and the Cold War caused consternation between India and Singapore, their relationship expanded significantly in the 1990s; Singapore was one of the first to respond to India's "Look East" Policy of expanding its economic, cultural and strategic ties in Southeast Asia to strengthen its standing as a regional power. Singapore, and especially, the Singaporean Foreign Minister, George Yeo, have taken an interest, in re-establishing the ancient Indian university, Nalanda University.

Singapore is the 8th largest source of investment in India and the largest amongst ASEAN member nations. It is also India's 9th biggest trading partner as of 2005-06. Its cumulative investment in India totals USD 3 billion as of 2006 and is expected to rise to US 5 billion by 2010 and US 10 billion by 2015. India's economic liberalisation and its "Look East" policy have led to a major expansion in bilateral trade, which grew from USD 2. 2 billion in 2001 to US 9-10 billion in 2006-a 400% growth in span of five years-and to USD 50 billion by 2010. Singapore accounts for 38% of India's trade with ASEAN member nations and 3. 4% of its total foreign trade. India's main exports to Singapore in 2005 included petroleum, gemstones, jewellery, machinery and its imports from Singapore included electrónic goods, organic chemicals and metals. More than half of Singapore's exports to India are basically "re-exports"-items that had been imported from India.

South Korea

The cordial relationship between the two countries extends back to 48AD, when Queen Suro, or Princess Heo, travelled from the kingdom of Ayodhya to Korea. According to the Samguk Yusa, the princess had a dream about a heavenly king who was awaiting heaven's anointed ride. After Princess Heo had the dream, she asked her parents, the king and queen, for permission to set out and seek the man, which the king and queen urged with the belief that god orchestrated the whole fate. Upon approval, she set out on a boat, carrying gold, silver, a tea plant, and a stone which calmed the waters. Archeologists discovered a stone with two fish kissing each other, a symbol of the Gaya kingdom that is unique to the Mishra royal family in Ayodhya, India. This royal link provides further evidence that there was an active commercial engagements between India and Korea since the queen's arrival to Korea. Current descendants live in the city of Kimhae as well as abroad in America's state of New Jersey and Kentucky. Many of them became prominent and well-known around the world like President Kim Dae Jung, Prime Minister Jong Pil Kim.

The relations between the countries have been relatively limited, although much progress arose during the three decades. Since the formal establishment of the diplomatic ties between two countries in 1973, several trade agreements have been reached. Trade between the two nations has increased exponentially, exemplified by the $530 million during the fiscal year of 1992–1993, and the $10 billion during 2006–2007. During the 1997 Asian financial crisis, South Korean businesses sought to increase access to the global markets, and began trade investments with India.

The last two presidential visits from South Korea to India were in 1996 and 2006, and the embassy works between the two countries are seen as needing improvements. Recently, there have been acknowledgements in the Korean public and political spheres that expanding relations with India should be a major economical and political priority for South Korea.

Much of the economic investments of South Korea have been drained into China; however, South Korea is currently the fifth largest source of investment in India. To the Times of India, President Roh voiced his opinion that cooperation between India's software and Korea's IT industries would bring very efficient and successful outcomes.

The two countries agreed to shift their focus to the revision of the visa policies between the two countries, expansion of trade, and establishment of free trade agreement to encourage further investment between the two countries. Korean companies such as LG and Samsung have established manufacturing and service facilities in India, and several Korean construction companies won grants for a portion of the many infrastructural building plans in India, such as the "National Highway Development Project". Tata Motor's purchase of Daewoo Commercial Vehicles at the cost of $102 million highlights the India's investments in Korea, which consist mostly of subcontracting.

Taiwan

The bilateral relations between India and Taiwan (officially *Republic of China*) have improved since the 1990s despite both nations *not* maintaining official diplomatic relations, India recognizes only the People's Republic of China and not the Republic of China's contention of being the legitimate government of territorial China-a conflict that emerged after the Chinese Civil

War (1945–49). However, India's economic & Commercial links as well as people-to-people contacts with Taiwan have expanded in recent years.

Thailand

India's Look East policy, saw India grow relations with ASEAN countries including Thailand, and Thailand's Look West policy, also saw it grow its relations with India. Both countries are members of BIMSTEC. Indian Prime Ministers Rajiv Gandhi, P. V. Narasimha Rao, Atal Bihari Vajpayee, and Manmohan Singh, have visited Thailand as have, Chatichai Choonhavan, Thaksin Shinawatra, and Surayud Chulanont, visited India. In 2003, a Free trade agreement was signed between the two countries. India, is the 13th largest investor in Thailand. The spheres of trade are in chemicals, pharmaceuticals, textiles, nylon, tyre cord, real estate, rayon fibres, paper grade pulps, steel wires, and rods. However, IT Services, and manufacturing, are the main spheres. Through Buddhism, India, has culturally influenced Thailand. The Indian epics, Mahabharata, and Ramayana, are popular and are widely taught in schools as part of the curriculum in Thailand. The example can also be seen in temples around Thailand, where the story of Ramayana and renowned Indian folk stories are depicted on the temple wall. Thailand, has become a big tourist destination for Indians.

Vietnam

India supported Vietnam's independence from France, opposed U. S. involvement in the Vietnam War and supported unification of Vietnam. India established official diplomatic relations in 1972 and maintained friendly relations, especially in wake of Vietnam's hostile relations with the People's Republic of China, which had become India's strategic rival.

India granted the "Most Favoured Nation" status to Vietnam in 1975 and both nations signed a bilateral trade agreement in 1978 and the Bilateral Investment Promotion and Protection Agreement (BIPPA) on March 8, 1997. In 2007, a fresh joint declaration was issued during the state visit of the Prime Minister of Vietnam Nguyen Tan Dung. Bilateral trade has increased rapidly since the liberalisation of the economies of both Vietnam and India. India is the 13th-largest exporter to Vietnam, with exports have grown steadily from USD 11. 5 million in 1985-86 to USD 395. 68 million by 2003.

Vietnam's exports to India rose to USD 180 million, including agricultural products, handicrafts, textiles, electronics and other goods. Between 2001 and 2006, the volume of bilateral trade expanded at 20-30% per annum to reach USD 1 billion by 2006. Continuing the rapid pace of growth, bilateral trade is expected to rise to USD 2 billion by 2008, 2 years ahead of the official target. India and Vietnam have also expanded cooperation in information technology, education and collaboration of the respective national space programmes. Direct air links and lax visa regulations have been established to bolster tourism.

India and Vietnam are members of the Mekong-Ganga Cooperation, created to develop to enhance close ties between India and nations of Southeast Asia. Vietnam has supported India's bid to become a permanent member of the U. N. Security Council and join the Asia-Pacific Economic Cooperation (APEC). In the 2003 joint declaration, India and Vietnam envisaged creating an "Arc of Advantage and Prosperity" in Southeast Asia; to this end, Vietnam has backed a more important relationship and role between India and the Association of Southeast Asian Nations (ASEAN) and its negotiation of an Indo-ASEAN free trade agreement. India and Vietnam have also built strategic partnerships, including extensive cooperation on developing nuclear power, enhancing regional security and fighting terrorism, transnational crime and drug trafficking.

Americas

India's commonalities with developing nations in Latin America, especially Brazil and Mexico have continued to grow. India and Brazil continue to work together on the reform of Security Council through the G4 nations while have also increased strategic and economic cooperation through the IBSA Dialogue Forum. The process of finalizing Preferential Trade Agreement (PTA) with MERCOSUR (Brazil, Argentina, Uruguay, and Paraguay) is on the itinerary and negotiations are being held with Chile. Brazilian

President Luiz Inacio Lula da Silva was the guest of honour at the 2004 Republic Day celebrations in New Delhi.

Argentina

Formal relations between both the countries were first established in 1949. India has an embassy in Buenos Aires and Argentina has an embassy in New Delhi. India has expressed its desires to agree with the Argentinian claims on British colonies in Southern Atlantic Ocean and other territorial border disputes with Chile.

Brazil

A group called the Filhos de Gandhi (Sons of Gandhi) participates regularly in the carnival in Salvador. Private Brazilian organizations occasionally invite Indian cultural troupes.

In recent years, relations between Brazil and India have grown considerably and co-operation between the two countries has been extended to such diverse areas as science and technology, pharmaceuticals and space. The two-way trade in 2007 nearly tripled to US$ 3. 12 billion from US$ 1. 2 billion in 2004. India attaches tremendous importance to its relationship with this Latin American giant and hopes to see the areas of co-operation expand in the coming years. Both countries want the participation of developing countries in the UNSC permanent membership since the underlying philosophy for both of them are: UNSC should be more democratic, legitimate and representative-the G4 is a novel grouping for this realization. Brazil and India are deeply committed to IBSA (South-South cooperation) initiatives and attach utmost importance to this trilateral cooperation between the three large, multi-ethnic, multi-racial and multi-religious developing countries, which are bound by the common principle of pluralism and democracy.

Canada

Indo-Canadian relations, are the longstanding bilateral relations between India and Canada, which are built upon a "mutual commitment to democracy", "pluralism", and "people-to-people links, " according to the government of Canada. In 2004, bilateral trade between India and Canada was at about C$2. 45 billion. However, the botched handling of the Air India investigation and the case in general suffered a setback to Indo-Canadian relations. India's Smiling Buddha nuclear test led to connections between the two countries being frozen, with allegations that India broke the terms of the Colombo Plan. Although Jean Chretien and Roméo LeBlanc both visited India in the late 1990s, relations were again halted after the Pokhran-II tests.

Colombia

Both countries established diplomatic ties on January 19, 1959. Since then the relationship between the two countries has been gradually increasing with more frequent diplomatic visits to promote political, commercial cultural and academic exchanges. Colombia is currently the commercial point of entry into Latin America for Indian companies.

Mexico

Mexico is a very important and major economic partner of India. Mexico and India, both have embassies in the other country. Octavio Paz worked as a diplomat in India. His book *In Light of India* is an analysis of Indian history and culture.

Paraguay

India and Paraguay established diplomatic relations on September 13, 1961. India is represented in Paraguay through its embassy in Buenos Aires, Argentina and an honorary consulate in Asuncion. Since 2005, Paraguay has had an embassy in New Delhi.

INDIA AND ASEAN: AN FTA AND BEYOND

The ASEAN-India Free Trade Agreement (AIFTA), which has been concluded after protracted discussions, is a strategic event that holds promise for both parties. The agreement is noteworthy as it completes ASEAN's links with Asia's two major emerging powers and two of the fast growing economies in the world, China and India. The FTA signals India's readiness to contribute to the development of the region, and seek benefits from the process.

There is no doubt that ASEAN welcomes India's involvement in the region. A quick scan of recent trade figures, precisely because they lack lustre, suggests that India is looking beyond the present in concluding this agreement. This gives cause for optimism.

India's trade with ASEAN has not been spectacular. India has been running a deficit with ASEAN in the last decade, and the deficit has been growing. India's trade deficit with ASEAN has increased from about US$2 billion in 1998 to around US$15 billion in 2007.

The widening trade deficit is a reflection of India's trade trends with ASEAN. In 2004-05, India's total imports from ASEAN were worth roughly $9 billion, with exports amounting to $8 billion. In 2007-08, total imports ($22 billion) continued to exceed exports ($16 billion), with a trade deficit around $6 billion. But total trade between the two has been increasing rapidly.

India has been willing to extend tariff reduction commitments on 89 per cent of its tariff lines through the AIFTA. India has also signalled its intention to lower tariffs on highly sensitive items like palm oil, tea, coffee and pepper. The import duties on these commodities will be lowered to around 40-45 per cent by 2019. The stance that India has taken on these agricultural commodities, in the face of domestic resistance, indicates the store the government puts on the agreement. It is also an indication of India's long-term economic interest in ASEAN and the synergy that it envisages it could develop with the region over time.

In the last decade, India has not had trade surpluses with most of the ASEAN member countries. Notable exceptions are Cambodia, Laos, Brunei, the Philippines and Vietnam. While India may want to expand its trade with these countries, there is little doubt that, as India opens its economy, and as its business interests expand, there is much scope for its companies to grow in this part of the world. If, at this point in time, India does not evince adequate interest in ASEAN, India may lose market share to China. India can ill afford to suffer a late-mover disadvantage.

India is keen to establish its commercial presence in ASEAN. India has an active interest in exporting chemicals, pharmaceuticals and refined petroleum products. These are areas where India may choose to explore possibilities in ASEAN. ASEAN countries are an important base for export-oriented manufacturing, particularly in electrical and electronic products, automobiles and related equipment, as well as other light manufacturing goods.

Indian companies could compensate for their current lack of competitiveness in these areas by forging partnerships with ASEAN firms. The agreement will make access to ASEAN markets easier; it also provides a platform for Indian companies that want to engage with ASEAN companies by offering their expertise and technological capabilities in exporting to third country markets.

Significant outcomes can be expected, out of the AIFTA, via trade in services and investment. Indian business is coming of age, and there is evidence that the increasing maturity is accompanied by growing confidence in investing globally.

The larger Indian multinational companies have already begun to spread their wings in the developed economics. ASEAN is likely to be a favoured target for the less ambitious (and more cautious) companies. Aside from manufacturing, chemical and pharmaceutical products, ASEAN countries offer opportunities in the services sector.

The horizons here are broad and deep. Obvious candidates are banking and financial services, with initial forays already being made into Singapore. But the list could easily extend to insurance, out sourcing, tourism and logistics. India could leverage on its massive Muslim population (160 million, and the third largest in the world) to connect with Islamic banking and finance and the halál food market.

Perhaps the most exciting aspect of India's engagement with ASEAN is its importance to establishing a cooperative Asian economic community.

Indian cooperation with ASEAN in science, technology, research and development, and capacity building can provide a foundation for broader cooperation in building an Asian economic community. As India joins the club of major players who have signed FTAs with ASEAN (Japan, China, Korea, Australia and New Zealand), it clears the path for a more integrated Asian economic community.

INDIA-ASEAN COOPERATION IN SERVICES - AN OVERVIEW

The world economy has fast turned into a 'service economy' since the 1990s. Services revolution across the globe has changed the business map and the way business is conducted.

Phenomenal growth of services sector has outstripped the growth in real GDP in a number of economies from Asia. While developed countries still account for the lion's share of services in world GDP and trade, developing countries have recently started to carve out an increasingly larger share of the pie for themselves.

Available information on trade in commercial services by country in 2004 indicates faster growth in commercial services trade in the Asian economies than in the North American or European economies. This high growth of services has been aided by the expansion of trade in services due to increased tradability of a variety of business and other services. Amongst the different services sectors, trade in business and professional services including data processing, accounting and related financial services, ITeS (viz. BPOs), computer services, management consulting, hardware consulting, legal, and architectural and engineering services have witnessed phenomenal expansion in recent years. This, however, could largely be attributed to a number of services sector firms from the US & EU, who have taken recourse to off shoring and out sourcing of their non-core activities to take advantage of the low-cost high-skilled professionals from the developing countries.

Over the last decade, international trade in services has been growing at a somewhat higher rate than trade in goods (merchandise trade), though services constitute at best a fourth of total (goods and services) international trade; between 1990 and 2000, global exports of services registered a growth of over 7% as compared to a growth rate of 6% in goods. Rapid advancement in technology and innovations (especially in communication, transportation, and information processing) accompanied by an increased integration of financial markets have increased the tradability of services, which has further facilitated the expansion of crossborder trade in services. Further, existence of two-way spillovers from growth in both manufacturing and service sectors indicate the sustainability and further strengthening of the growth and trade prospects of services; demand is expected to be coming from both producer services as well as consumer services. In particular, high growth developing regions as the Asia-Pacific stand to gain the most from consolidation of the above trends, from the perspective of both employment generation and stabilisation of growth prospects in the region.

General Economy and Policy Initiatives in ASEAN & India

Though the region boasts of centuries-old politico-economic and cultural ties, it is the period since the early 1990s that has witnessed a perceptible shift in positive direction in the relations between India and the Members of ASEAN) which is rather different from the situation prevailing during the Cold War era; this has been aided to a large extent by India's 'Look East' Policy, enunciated in 1991. The economic and political interactions have increased manifold eversince, in particular after India was invited to be a full dialogue partner with ASEAN at the Fifth ASEAN Summit in Bangkok in December 1995 and India's becoming a Member of the ASEAN Regional Forum (ARF), and the two parties have agreed to explore avenues of taking advantage of the emerging economic opportunities for mutual benefits.

As a precursor to attaining the stated long-term objective of a India-ASEAN Regional Trade and Investment Area (RTIA), and recognising the need to further promote and facilitate their cooperation and utilisation of greater business opportunities provided by the India-ASEAN RTIA, India and the ten Member countries of ASEAN signed the India-ASEAN Framework Agreement on Comprehensive Economic Cooperation (CECA) in Bali, on 8 October, 2003. This forward-looking Agreement is aimed at forging a closer economic partnership in the 21st century between the ASEAN Member countries and the Republic of India by minimising barriers and deepening economic linkages between the trading partners, lowering costs, increasing intra-regional trade, investment and productive efficiency, and carries forward the historical economic and commercial ties established between the peoples of the two regions since time immemorial. The CECA is expected to create a large market of over 1. 5 billion people, with a combined current GDP of $1. 2 trillion, and will cover agreements in investment and services, in addition to trade in goods. Accepting that the total size of the market is an important determinant of realisation of the potential gains from a RTA, the India-ASEAN CECA is a step forward in the attempt by the East Asian economies to carve out a trading block which can somewhat counter the distortions created by the existing trading blocks in the Western hemisphere, viz. NAFTA and the EU25.

The combined GDP of ASEAN Members in 2004 was US$ 800, 735 million, approximately 1. 17 times India's recorded GDP in the same year, and is poised for sustained growth. The region's economy has finally come out of the shadow of the Asian Crisis of 1997, and is expected to continue its upswing; most economists believe that the region will expand at an average 5-6% for the next few years. The growth is likely to be a broad-based one, with both domestic and external demand providing the impetus for expansion. Within the ASEAN and for individual Member countries, integration has been facilitated mainly by trade, in particular in the manufacturing products (and unfortunately also in a narrow range of commodities); trade openness of the region has been very high in the last three decades or so, and on an average for the region, is over 150% of the combined GDP of the Members.

However, intra-regional trade continues to be small at less than 30%6 of total ASEAN trade, and the Members are often dependent on the US and EU for their export markets; this is a crude indicator of the imperfect integration that ASEAN Members have achieved so far. Hence, the key to ASEAN's economic competitiveness and future growth is expected to lie in 'economic integration' with the rest of Asia, an agenda which the Members are following vigorously by forming groupings like ASEAN) with several countries, ASEAN) with China, Korea and Japan, and an East Asian Community (EAS); necessary policy reforms are being undertaken to complement the growth and export targets of Members and for effecting the regional integration.

Within the regional block, the ASEAN Members are working towards realising the aim of establishing an ASEAN Economic Community (AEC) by the year 2020, when ASEAN will be a single market and production base, with free flow of goods, services (people) and investment and freer flow of capital. The ASEAN Leaders have reiterated this at their Bali Summit in October 2003, when they adopted the landmark Bali Concord II in which the AEC, the ASEAN Security Community and the ASEAN Socio-Cultural Community are affirmed as the three key pillars supporting the ASEAN Community. ASEAN is formulating detailed medium to long-term programs and activities for achieving the AEC. The ASEAN Economic and Investment Ministers met in Sentosa (Singapore) in April 2004 to review the progress made in the implementation of various initiatives mandated by the ASEAN Leaders to strengthen the AEC, and endorsed a plan for finalising the roadmaps for the integration of 11 priority sectors which ASEAN enjoys competitive advantage. These 11 priority sectors are automotive, wood-based products, air travel and tourism, e-ASEAN, electronics, rubber-based products, textile and apparels, agro-based products, fisheries, information and communications technology (ICT) and health-care.

The respective Country Coordinators in these 11 priority integration sectors are as follows:

(i) *Indonesia*: wood-based and automotive products;

(ii) *Malaysia*: rubber-based products, and textiles and apparels;

(iii) *Myanmar*: agro-based products and fisheries;

(iv) *The Philippines*: electronics;

(v) *Singapore*: e-ASEAN and health-care;

(vi) *Thailand*: air travel and tourism.

The Ministers, in November 2004, at the 10th ASEAN Summit in Vientiane have signed the legally-binding agreements to implement the measures to integrate the 11 priority sectors, expected to be completed by 2012, and the roadmaps for integration of these sectors have been clearly outlined. These would cover some 4273 tariff lines at a 6 digit level in 12 key product categories. To settle differences and disputes in implementing the economic agreements, the Ministers also endorsed the provisions for establishing the ASEAN Dispute Settlement Mechanism (DSM). Simultaneously, the Ministers also decided to recommend to their Leaders to go for a free trade agreement (FTA) with Australia and New Zealand. Already, through bold, pragmatic and unified strategies, ASEAN has established strong economic linkages with major trading partners like China, India, Japan and the Republic of Korea, creating closer economic partnerships aimed towards ending up as FTAs, to boost market access for ASEAN exports and provide businesses with greater choice of capital and intermediate products.

Scoping studies are currently on for an ASEAN-US Trade and Investment Framework Agreement. ASEAN Member states are also individually negotiating bilateral/regional FTAs with different countries, all in various stages of negotiation

Hence, one finds a veritable mushrooming of the preferential agreements being negotiated by the ASEAN Members, as a group, and also individually. However, none of the existing bilateral and regional agreements of ASEAN and its Members in services offer access to trade partners that go beyond the existing unilateral liberalisation in concerned sectors in partner countries.

As discussed earlier, ASEAN integration is mostly focussed on liberalisation of trade in goods; agriculture and services continue to remain largely protected by Members through strict domestic regulation requirements and other conditionalities, for both intra-ASEAN trade and also trade with the rest of the world. However, keeping the need for a comprehensive integration in mind, under the ASEAN Framework Agreement on Services (AFAS), the ASEAN market for services is also being liberalized and integrated, with several sectors at various stage of negotiation. So far, the ASEAN countries have engaged in three rounds of services negotiations producing four packages of commitments on services sectors.

The sectors in which Members have taken commitments in ASEAN are: tourism and air-transport services, business services (including professional services), construction services, financial services, health-care services and ICT & telecommunication services. In August 2005, ASEAN started the fourth round of services negotiations, in order to achieve "higher quality and deeper level of services commitments" with the explicit aim to accelerate the integration of four important services sectors for the Members, namely travel, tourism, health-care and e-Asian. "The other services sectors, including professional services, are targeted for liberalisation by 2020, although consideration is being given to advance the timeline to 2015 with flexibility for sensitive sectors". The Forum reiterated the commitments made earlier at Vientiane for a speedier liberalization progress of the regional service market. In the 10 ASEAN Summit in 2004 at Vientiane, it was agreed that:

"Member States shall integrate Trade in Services by :

(a) setting clear targets and schedules for progressive liberalisation for each round of negotiations towards achieving freer flow of trade in services earlier than 202011;
(b) accelerating the service liberalisation for the priority sectors by 2010;
(c) accelerating the development of Mutual Recognition Arrangements by 1 January 2008;
(d) applying the ASEAN-minus-X formula; and
(e) promoting joint ventures and cooperation, including third country markets. "

The most recent target for a possible end-date for a free-flow of services within ASEAN is 2015, though from the experience of the last 40 years of ASEAN integration, this seems hugely optimistic. However, in order to achieve this goal, ASEAN Members have agreed to set clear targets and schedules of services liberalisation for each sector and each round. They have also decided to proceed with a WTO-plus modalities of liberalisation in order to speed up integration, wherein, unlike the established method in GATS, liberalization modalities to be chosen can vary from request-offer to formulae and sectoral approaches of liberalisation, depending on the feasibility of effecting such modalities given the sensitivities of different services sectors in the Member countries. Evidently, the sectors in which Members have common interests and in which trade within ASEAN is deepening, will be natural candidates for rapid formulae based liberalisation.

Members have also agreed to take deeper inter-ASEAN commitments in mode 3 and reconcile the relevant services sectors into the common investment policy being worked upon to facilitate the regional integration process. Additionally, the relevant service sectors that are covered in the fast-track 'priority sectors' integration mode (to be achieved by 2010) are broadly: air-travel, ICT (especially e-commerce) and health-care. Further, given its importance as a critical business infrastructure and input, financial services are also being liberalised by most of the ASEAN Members as a priority sector. ASEAN is also in the process of concluding MRAs for qualifications in major professional services areas like engineering, accountancy, architecture, surveying and nursing services, in order to facilitate free movement of professionals, skilled labour and talent.

Another important area of intra-ASEAN cooperation is closer regional integration through integrated and efficient infrastructural linkages for transportation, telecommunications and energy. Concrete measures are taken towards the realization of the ASEAN Highway and Singapore-Kunming Rail Link (SKRL). ASEAN transport facilitation agreements covering transit and inter-state transport of goods, as well as multimodal transport operations, to support AFTA and improve transport logistics in the region are being implemented. An ASEAN action plan for open-sky arrangement is being formulated. The ASEAN Power Grid and the Trans-ASEAN Gas Pipeline Networks are being institutionalized. In the implementation of e-ASEAN Agreement, concrete steps are being taken in advancing ICT market integration and trade facilitation, promoting universal access to ICT infrastructure and services, developing ICT skills and competencies and creating a more secure cyberspace in ASEAN. All these areas therefore present opportunities for curving out closer integration in the context of the proposed India-ASEAN CECA. And despite the concerns over the diverse historical experiences, legal systems, cultural backgrounds and economic development which act as a deterrent for harmonising the mental and operational maps of the trade partners, there does seem to be a growing convergence of strategic interests which needs to be put to optimum use without delay.

In the case of India, services have been one of the thrust areas for over a decade. While agriculture continues to hold the most important position in the economy, given the high employment-generating ability and livelihood-insurer character of the sector in India, it is services that have become the growth engine in the economy in the last decade or so. Not only has the sector been growing at a steady pace of close to 10% for the last decade and contributing over half of India's GDP growth each year, services exports from India has seen double digit growth in the last decade and has continued to be one of the main sources of foreign exchange earning in the country. In 2004, exports of services from India grew by 16%. According to WTO International Trade Statistics 2005, India's share in world services trade stands at 1. 9% vis-a-vis a 1. 0% for merchandise trade; India also exhibits a strong revealed comparative advantage (RCA) in services relative to goods, with the competitiveness and contribution emanating primarily from the other business services category.

India's Foreign Trade Policy (FTP) 2004-09 recognises the importance of services in the overall trade performance of the country, by proposing to create a 'Served from India' brand, and setting up an exclusive export promotion council for services sector along with schemes to assist and promote home-grown service providers. The Council is expected to map opportunities for key services in key markets, and develop strategic market access programmes, including brand-building in co-ordination with sectoral players and recognised nodal bodies of the service industries.

Also, Common Facility Centres are proposed to be set up for use by home-based service providers, particularly in areas like engineering and architectural design, multi-media operations, software developers etc. to draw a vast multitude of home-based professionals into services export arena. It is expected that the new policy will help broad-base services exports from the country, to include as many of the 161 tradable services covered under the General Agreement on Trade in Services and where payment for such services is received in free foreign exchange; service sector exports from India are currently dominated by software exports. The expectation is that services exports will grow to US$ 150 billion by 2009 in which software services will account for about US$ 65 billion.

India's services-led export boom in the last decade and the surplus of the increased invisible earnings had in fact fully offset the net merchandise trade deficit till last year, and is the consequence of a more liberalised policy regime in services as compared to manufacturing. The emergence of India as one of the fastest growing economies in the world during 1990s was attributable to a significant part to the rapid growth of its services sector, which grew at an annual average of 9%. In services, India pursued significant reforms, especially in telecommunications, and, to some extent, in financial services and infrastructure services, such as power and transport.

The result also was that, at over 17% annually in the 1990s (with exports of software and IT enables services growing at around 46% since mid-1990s), India's services exports have experienced one of the fastest growths globally in the last decade, compared to the world average of 5. 6%17. In 2004, India's service exports constituted 34. 4% of the country's global exports (goods and services) (at US$ 39. 64 billions out of US$ 115. 23 billion total exports), while service imports were 29. 61% of total imports (at $40. 95 billions out of $138. 29 billion total exports); however, globally, India remained a net importer of services (though, in 2004, the service trade deficit was only 5. 69% of the total trade deficit of US$ 23. 1 billion). In services, the areas of policy focus, liberalisation and high growth in India have been: software, ITeS (including financial IT services) & BPO, besides emerging areas as health-care (in particular diagnostics and surgeries), telecommunication, and more recently in professional services, distribution and government services. It should be noted here that unilateral service sector liberalisation in India has been most focussed in mode 3 (or commercial presence), and mode 4 access (movement of natural persons) is still restricted in many services sectors. India is also working hard to offset its current disproportionately low participation in bilateral and regional agreements with trade partners by engaging into discussions on economic and trade cooperation with a multitude of countries and regions across the world.

While retaining its support and commitment to multilateralism per se, most of these agreements under the forge-closer-regional-integration initiative are focussed on enhancing non-MFN merchandise trade opportunities with its key trade partners, as also improved market access for services and investment, and preferential liberalisation thereof.

India has signed limited free trade agreements with Sri Lanka (1998) and Thailand (2003) plus a number of preferential trade agreements (tariff concession schemes) with countries such as Afghanistan, Chile, N. Korea, Mongolia, Mauritius, Japan and Maldives; India also has transit agreements with its immediate neighbors in the SAARC region.

At the end of June 2005, the government signed a Comprehensive Economic Cooperation Agreement (CECA) with Singapore, what many consider India's first "comprehensive" FTA. By the end of 2005, India expects to upgrade its pact with Sri Lanka into a Comprehensive Economic Partnership Agreement.

Currently, other than the ASEAN, bilateral negotiations are going on with Bangladesh and Korea, about to start with Mauritius and the GCC, and India is also considering talks with Egypt, MERCOSUR and SACU (Southern African Customs Union). In the most recent development, there has been discussions on the feasibility of India's working out a Services-Only Agreement with the US & EU, the two largest trade partners of India in services.

The other area of gain and strategic cooperation lies in energy-trade and energy services cooperation. Taking forward the Asia-Pacific Energy Cooperation would be critical to the long-term growth and development in the two trade partners, as well as the Asian region as a whole. The Trade and Economic Relations Committee (TERC) headed by the Prime Minister of India Dr. Manmohan Singh, is strongly in favour of a rapid conclusion of the FTA negotiations to enhance economic relations with the neighbouring countries.

6

India Relations and Policy of China and Bhutan

India's strategic concerns about China arise from latter's emergence as the most influential player in Asia – one with the ability to shape the future balance of power. Despite a dominant Indian desire aimed at cooperation rather than competition with China, the vexed 5045 Kilometers undemarkated border complicates the relationship. China's continued military modernization and incremental upgrade of its military posture in Tibet to enable rapid force deployment, backed by logistics capability and communication infrastructure are worrisome.

Chinese land threats to India get greatly compounded as Bhutan and Nepal fall into the Chinese sphere of influence. The disputed borders with Bhutan sit at the centre of Sino Indian Eastern sector. As long as Bhutan continues to favour India, Chinese military adventurism in Chumbi valley and Tawang would be attritional frontal wars, if and when they take place. However, should territories of Nepal and Bhutan be included in the Chinese calculus, cutting off the land routes through the Siliguri corridor would become a reality – isolating the entire eastern sect. It would also complete China's containment policy towards India where China is leveraging economic and military relationships with India's neighbors.

Restoration of diplomatic relations between China and Bhutan is an inevitability which India is extremely weary of. In managing its periphery India has hostile neighbours in Pakistan and China land locking it from West and North. Nepal, Bangladesh Myammar & Sri Lanka are countries where India has ceded strategic space to China through acts of omission and commission in dealing with its smaller neighbours.

Strategically, Bhutan sits at a critical location across the Himalayas where Indian influence has thus far been maintained from the paradigms of providing depth to Chumbi Valley leading to Siliguri Corridor and Tawang-the centre of Tibetan spiritual abode in India. Should Bhutan diplomatically ally with China – these two Indian vulnerabilities will be greatly exposed with attendant military ramifications. Access to Chumbi Valley through Bhutan, in addition to the traditional routes would severe & isolate North East in the event of a war with China. Simultaneously, Bhutan would open the Westen flank of Tawang-Tenga sector exposing the threat to plains of Assam.

The Chinese Premier Wen Zia Bao and Bhutanese Prime Minister Jiome Thinley's much touted meeting on the side lines of R_{10+20} Summit recently seems to have come about in pursuit of Bhutan's ambition to a non permanent seat in the UNSC in 2013 against South Korea.

India is supporting Bhutan and China wishes to exploit this opportunity too.

A China-Bhutan reconciliation can only come with the settlement of the bdy issue where China seeks the Dhoklan plateau overlooking Chumbi Valley while making tradeoffs in the grazing grounds in North Bhutan.

This complicates the China threat theory. Simultaneously, China, according to reports, has plans to extend its railway network from Lhasa to Zangmu, as well as Shigatse and possibly to Yadong at the opening of the Chumbi Valley.

Indian economic investments in Bhutan are exemplified by Bhutan becoming a hydropower exporter to India. By 2020, India expects Bhutan to export 10000 MW of power to India. In addition there are a large number of other economic programmes afoot. In initiating diplomatic ties with China thus, Bhutan shall have to make some stark strategic choices. Replacing India with China world mean economic and ecological tradeoffs which may be detrimental to Bhutan's index of happiness while assuming centrality in Sina Indian territorial conflict.

How far is Bhutan ready for becoming a pawn in Chinese hands thus remains to be seen. The ultimate formula to settle the boundary dispute would dictate the extent of this engagement between the two. Bhutan's strategic choices are thus of great geostrategic and military concerns to India. How it makes them would depend on the range and depth of Indo-Bhutan relations.

Alternatively, Bhutan may provide the Continental Bridge to China to link the region as it has done to dominate CAR and Afghanistan by resolving its boundary disputes with Tajikistan.

INDIA'S CHINA DEBATE

The Indian political establishment is fond of arguing that there is a distinct continuity that defines Indian foreign policy. One can relate this easily to the standard structural-realist theory of international politics, according to which states fashion their foreign policies in response to the systemic constraints imposed by the international system, and domestic politics is not an important variable in this process. In a certain sense, this holds true for Indian foreign policy in general. There have been relatively few dramatic shifts in Indian foreign policy over the years and these shifts have been engendered by larger systemic forces, such as the end of the Cold War and the disappearance of the Soviet Union.

In so far as India's China policy is concerned, there is visible continuity in the official position of India. There is a consensus across Indian political spectrum for improving bilateral ties with China and for resolving Sino-Indian differences through dialogue. However, this official policy hides a broader debate in India about how to deal with China. It has been pointed out that there are three broad views in India on how to deal with China and they have been classified as the pragmatists, the hyperrealists, and the appeasers.

The pragmatists view China as a long-term threat and as a competitor but argue that this competition can be managed by engaging China economically and balancing against China by emerging as a major power in the international system. The hyperrealists view China as a clear and present danger and would like India to contain China by for gin galliances around China's periphery and by strengthening its military capabilities. The appeasers view China as a friendly and benevolent neighbour and would like India to engage it whole-heartedly since China, in their opinion, is not a threat to India in any way.

Along similar lines, Steven Hoffman has also delineated Indian perceptual positions on China. He has outlined three ideal types which he classifies as the Mainstream position, China-Is-Not-Hostile position, and China-Is-Hostile position. These ideal types closely correlate with the pragmatists, the appeasers, and the hyperrealists of the above-mention edtypology. The Mainstream Indian perspective on China, according to Hoffman, views China as a potential threat to Indian security threats but hopes that effective Indian diplomacy can avert any major problems in the future. The China-Is-Not-Hostile perspective holds that China is a rational and peace-loving state that does not have malevolent intentions vis-à-vis India. In marked contrast, the China-Is-Hostile position views China as a short and long-term strategic rival of India and calls for Indian diplomatic assertiveness vis-à-vis China.

The common perception in the early years of independent India was that India had lost its great power status due to internal strife and discord, coupled with a stagnating economy which did not keep pace with the technological advancements of its competitors. It was assumed that the global balance maintained by the superpowers through the Cold War could be used to contain external dangers and thus military preparedness could wait. This belief was shattered by the 1962 border conflict with China.

The India-Pakistan war of 1965 revealed the extent of Sino-Pakistan collusion and the unwillingness of the superpowers to pull India's chest nuts out of the fire. Subsequent enhanced reliance on a single superpower limited India's choices till a paradigm shift took place with the collapse of the Soviet Union.

This experience also conditions the domestic debate in India: The Communists caution against an alliance with any power which limits India's ability to foster mutual trust and forge amicable relations with its neighbours while the Congress has drawn attention to thee mergence of a global market and a globalising polity that makes a policy of universal global engagement most appropriate. The debate is clothed in clichés easily understood by their respective constituencies.

This debate has been going on for quite some time. Though the multiplicity of views reflects Indian democracy at its best, in many ways it also impedes the formulation of a long-term strategy. The consequence is that the Indian government, realising that there are a plethora of views on China, has taken the path of least resistance, a policy that keeps most groups satisfied, if not happy, even though it is a policy only in name.

Power Matters

The success and failure of a nation's foreign policy is largely a function of its power and the manner in which that power is wielded. Power and its pursuit lie at the heart of inter-state relations. A state's power in the international system can be defined as a function of the material capabilities that it possesses. Despite all the talk of India as a rising power, on all indicators of power, economic and military, India remains behind China in terms of capabilities. While India's economic and military capabilities have no doubt increased substantially in recent times, with its GDP being fourth in the world in purchasing power parity and its military the third largest in the world, China's capabilities have continued to remain ahead of India's. 31 More importantly, India is yet to master the ability "to integrate the creation, deployment and use of military instruments in support of national objectives." 32 Military power, more often than not, affects the success with which other instruments of statecraft are employed. As has been observed by Robert Art, military power always lurks in the back ground of inter-state relations, even when nations are at peace with each other. 33 It affects the influence that states exert over one another, thereby shaping political outcomes. In stark contrast to India, China has shown a willingness to use force quite readily in pursuit of its national goals while always insisting that it is defensive in nature. Chinese leaders tend to rationalize even their offensive military operations as purely defensive and measures of last resort (this logic has also been applied to the 1962 Sino-India war), to an extent where defence can even include a pre-emptive strike.

Indian foreign policy's failure to achieve its objectives vis-à-vis China has a lot to do with India's as yet underdeveloped power capabilities. China's rising power and the effectiveness with which it has wielded it has allowed it to achieve most of its strategic objectives vis-à-vis India. In fact, one of the reasons why China does not consider India to be its rival is because of its low opinion of Indian capabilities. Power matters and in international politics, weakness begets failure while strength begets strategic clout. Unless India achieves higher rates of economic growth and modernises its military, both quantitatively and qualitatively, and learns to use its military instruments in pursuit of national objectives, its foreign policy will struggle to achieve the results it desires.

Outcome: Does it Serve Indian Interests?

As a consequence of various constraints that have impeded that evolution of a long-term China policy in India, Indian foreign policy remains mired in confusion. Leaving aside the question of the ability of the Indian elites to think strategically on national security, in the case of India's China policy, one is not even sure if the Indian political and foreign policy establishment understands the basic forces that shape and configure global politics. India's inability, or rather unwillingness, to see the world as it is instead of as it should be, has become the major bane of foreign policy.

India's lack of direction in its China policy is clearly revealed by the manner in which it has dealt with China in the past few years. While Sino-Indian bilateral relations have apparently improved, it is not clear if India has any idea as to what ends it wants to harness this improvement and what its strategic objectives with respect to China are. This has resulted in policy flip-flops that have undermined India's regional and global diplomatic stature.

Former Indian Defence Minister George Fernandes described China as India's "potential enemy number one" and former Prime Minister Atal Bihari Vajpayee explained to the world powers that Indian nuclear tests were a response to the threat posed by Chinese nuclear weapons and Sino-Pakistan nuclear and missile collaboration. But some five years later, China became a "good neighbour" for the same Indian government when Prime Minister Vajpayee visited Beijing. What brought about this remarkable transformation, of course, remains unclear till date. The Man mohan Singh government came to the office declaring that it wants to have friendly relations with China, which, of course, is a reasonable foreign policy objective. But without a clear articulation of India's national security objectives, such declarations remain just pious rhetoric that has never been in short supply in India-China relations. Pursuit of friendly relations with China seems to have become an end in itself when it should be a means towards achieving India's larger strategic objective of emerging as a major regional and global player. Diplomacy without an overarching conceptual frame work of foreign policy often becomes a technical exercise in splitting differences, thus acquiring shades of what many might consider appeasement.

India's China policy is in many ways symptomatic of a larger misunderstanding in the Indian political establishment with regard to what the nation's foreign policy should be. For the left-liberal strand, foreign policy is merely an extension of domestic policy. As such since India is as ecular, democratic, and peace-loving nation, India's pursuit of its relations with other states should merely be a reflection of these virtues. This has shaped much of the moral rhetoric in foreign affairs in India for the better part of the last 50 years and still continues to shape the understanding of global affairs within the major political formations on the left of the Indian political spectrum. The Indian discourse on foreign policy, in the words of one of the most astute observers of Indian foreign policy, "has remained frozen in a rhetorical trap, reminiscent of our class X essays in the earnest, third-worldist, allegedly non-aligned seventies." A vivid example of this attitude is the rather extreme positions on national security taken by the Communist Parties consistently. While emphasising their fraternal ties with China's ruling Communist Party time and again, they have called for an end to all military cooperation with the US and Israel, asking the Indian government to return to a policy of genuine non-alignment. Their complete silence on Chinese activities adversely affecting Indian national security interests even as they continue to denounce the US as a global imperialist has befuddled many.

Prime Minister Man mohan Singh has also articulated a vision of Indian foreign policy, according to which foreign policy exists to push pragmatic economic goals, especially as India integrates more and more with the global economy, and also to build a world of open inclusive nations. This understanding of Indian foreign policy unambiguously identifies India with other liberal democracies of the world. The Prime Minister also suggested that the global environment has never been more conducive for India's economic development than it is today and the world wants to help India to achieve its full potential. He argued that India should engage other great powers such as the US and China to the fullest and neither should be treated as an adversary. While there is much to commend in this articulation of Indian foreign policy agenda, particularly the exhortation that India should rise and take full advantage of the opportunities presented by the changing global economic milieu, it is rather naïve in its assertion that foreign policy is nothing more than an outcome of economic policy and that international politics is nothing but a sum total of global trade and economic cooperation.

It is in fact an offshoot of the liberal fallacy that assumes that only if nations were to trade more with each other, the world would become more prosperous and peaceful. In the case of Sino-Indian relations, many have argued that once economics becomes the driving factor, it will us her in a 'paradigm shift' in Sino-Indian bilateral relations. The understanding here being that in the short-term there is no threat to Indian interests from China and it is only a potential long-term threat or challenge to vital Indian interests. There is also the attendant belief that by embedding India-China relations into an expanding structure of economics ties future problem scan be averted. In many ways, this has become the dominant narrative of Sino-Indian relations in recent years.

K. Subrahmanyam has argued that China's desire for increasing its bilateral trade with India and collaboration in sectors such as information technology can be effectively leveraged by India in shaping China's attitudes vis-à-vis India. In a recent study, Jairam

Ramesh, an influential member of the ruling Congress Party, has come up with the concept of "Ch india" that denotes synergy between the two Asian giants. He views closer economic cooperation between China and India as the best way to build trust and friendship, leading to a long-lasting peace between the two states. The problem with these assumptions is that not only is there little empirical evidence to prove that more trade leads to peace and tranquillity, but also that while politics and economics are certainly inter-related, the international economic system rests upon the international political order and not vice-versa. Indian foreign policy cannot be conducted on the naïve assumption that greater economic integration with the world would some how solve all its foreign policy problems.

At the other end of the political spectrum, the Indian right, because of its preoccupation with establishing a "Hindu" nation and minority bashing, has extended its narrow sectarian view to foreign policy. The consequence has been its obsession with Pakistan as evil incarnate in its foreign policy agenda and its inclination to view the world in black and white, friends and enemies, evil and noble. While undoubtedly pursuing pragmatic economic and foreign policies when in power, the Indian right, as represented by the BJP, seems to be under tremendous pressure to revert back to its extremist views, now that it is out of power. Where India's multiculturalism and pluralism should be leveraged as India's strengths in negotiating with an increasingly polarised outside world, the Indian right, with its resistance to India's plural heritage, has been more interested in turning India into a mirror image of Pakistan.

Then there is the great Indian bureaucracy which suffers from the same myopia that Henry Kissinger long back diagnosed for the US foreign service— that it views its role as merely a solver of concrete issues as they come about and a negotiating instrument rather than one of shaping events and conceptualising strategy.

Shaped by these forces, Indian foreign policy has merely been one of responding to events around it rather than anticipating them and evolving coherent long-term strategies to deal with them in the best interests of the country. A nation's foreign policy, to be effective, should ultimately rest on philosophical assumptions as to the nature of world order and the relationship of order to progress and national interest. In the absence of such a conceptual framework, incoherence would loom large as the diplomatic back and forth would become an end in itself and rather than shaping events, the state would end up reacting to developments around it as in the case of Indian foreign policy. The greatest casualty of this larger foreign policy malaise has been India's China policy. From Hindi-Chini bhaibhai to potential enemy number one to great friend, India just does not know how to deal with its neighbourhood dragon that has played its cards so skilfully vis-à-vis India. It can be argued that successive Indian governments have, in fact, been following a coherent policy towards China, i.e., cooperation with China to build Indian capability till such time when India is able to challenge China's primacy openly. If indeed this is the guiding framework, then India is in for a rude shock, as the current Chinese policy towards India will essentially preclude India's emergence as a global or even regional power of any reckoning.

There is nothing really sinister about China's attempts to expand its own influence and curtail India's. China is a rising power and as such will do its utmost to prevent the rise of other power centres around its periphery. This is not very different from the stated US policy of preventing the rise of other powers that might threaten its position as a global hegemon. Just as the US is working towards achieving its strategic objective, China is pursuing its own strategic agenda. In many ways, it is natural for China to view India as a potential rival: for foreign capital, export markets, political influence, and aspirations for regional leadership.

There is also nothing extraordinarily benign in China's attempts to improve its bilateral relations with India in recent times. After limiting India's influence in various ways, China would not like to see India coming close to the US in order to contain China. In this geopolitical chessboard, while both the US and China are using India towards their own strategic ends, India has ended up primarily reacting to the actions of others. And the primary reason for this is the failure to recognise the forces that drive international politics in general and come up with a coherent strategy towards China, in particular.

With the US largely preoccupied with its war on terror and Iraq, China has increasingly asserted its pre-eminence in Asia. It has started to act like a traditional great power, pursuing its regional interests in a proactive manner and transforming its diplomatic relations with smaller neighbours. According to informed observers, this points to a well-conceived grand strategy at play – a strategy that would make it possible for China "to continue its economic growth, technological modernisation, and military build-up without provoking other countries to a costly rivalry."

However, notwithstanding China's attempts at reassuring its neighbours, China's growing power and muscle flexing as in the Taiwan Straits has led other regional powers to re-evaluate their strategic options. Japan has recently sought to broaden the scope of its security ties with the US and for the first time has explicitly discussed joint US-Japanese cooperation in the event of a crisis in the Taiwan Straits. In the face of a rising China that offers new opportunities, some in Australia have demanded that the government review its 50-year-old treaty with the US. 45 China's rise has also engendered a cautious wariness in Russia, despite Moscow's improving ties with Beijing. There is nothing surprising in China wielding its increasing economic and military clout in the region to gradually extend its influence and most other regional powers seem to have realised this. The only exception seems to be India, which seemingly believes that only if the two nations would trade more, all problems in their bilateral relationship would take care of themselves.

It is the structure of global politics that by definition makes Sino-Indian competition inevitable. There are two options for India – either play the game of global politics by the rules laid down by its structure or resign itself to a secondary status in the global hierarchy. Given that Indian decision-makers are already talking of India as a global player in the making, they cannot but take the rules of the game that is global politics, seriously. Of course, a Sino-Indian competition that can be diplomatically managed would be in everyone's interest. But historically, rising powers have tried to reshape their strategic environment to reflect new realities of power and this has provoked conflicts. Many in India share the idea that only if India provokes China would China threaten India. This might seem comforting as it gives India a false sense of control over the unfolding of events. But China could be provoked by its own strategic environment if that is not seen to be commensurate with its rising prowess and expectations, regardless of India's actions. India's weakness, in that case, would do more harm than good. The best that India can do is to first put its own house in order. India needs to develop its economic and military might without in any way being apologetic about it. It needs to clearly articulate its national interests and engage China on a host of issues, from the border problem to the alleged dumping of cheap Chinese goods in the Indian market. India needs to recognise that appeasing China is neither desirable nor necessary even as a direct confrontation with China is not something India can afford, at least in the near future. A stable foundation for the future of India-China relations cannot be laid by feigning total ignorance of Chinese activities that have adversely affected Indian national interests in the past. In all likelihood, Chinese attitudes towards India will change radically in India's favour as the US strategy of strengthening India as a balancer in the Asian balance of power gathers momentum. This should present India a strategic opportunity to recalibrate its China policy and leverage its relationship with one power vis-à-vis the other.

BHUTAN'S TRIANGULAR RELATIONS

The King of Bhutan was the guest of honour in this year's Indian Republic Day celebration on January 26. In the banquet in honour of His Majesty, Pranab Mukherjee, the President of India observed that India gives topmost priority to Bhutan's sovereignty and its independent way of development. His Majesty the King, on his turn, said Bhutan has not walked alone in its national development. It has walked along with India. It was Jawaharlal Nehru who had founded Bhutan's relation with India when he travelled to its capital on elephants and horses. Nehru had a romantic approach to Himalaya and Bhutan. Nehru was a democrat but he accepted Bhutan's absolute monarchy as it was. History has passed a long way.

We can not ignore that Bhutan was the first country to recognize the People's Republic of Bangladesh. It was the same year Bhutan entered the United Nations and opened its gate to the world. Bhutan's independent foreign policy has always been respected by its neighbours. This was reflected when Bhutanese Prime Minister Mr Tinley, a visionary like Nehru, met the Chinese Prime Minister Wen Jibao at the Rio climatic summit last year. There was talk of Sino-Bhutanese diplomatic relation and Bhutan wants to make it clear that it is not aimed against India. Bhutan provides the shortest way from the sub-continent to China.

Bhutan is no more the impassable mountain Kingdom that Nehru visited. It has highly developed infra-structure that includes air port and national network of high ways spread from the east to the west, north to the south. The Bhutanese have one of the highest living standards in South Asia and has fairly equitable social distribution of wealth by its Buddhist codes. One scholar Purobi Bose who had happened to be in Bhutan, told me in Sweden that both Sweden and India could learn from Bhutan. I do not like to touch the eternal social disparity in India but Sweden has quite worthy social care. But Purobi Bose, in her research felt that Bhutanese system was more caring. Bhutan with sixteen thousand square miles is as big as Switzerland.

But whereas Switzerland has seven million people, Bhutan has only seven hundred thousands. But it has a multi-cultural and multi-lingual affinity like Switzerland, though that has been affected by the developments of the recent years. Many Nepalese, Bengalese and Tibetans had to leave Bhutan because of what they felt Bhutanese xenophobia. Many of them were from educated middle class who formed their own communities in USA, Australia or New Zealand. But they proudly feel themselves to be Bhutanese and aspire to return to a multi-cultural and multi-ethnic democratic Bhutan. Obviously India does not want to interfere in the internal affairs of Bhutan but it does not want Bhutan to shelter Indian terrorist groups. Bhutanese army with iron hand crushed such groups few years ago. India expects same from Bangladesh. His Majesty met with the Indian army chief and national security adviser. Indian national security adviser and Defence Secretary visited China and had high level talks to strengthen the strategic partnership with that country which is a regular feature. Sino-Bhutanese ties should aim at strengthening that partnership not weakening it. We do not live in the seventies when there was conflict between China and Russia. Today both China and Russia are partners with India in BRICS spread over five continents of the emerging world.

Newly named US foreign secretary Kerry has promised partnership with China for peaceful development of the globe. It has been India's policy when India developed Panchasheela or Five Principles with Nehru, Chou en Lai and Shoekarno. We feel India's support to our liberation war against genocide was glorious manifestation of Panchasheela. But we can not ignore Felani hanging on the fence or persecution of ethnic minorities in Bhutan. We should remove all the fences and seek the Sarba Satyam, the supreme truth, as our great scholar from our ancient capital Vikrampur Atish Dipankar preached. He is equally respected in India, China, Bhutan and Bangladesh. Bhutan's triangular relation with China and India should be guided by Panchasheela and Sarba Satyam. Supreme truth is love. Love between nations is the supreme truth.

On our part we welcome brotherly relations between our neighbours and destruction of all fences both physical and mental inherited from colonial legacy. All nations big and small have equal rights in our planet that should not be lost in triangle.

In Bhutan, China and India Collide

As the world's newest democracy, the Buddhist Kingdom of Bhutan has won praise around the world. Its recent transformation-from a century of monarchy to a multi-party democracy-has all the trappings of cinema: an enlightened king steps aside for his dashing, Oxford-educated son who represents a future of peace and prosperity.

But all's not entirely well in Shangri-la. Bhutan, sandwiched between two Asian giants, China and India, is increasingly embroiled in other nations' realpolitik and has been recently subjected to military incursions that are reverberating around the region. Despite the dazzle of democracy, the often-cited "gross national happiness" of bucolic Bhutan is truly at stake. Delhi and Beijing are watching the kingdom intensely, and recent moves suggest that Bhutan may become either a strategic pawn or a malleable "buffer" zone between the two expanding powers.

This month, the Wall Street Journal wrote that King Jigme Singye Wangchuk, the "Dragon King" who ascended the throne in 1972 at the age of 16, "deserves to go down in history as his country's George Washington, John Adams and Thomas Jefferson".

In 1998, Wangchuk voluntarily reduced his powers and declared that Bhutan would become a constitutional monarchy. He ordered legal experts to study constitutions of all the world's great democracies and the final version, which was mailed to every home in the country, begins with "We the people". In December 2006, he abdicated and a year later the first general elections were held in the country's 20 *dzongkhag* (districts). Elections for the lower house of Parliament commence next month, and in the foreseeable future the monarch will become a ceremonial head of state.

The outcome of the elections will impact India and China, both of which have strategic footholds in the landlocked Himalayan kingdom. Bhutan does not have diplomatic relations with China, the United States, Russia, the United Kingdom or France. This is possibly done so Bhutan is not seen as an enemy to China, these nations all being members of the United Nations Security Council.

Informal contact with the US is made through the American Embassy in New Delhi. As Bhutan is close to India's restive northeastern states, any sort of negative development in the Himalayan kingdom is considered critical to India's strategic interest.

India's relationship with Bhutan is based on the Perpetual Peace and Friendship agreement signed in 1949. The pact was tested when Bhutan, under Indian pressure, launched "Operation All Clear" to flush out Indian militants operating inside Bhutan on December 15, 2003. The Bhutanese army, aided by Indian forces, completed the operation in January 2004.

There is a fear of China in Bhutan. There are unresolved border disputes going back centuries and the issue was only addressed in Beijing in 1984. Bhutan has traditional trade relations with Tibet, but Bhutan closed its northern borders with China after an influx of Tibetan refugees in 1960. With that the age-old cross-border trade came to a halt and there have been no official trade or business relations with China ever since. In 1998, Bhutan and China signed an Agreement to Maintain Peace and Tranquillity on the Bhutan-China border, marking the first and only Sino-Bhutanese peace agreement to this day.

In recent months, Bhutan's relations with it powerful neighbours have had a twist. Chinese forces are alleged to have intruded several times into Bhutanese territory at the tri-junction with India. Over the past six months, the Chinese have increasingly made inroads in the strategically important area. The incursions into Bhutan are precariously close to India's "chicken's neck"-the vulnerable Siliguri Corridor which links the northeast passage.

At the moment, Indian military strength is depleted in its eastern region as one of the divisions normally based in the hills of West Bengal is currently deployed in Kashmir. The other division, located distantly at Binaguri, would be ineffective if the Chinese sliced through Bhutan to sever the Siliguri "neck".

Although the ruling United Progressive Alliance government government in India has publicly dismissed these intrusions as "nothing serious", experts view these "aggressive" Chinese moves as a deliberate strategy to put pressure on India and strengthen China's claims on disputed areas along the "Line of Actual Control". The Indian army has been alarmed at the increasing Chinese forays into Bhutan, which are also close to the strategic Chumbi Valley-another vital junction between India, Bhutan and China.

Trouble is mounting on China's border with Bhutan. The intrusions of Chinese forces, analysts say, has more to do with India than Bhutan. The official statement of Indian army chief General Deepak Kapoor is that Chinese forays into Bhutan are a "matter between the two countries". But, in contradiction, the Indian army recently moved 6,000 troops to the Sino Indian-Bhutanese junction from the troubled states of Jammu and Kashmir. In November 2007, Chinese forces demolished several unmanned Indian forward posts near two military bunkers in the border region of Bhutan's Dolam Valley. This has drastically distorted the Sino-Bhutanese border at Sikkim and puts Chinese forces only a few kilometres from North Bengal's Siliguri Corridor. China has always laid claim to Dolam and there is rampant suspicion that it is now extending its claim. So far, India has treaded softly and has been tight-lipped for political and diplomatic reasons.

The Dolam Valley incident has exacerbated fear in Bhutan. The general feeling is the more Bhutan proximates itself with India the more it faces trouble from China. The newly elected government, from February, will be hard-pressed to remain equally distance from both the countries.

There is a strong feeling in Thimphu that Bhutan is becoming a buffer state. The outcome of the elections will likely determine the future of the relationship between India, China and Bhutan. It is believed that China's strategy is to drag India more and more into a Bhutanese gambit and benefit by pinning more Indian troops into border areas. Bhutan stands a great chance of becoming a tiny pawn in a big game between the two Asian giants.

CHINA'S POLICY OF SUBDUING INDIA'S QUEST FOR POWER

Subduing India's quest for power is one of China's many goals in modernizing its armed forces. A US Congressional report which says, China is developing a capability to project air and naval forces beyond its coastal areas, has among its goal "subduing India's quest for power", securing unification of Taiwan, preventing Japan's rise as the strongest Asian power, ensuring Chinese influence over the Korean peninsula and supporting Beijing's claims in the east and south China seas. China's foreign and defence policy initiatives, military analysts say, are quite obviously designed to marginalise India in the long-term and reduce India to the status of a subregional power. For many decades now, despite Indian protestations to that country, China has been pursuing a carefully orchestrated plan for the strategic encirclement and containment of India and has been gradually enlarging its sphere of influence towards South East Asia and the Bay of Bengal. China's strategic manoeuvring and its intransigence in resolving the long-standing territorial and boundary dispute with India are a source of soft potential conflict.

China continues to be in occupation of approximately 30 thousand square kilometres of Indian territory in Aksai Chin since the 1962 war and lays claim to large areas of Indian territory in the eastern sector. Pakistan has also ceded a part of occupied Kashmir to China through this China built the Karakoram highway that now provides a strategic land link between China and Pakistan.

Despite the Border Peace and Tranquility Agreement (BPTA) of 1993, the Confidence Building Measures (CBMs) in the Military Field agreed in 1996 and over a dozen meetings of the Joint Working Group and the Experts Group, even the LAC is yet to be demarcated. Political observers say, perhaps the real reason that compels China to drag its feet in resolving its dispute with India is to enable Pakistan to continue to destabilize India through its proxy war without fear of major military retaliation due to the specter of a two front war. The only conclusion that can reasonably be drawn is that China is deliberately stalling further progress on these substantive issues as its suits China to put them on the back burner for the time being.

India is also watchful of China's increasing military involvement in Myanmar which has the potential to impinge on India's trade and maritime interests. China's wooing of Nepal and Bhutan, its sale of sophisticated military technology to Pakistan, Bangladesh and Myanmar, and the possibility it acquiring naval bases, and overland and air-routes to such bases in the countries around India, are areas of concern for India's security. Even through China's navy is still decades away from acquiring the long-range capability necessary to operate with some degree of assurance and freedom in the Indian Ocean, these aspects need to be constantly monitored and vectored into India's calculations.

Since the Gulf War of 1991, China has stepped up its efforts to modernize the People's Liberation Army (PLA). The PLA army has been engaged in raising a large number of rapid deployment divisions and in improving mobility and logistics support capability, while simultaneously upgrading its ability to undertake operations, improve air defence capability and institute state-of-the art command and control systems. In this context, Chinese aspirations to gradually upgrade the PLA navy, to acquire deep penetration strike and strategic lift transport aircraft for the PLA air force and to obtain mid-air refueling capability for long range operations, are also relevant. All these endeavours aim at creating a modern fighting force capable of undertaking swift offensive operations in area away from China's borders in keeping with China's strategy of fighting a limited war under high-tech conditions. It is noteworthy that the upgradation of the military logistics infrastructure in Tibet is continuing at a steady pace. China has been actively engaged in building new roads, supply lines and airfields close to the Indian frontier.

POLICY TO BOX RESURGENT INDIA

In establishing close political and military nexus with Pakistan directed against India, China is seeking to box India into the geographical confines of South Asia to stultify its stature as an emerging global power. As remarked by P.R. Chari, Director, Institute of Peace and Conflict Studies, New Delhi, since the United States too is interested in bolstering the entity of Pakistan, despite its drift into social chaos and financial bankruptcy, an axis of powers-Pakistan, China and the US, with palpable anti-India compulsions is visible. Undoubtedly, China has developed close military relationship with Pakistan since 1965 largely designed to restrain Soviet expansion into the Indian Ocean via Afghanistan, but Pakistan has used the weapons, nuclear and missile technology acquired from China to bolster its defences against India and to allow it to be used by China to erode India's stature as a regional military and economic power.

India, aspiring to become a global power, is increasingly perceived as a potential giant on the strength of an expanding economy and market especially by the major industrial nations. In the Asian context, India is undoubtedly a force to be reckoned with and its demonstrated nuclear capability has enhanced its military stature even if the G-7 countries had been condemnatory of its underground nuclear weapons tests in may, 1998. Over the two years, much to the chagrin of China which is insisting on India [and Pakistan] honouring the UN Security Council Resolution and sign CTBT, the international community is gradually reconciling itself to the reality, though there is an understandable concern that the embittered Indo-Pak relationship may end up in a nuclear holocaust. Japan, Australia, Germany, Russia and even the US after the visits by President Clinton and Mr. Vajpayee to each other's country, are inclined to lift sanctions imposed after the Pokhran II nuclear tests. The Clinton visit to India in March last year has, apart from generating warmth in Indo-American relations, aroused rethinking on the part of countries like Japan and Britain to reassess their bilateral ties with India. A global partnership and security dialogue between India and Japan is something which China will carefully evaluate for its strategic impact on Asian security. There is, therefore, no scope of the Russian blueprint of strategic partnership between Moscow, New Delhi and Beijing in matters of international security and the establishment of a multipolar world of peace, security and development. Such a strategic partnership is envisaged by Russian President Putin who has visited China and India and spoke out his mind on this idea to the leaderships there.

It is plainly evident that the strategic direction of India's missile and nuclear programme is against China, however strong the denials of such a fear expressed by Defence Minister George Fernandes after Chinese protestations in the past. China's current nuclear posture of "creeping proliferation" would eventually include China. India could also profitably reevaluate its policy of dealing with Taiwan in the present gingerly fashion and deepen its relations with Vietnam as part of an extra-regional strategy.

INDIA BHUTAN CHINA STRATEGIC TRIANGLE

India Bhutan and China are part of a strategic triangle in the Eastern Himalayas with the inverted apex jutting in the form of the all important Chumbi Valley in Yadong (Yatung) county of Tibetan Autonomous Region (TAR). Given proximity of the Chumbi Valley to India's jugular to the North East the 20 kms wide Siliguri corridor, the two arms of the triangle resting on Indian state of Sikkim in the West and Bhutan in the East assume importance.

Chinese plans to extend the Qinghai Tibet railway to Xigaze and Yadong close to the Sino Indian border have added to concerns in India with tardy communication links on the Eastern frontier.

Given the strategic significance, India has been able to maintain balance primarily through the Indo Bhutan Treaty of Friendship first signed in 1949 and revised on mutually agreed terms in 2007.

Thus two arms of the triangle could be said under Indian control and influence, even as China holds the base. This equation may be upset in case China is able to gain greater access to the Bhutanese arm of the triangle with a reset of the Sino Bhutan boundary, negotiations for which are underway. Given the difficult terrain on the Western arm of the Chumbi Valley and scope for expansion is primarily in the East. These fears were attenuated with the first ever summit held between the prime ministers of Bhutan and China in Rio recently. An over view of the relationships would therefore be in order and is covered as per succeeding paragraphs.

Indo Bhutan Treaty of Friendship in 2007 has led to greater diplomatic freedom to Thimpu opening prospects of engagement across the board.

The most significant change in 2007 was mutual reaffirmation of sovereignty and territorial integrity in the preamble of the Treaty which was not there in the 1949 text. More over Article 2 of the 1949 Treaty stated that Bhutan will be guided by the advice of India on external relations.

The Article read, "The Government of India undertakes to exercise no interference in the internal administration of Bhutan. On its part, the Government of Bhutan agrees to be guided by the advice of the Government of India in regard to its external relations". This has been reviewed of the 2007 Treaty reads, "__the Government of the Kingdom of Bhutan and the Government of the Republic of India shall cooperate closely with each other on issues relating to their national interests. Neither Government shall allow the use of its territory for activities harmful to the national security and interest of the other". The sum total of implications of the change is greater freedom of choice to Bhutan in management of sovereignty and external relations.

This background is essential to understand the nuances of the first ever bilateral held between the Chinese Prime Minister Wen Jiabao and Bhutan's Prime Minister, Jigmi Y. Thinley on the side lines of the Rio Conference on Sustainable Development in June 2012. While Bhutan has been expanding foreign relations over the years and in 2011 chaired South Asian Association of Regional Cooperation (SAARC), there was no formal diplomatic relations or summit level contact with Beijing.

Having greater autonomy post 2007 Treaty, it is inevitable that there would be greater traction for Bhutan to establish diplomatic relations with China the only nation other than India with which it shares a land border. Proposal for diplomatic relations was first discussed between the two countries in 1998 during the 12th Round of border talks.

Significantly, Bhutan and India are the only two countries with which China has not resolved land borders. There are two areas of dispute, one falling in North West Bhutan covering 269 sq km and the other Central Bhutan covering 495 sq km. The North West area comprises Doklam (89 sq km), Sinchulumpa (42 Sq km), and Shakhatoe (138 Sq km) in Samste, Haa and Paro districts and Central parts the Pasamlung and the Jakarlung valley in the Wangdue Phodrang district. The 1998 agreement between Bhutan and China entitled, "Maintain Peace and Tranquility on the Bhutan-China Border Areas," provides the framework for stability on the border. However despite this there have been reports of intrusions by Chinese troops in Bhutanese territory. In November 2007 some reports indicate dismantling of unmanned posts in the Dolam Valley. Bhutan's media reported a number of intrusions in 2009.

At the same time Bhutan and China have held 19 rounds of talks on the boundary dispute so far the last one being held in January 2010 after a gap of four years where a joint field survey was agreed upon. This was to be carried out of disputed areas in Doklam, Charithang, Sinchulumpa and Dramana in Bhutan's North West and Pasamlung and the Jakarlung valley in the Wangdue Phodrang district in Central Bhutan. It is reasonably well established by now that China is looking for a package deal with Bhutan seeking areas in the North West while establishing Bhutan's claims in the Central region. This offer was first made in the sixth round of talks held in August 1990. Chinese quid pro quo does not take into account that the territory is a part of the sovereign state of Bhutan and strategic interests seem to be pushing Beijing to offer a package to the southern neighbor. Herein lies the rub where India's interests come in given proximity of the North West areas to the Chumbi Valley. In case Bhutan seeks to appease China to move the trajectory of relations forward, it would most certainly cause concern in Delhi and may even be objected to.

In the light of this legacy the Wen Jiabao – Thinley meet seems to be an opening gambit by both sides to test the waters on how far they can push the envelope without India blocking the package deal altogether. Premier Wen Jiabao as per a report by the AFP stated, "China is willing... to establish formal relations with Bhutan, resolve the border issue between the two nations at an early date, strengthen exchanges in all areas and advance Sino-Bhutanese relations to a new stage." A report in the Hindu of 27 June also quoted Mr. Wen saying that China was "willing to complete border demarcation with Bhutan at an early date." Mr. Thinley was quoted by Xinhua the official Chinese news agency to have expressed that Bhutan wishes to forge formal diplomatic ties with China as soon as possible. Bhutan has also sought China's support in elections to the non permanent seat in the United Nations Security Council being vacated by India in 2013.

South Asia experts from Chinese think tanks, China Institutes of Contemporary International Relations (CICIR) and Chinese Academy of Social Sciences (CASS) as quoted by the Hindu in a report on 26 June 2012 have been quick to speculate that Bhutan would not have taken these initiatives without India's express, "approval or agreement."

The official web site of the Cabinet Secretariat of the Royal Government of Bhutan however makes muted remarks on the bilateral summit and states, "The meeting [Wen Jiabao-Thinley] carries great historic significance as it marks the first meeting between the heads of the two governments. They discussed bilateral issues of mutual interest and multilateral cooperation including Bhutan's bid for a non permanent seat on UN Security Council for the term 2013-2014, elections for which are to be held in fall this year". No mention was made of either diplomatic relations or boundary issue.

Bhutanese writer, Kuenzang Choden writing in web site The Bhutanese on 22 June 2012, quotes Media Attache of Bhutan Prime Minister's office to refute any initiative by Prime Minister Thinley to propose establishment of diplomatic relations with China. He states, "local Chinese media had misreported that Bhutan and China will establish diplomatic ties." Kuenzang further goes on to quote a Foreign Ministry official who sought to remain anonymous indicating, "It is unlikely that Bhutan and China will have diplomatic relations soon. There are certain policies when it comes to the Permanent five of the United Nations Security Council."

There are obviously different versions being floated of deliberation during the summit. Has the Chinese media gone overboard in flagging the initiative for bilateral relations and resolution of boundary issue will not be clear but without a push from the officials accompanying the Prime Minister these reports are unlikely to have been published. Has Bhutan gone ahead with the move after approval from New Delhi as some Indian media reports and Chinese scholars seem to suggest or the Prime Minister of Bhutan has been misquoted by the Chinese media as Bhutanese authorities are indicating or this is an unilateral initiative by Thimpu, hence the foreign office cover up is not clear so far.

Suffice to say that first summit level contact between Bhutan and China has been established and the engagement will be taken forward to establish diplomatic relations and possibly even resolve the boundary issue in times to come. The trajectory may not be easy to determine at this juncture nor the time frame predictable. Settlement of boundary however is unlikely to happen soon. Given importance of the Chumbi Valley India is unlikely to agree to any concessions by Bhutan that leads to exchange of territory in this area providing further elbow room to China. Fears expressed by reports in the Indian media may therefore may be unfounded.

On the other hand Chinese keenness to extend the railway line to Yadung and secure the Bhutanese arm of the Chumbi Valley triangle may be as much due to fears of India cutting off the salient jutting threateningly towards the Siliguri corridor. This will overcome the vulnerability of the Siliguri Corridor providing it additional depth. This could be one explanation for given the operational challenges of launching a major thrust through the Chumbi Valley to cut off the Siliguri corridor and India's build up of forces on the Eastern front, Chinese offensive in the area will be posed major operational challenges.

What ever it be, given mutual apprehensions, strategic stability in the India Bhutan China triangle would require statesmanship of a high order. This will depend on how the political and military leadership of the three countries and especially New Delhi and Beijing are able to manage the same ensuring Thimpu's sovereignty and autonomy. The Indian government has done well not to over react to media reports and would be seeking full details of Chinese interaction from Bhutan to chart out a future course of action. This will no doubt be done keeping in view larger national interests of managing relations with China amicably yet not compromising on basic national security interests, thus implying any attempt to extend the Eastern arm of the inverted apex of the Chumbi Valley will be fiercely resisted by New Delhi.

INDIA'S LOSS IS CHINA'S GAIN

Indian concerns about rising Chinese influence in Africa, the Middle East, South America, and Central Asia are derived from the Indian perception that it is losing out to China in the energy race. The Chinese have an upper hand over India in bidding, because they can clinch a deal at any cost, while Indian public sector companies need to ensure that the investment provides at least a 12 per cent rate of return. The Chinese companies not only enjoy a head start over their Indian rivals but also have deeper pockets.

India is only a recent entrant into the global bidding process, because it was only in 2002 that the Indian government deregulated the domestic oil sector. For China, buying foreign oil and gas fields for energy security has become a central mission, and the Chinese government has allowed its oil majors unprecedented freedom to achieve that goal.

China has realized that its energy interests lie in geopolitical relations and has thus decided to focus on the same much more intently to address its security needs. And in that pursuit, Chinese oil companies have used all sorts of government aid, including nonoil commitments, transfer of missile technologies, the veto of UN sanctions against countries where China has oil interests, and even education and development aid, to lure energy rich states.

With energy in mind, China has systematically raised its investment profile across Africa in the last few years. China is aggressively wooing Africa with Chinese president Hu Jintao himself leading from the front. He had visited Africa thrice in the last two years, propagating a strategic partnership between China and Africa. The largest China-Africa gathering since the founding of Communist China in 1949 was held last year, where the Chinese and African leaders signed deals worth $1.9 billion, covering telecommunications, infrastructure, insurance, and mineral resources as well as assurances from China that it would not monopolize Africa's resources as its increases its influence across the continent. China also agreed to extend $1.5 billion in loans and credits to Africa, forgive past debts, and double foreign aid to the continent by 2009. China and the participating nations from Africa also declared a strategic partnership and "action plan" that charts cooperation in the economy, international affairs, and social development.

China's third-largest national oil company, China National Offshore Oil Corporation (CNOOC), has bought a 35 per cent stake in a venture to explore oil in the Niger Delta and a 45 per cent share in the Akpo field in Nigeria. China's oil exploration activity has also increased in East Africa, with China investing in the exploration of oil and gas reserves in Kenya. China's earliest and most successful oil security ventures in Africa are in Sudan. After investments in the mid 1990s that included sending large numbers of Chinese engineering construction teams, Sudanese oil began pumping in 1999, becoming China's first successful overseas effort to produce a significant output.

While the United States and the European Union imposed sanctions against oil producer Sudan, China supported the removal of sanctions. Sudan is one of China's largest trading partners, accounting for almost 10 per cent of China's oil imports. The CNPC owns a 40 per cent share in the Greater Nile Petroleum Operating Company, the main international consortium extracting oil from Sudan.

Chinese energy investments have also made a significant impact in Libya, where a $300 million, ten million-barrel crude purchase agreement was made. In Algeria, China has made agreements to explore for oil and has provided loans so that Chinese telecom companies can update Algeria's telecom systems.

China has also cemented ties with Angola, which exported 25 per cent of its output to China in 2001. Angola's future exports are unlikely to decrease after China provided a seventeen-year, $2 billion oil-backed loan in 2005, which the Angolan government is using to rebuild national infrastructure ravaged by years of civil war. Although the Indian government also promised a $200 million rail line in Angola (over the $620 million for the oil blocks), China National Petroleum Corporation managed to snatch it away, because the Chinese government offered a composite $2 billion in aid for a variety of projects in Angola. Similarly, China managed to retain its 50 per cent stake in Yadavaran, Iran, because there was reportedly an informal arrangement for the transfer of missile technology to Iran.

A Chinese oil company also won the bid for acquiring the assets of the Canadian oil firm, Encana Corporation, in Ecuador after India decided to withdraw from the deal at the last minute. Even with regard to the much-touted China-India joint bid in Syria, the fact remains that the Syrian fields are not very desirable, with production falling from 390,000 barrels a day in 1995 to about 177,000 barrels per day in 2005. There are enormous political risks in investing in a country such as Syria. China and India seem to have made a practical decision to work together so as to share the risk and to keep the cost of the acquisition down.

While India and China may go in for more overseas bids for foreign energy projects to avoid cut-throat competition, a lasting cooperative arrangement is highly unlikely. China is already way ahead of India in this process, and while it may try to assuage some Indian concerns by partnering with it on projects such as the Syrian one, it is unlikely to gain much. India needs to cooperate with China more than vice versa, because it is difficult for India to win over China when they bid for assets.

Given that the Chinese are a much larger participant in the global oil market, it is not clear what advantages it would be deriving from cooperation. Moreover, the Indian government's energy strategy still lacks clarity and bureaucratic problems remain endemic. This was reflected in the manner in which the Indian government decided to reject at the last minute the ONGC's apparently winning bid for an up to $2 billion stake in a Nigerian oil field, thereby damaging the credibility of Indian companies in the international market. In the long term Chinese companies may see more to gain from forming ventures with experienced majors like BP, Royal Dutch Shell, and Exxon Mobil Corporation as opposed to teaming with the Indian counterparts.

The problems that India faces in its search for energy security are much more complicated than China's. Many of the countries that India is courting share ideological affinities with China. Not only are states such as Venezuela, Sudan, Syria, and Iran known for their anti-U.S. and anti-West posturing, but they are also more than willing to join the Chinese bandwagon.

Moreover, some of them are open supporters of radical Islamist ideology. This creates problems for India, which has long been battling Islamic radicals in its own territories aided and abetted by outside powers. The Chinese government's autocratic character has retarded the spread of radical Islam in China, relative to the traction extremists have found in the more permissive Indian society. India is also increasingly reluctant to partner with those states that have an explicit anti-West orientation in their foreign policies. This creates problems for Indian diplomacy that do not afflict China.

CLOSER RELATION OF INDIA, CHINA AND BHUTAN

Till the 1960s, the official, economic and military capacities of the Bhutanese leadership to enhance the kingdom's international relations were severely limited by the country's geographical isolation, lack of modern communications and general economic backwardness. As it is, Bhutan being a landlocked country, with enormous mountainous barriers, was far away from mainstream international commercial and political activities. Its leadership and officials may also have been unaware or unconcerned with the world beyond the immediate border regions. They seem to have had no need to venture beyond relations with bordering countries, and that too, only when its own interests mattered. There was almost a complete absence of all forms of communications starting with motor roads, telephones and news media. Even for communications within the country this was possible to some extent only from 1956-57 onwards when wireless sets powered by generators run on imported petroleum carried on human or animal backs to various centers, began to replace mail runners.

Motor roads were constructed into the interior areas of Bhutan from the Indian border from 1961 onwards. Nationwide and viable telephone services were possible only when the Japanese assisted Bhutan with satellite and digital communications as late as the 1980s. The earlier system set up in a tardy fashion was only to meet basic official needs after development plans were begun and could hardly be termed functional or modern, and even then not available for private use. Up to 1985, the Bhutan embassy in Delhi had to communicate with Thimphu by wireless, and this communication was extended to the Permanent Mission of Bhutan to the United Nations in New York through "telex" by the Delhi embassy. As the Bhutanese Ambassador in New Delhi in 1985, the author recalls informing Thimphu about Mrs. Indira Gandhi's tragic assassination through the embassy's wireless facility as phone calls were not possible.

Radio broadcasting began in the country in 1973 as a "youth broadcasting" service through the personal initiative of Karma Tenzing, a graduate from the United States and an officer of the Ministry of Trade, Industries and Forests who seemed to do it out of sheer nationalistic and patriotic feelings. A few years later the government converted this service to a national one and named it Bhutan Broadcasting Service (BBS). Bhutan also did away with its own restrictions on satellite television and the Internet as late as 1999.

During and prior to the rule of the third King there were certain historical legacies and threats, though considered distant and even absurd today, could not be easily ruled out and had to figure in the strategies followed by Bhutan's leaders. The first was the fear of China and the possibility of this giant neighbor compromising Bhutanese sovereignty. In 1910, when China intervened in Tibet it declared that the Himalayan region including Bhutan, Sikkim, Nepal and Ladakh were parts of China.

This fear of China could be said to have manifested in the Treaty of Sinchula with the British, which essentially made Bhutan a "protectorate" of Britain. Henceforth, Bhutan's relations with the outside world would be conducted on the "advice" of Britain, and after the 1949 treaty, by independent India. The concerns over Chinese intentions were again enhanced after the Chinese army intervention of Tibet in 1951 and the violent suppression of the Tibetan revolt in 1959 after which Bhutanese-Tibetan relations of the past effectively came to an end. Bhutan closed its borders and avoided doing anything to antagonize China.

After the 1962 Sino-Indian war over their boundaries, China may have become much more amenable and enthusiastic in giving recognition to Bhutanese sovereignty if only to compromise the 1949 Indo-Bhutan Treaty and India's foothold in the kingdom. At the same time, India may also have been more forthcoming in recognizing and giving more substance in its relations to Bhutanese sovereignty. There was therefore some advantage in Bhutan's geopolitical situation in strengthening its sovereignty.

A more substantive relationship with the Chinese at the time would have been inconceivable for Bhutan. Given the Chinese threats and its announced views of the Himalayan kingdoms, the absorption of Bhutan into Tibet, and therefore, China, loomed as a fearful possibility. The Cultural Revolution of Chairman Mao Zedong would have destroyed all of Bhutan's traditions and the young monarchy. Bhutan would have no longer existed as a distinct cultural and political entity. While considering this possible relation with China in the early 1960s it should be remembered that this was not mere conjecture. There were strong views among some prominent members of the then Bhutanese leadership that Bhutan should move closer to China rather than India, especially from ethnic and cultural points of view.

These persons, who fortunately were in the small minority, failed to comprehend that when it comes to safeguarding a nation's sovereignty and independence, ethnicity or racial policies and approaches may not prove to be in one's true interests. One needs to simply look at the histories of Asia, Africa and Europe.

The Indians and the Pakistanis, the Japanese and the Koreans, the Chinese and the Japanese, the Chinese and the Tibetans, the Chinese and the Taiwanese, the Kuwaitis and the Iraqis, don't really get along politically despite racial and cultural similarities. In the 21st century, Africa has faced history's most serious problems in Rwanda, Sudan, Nigeria, Uganda and elsewhere.

Again, if Bhutanese consider themselves closer to Tibetans, it should be remembered that the latter have demonstrated attitudes of condescension towards Bhutanese. So a one-sided approach will not succeed.

Therefore in national politics, the urge to reach out to other peoples based on preconceived notions that ethnicity and race will better serve one's interests may not be the best of politics for a nation, and leaders and people with such notions should be simply ignored and not permitted to play any significant national role.

A nation has to base its international politics on safeguarding its vital interests of sovereignty, independence and security–no matter with which entity or race or ethnicity its leadership may have to deal with. In Bhutan's case this has been glaring. India, rather than Tibet or China, has served Bhutan's interest the best.

Setting the Stage for Indo-Bhutan Relations

King Jigme Dorji Wangchuck ascended the throne in 1952 when Bhutan, Tibet and the region as a whole were going through trying times. In the north, the Chinese intervention in Tibet had acquired a violent and ominous character resulting in the fleeing of the Dalai Lama and thousands of Tibetans into India. The Chinese communists of the times seemed to be in no mood to make any compromises on their claims over Tibet. At the same time they were bent upon integrating the Tibetan region into the "motherland" by all means, including militarily.

The Cultural Revolution in China attempted to achieve this through the destruction, and if this was not possible, the dilution of Tibetan religion, culture, language, geographical boundaries and demographics. Thousands of Tibetans fled their homeland and scattered all over the Indian subcontinent and beyond to Europe, the United States and Canada.

The Cultural Revolution resulted in the tragic destruction of Tibet's ancient civilization that had for centuries influenced Bhutan and the Himalayan region including Mongolia and parts of China. The "it looks like me" revered statue of Guru Rimpoche in Samye, Tibet, was also destroyed during this period.

The Tibetans expected support from an international community that knew or cared very little about them or their struggle. The United States, through its Central Intelligence Agency (CIA), made some half-hearted attempts to provide training and arms to the Tibetan resistance movement but as soon as they felt that their interests were not threatened and Tibet was of little importance to them politically and economically, they dropped even the token assistance being provided. In fact, the resistance put up by Tibetans with CIA assistance may have only helped to make the Chinese reactions harsher. When US aid was abruptly cut off, the Tibetans suffered more as a result.

Neither was Nehru's India in any mood to aid the Tibetans militarily or in the United Nations. In fact, India initially inherited the British view that Tibet was an autonomous region under Chinese "suzerainty" as opposed to "sovereignty"–a legal position that British diplomats had devised to avoid Chinese wrath but seemingly to show some sympathy for Tibet's cause. India, of course, now fully recognizes the sovereignty of China over Tibet, as does China regarding India's Sikkim.

From the Indian perspective, Indian diplomats seemed to have had this concept that India's sphere of influence should be paramount south of the Himalayan range and that of China in the north. This was a colonial concept, but the hangover may persist in New Delhi. Prime Minister Jawaharlal Nehru's government in India after 1947 was in a dilemma on how to react to the developments taking place on the yet-to-be demarcated borders of the Himalayas with China.

Nehru seemed basically an idealist who believed that the Indians and Chinese, the two great civilizations and peoples of Asia, and who had both emerged from the yoke of colonialism, could not afford any rivalry. Now, as independent developing countries he expected that both would concentrate on socioeconomic development and deal with neighbours and other countries on the basis of respect for each other's sovereignty and national pride.

He was so carried away by the idea of friendship and cooperation that the term "Hindi Chini Bhai Bhai" was coined. Nehru's expectations were shattered in 1962 when the Chinese invaded parts of northern India and disputed India's concept of the borders with China as inherited from the British.

India, Bhutan and Nepal have to be nevertheless given the credit for the help provided and the generosity shown to the waves of Tibetan refugees. India has given a lot of space for Tibetan refugees to sustain their religion and culture in Dharamshala and other parts of India. In the case of Bhutan, those Tibetans who wanted to integrate into Bhutanese society found it easy in view of the ethnic and cultural similarities.

Officially Bhutan could not afford to antagonize the Chinese, and hence, had to curb all political activities of the Tibetans that were directed towards China. Internationally, Bhutan could say nothing about Tibet's status even if it wanted to, and politically it became expedient to accept Chinese claims over Tibet. After all, where did Bhutan stand when powers like the United States, the erstwhile Soviet Union, the United Kingdom, India and all major nations acquiesced to the fait accompli in the face of China's evolving global economic and political clout.

Despite the 1949 Treaty with Bhutan, the Government of India was unclear on how it should deal with Bhutan under the circumstances, especially with the Chinese takeover of Tibet and claims over the Himalayan region. Besides Bhutan and Nepal being a consideration, what was more important were the Chinese claims of what India considered its territories like the North East Frontier Agency (NEFA)–later renamed Arunachal Pradesh by Prime Minister Indira Gandhi of India, and Aksai Chin. The Indian army which had just emerged from the partition of their country and the grant of independence by the British, was still not well trained and equipped to meet a threat like that of Mao Zedong's revolutionary China.

In the case of India's relations with Bhutan, Pandit Jawaharlal Nehru provided an unambiguous interpretation in his public speech in Paro on September 23, 1958. He declared: "Some may think that since India is a great and powerful country and Bhutan a small one, the former might wish to exercise pressure on Bhutan.

It is, therefore, essential that I make it clear to you that our only wish is that you should remain an independent country, choosing your own way of life and taking the path of progress according to your will. At the same time, we two should live as friendly neighbours helping each other. Freedom of both Bhutan and India should be safeguarded so that none from outside can do harm to it." This statement of Nehru's has proved to be enduring for Indo-Bhutan relations, and was quoted by Prime Minister Dr. Manmohan Singh during his visit to Bhutan in May 2008.

An outsider's assessment of the thinking within the Indian leadership at least till now shows that India decided to accept Chinese claims north of the Himalayas, that is, in Tibet. As for Bhutan, Nepal and Sikkim, India felt that these should be under its sphere of influence both in international relations and security considerations.

The problem for India was and still seems to be, is that China has not conceded to this view of the region, and neither have these Himalayan entities all gone the way India wanted. Indira Gandhi's government managed to annex Sikkim by taking advantage of the political upheaval in that country begun by Kazi Lhendup Dorji Khangsarpa.

Nevertheless, China put off recognizing this annexation for a long time but has now given in to the fait accompli in exchange of India's consistent stand recognizing China's sovereignty over

Tibet. India avoided dealings with Taiwan and supported mainland China's seat at the United Nations just as trade and economic links between the two giants grew, and the enhanced position and role of China on the world stage.

This was formally done during Prime Minister Vajpayee's visit to China in 2003 and further confirmed when the Chinese presented India with revised maps showing Sikkim as a part of India.

Nepal has always tried to resist or minimize India's influence while still expecting all the trade and transit advantages in India, emphasizing when it could that this was an international right of landlocked countries. At the same time, Nepal from time to time attempts to play off India and China to its advantage, and which sometimes has backfired.

It also refused to accept any defence arrangements with India vis-à-vis China and instead made attempts to import Chinese weaponry including ground to air missiles, which India felt was not in keeping with the treaty relationship between the two countries.

This attitude of Nepal has resulted in constant friction in Indo-Nepal relations, and at times has reached seritous proportions when at one time Prime Minister Rajiv Gandhi even decided to close down all transit routes and trade between the two countries–reportedly "to teach Nepal a lesson."

The most recent attempt by Nepal to play off India and China came when the newly elected Prime Minister, Pushpa Kamal Dahal, or more popularly known by his revolutionary name, Prachanda, snubbed New Delhi and made his maiden visit to Beijing in August 2008.

When undertaking the boundary negotiations with China, these same principles seemed to find no place in negotiations with the Government of India.

The Bhutanese cabinet in the 1970s frequently questioned the Survey Department as to how the boundaries with India had been finalized without explicit cabinet consent let alone through deliberations and approval in the National Assembly. The cabinet never resulted in a satisfactory conclusion except to be informed that the basis would be the boundary line finalized with the British, which were most likely unilaterally drawn up by colonial surveyors as in the case of most boundaries in the subcontinent.

On the other hand, the border discussions and the periodic outcomes between Bhutan and China have rightly been subjected to lengthy debates in the National Assembly with displays of large detailed maps and sand models at the Royal Bhutan Army headquarters in Lungtenphu, Thimphu.

For the sake of mentioning it, the author had been made responsible by the fourth King to lead the border negotiations with China for the first time in Bhutan's history in the summer of 1984.

7

Indian Foreign Policy in the 21st Century

The first eight years of the 21st century has seen India rise from the international wilderness to be a significant player in the global environment. As India acquires greater prominence, it becomes consequential to evaluate the foreign policy of the world's largest democracy for its engagement within its neighbourhood and globally.

INDIA'S FOREIGN POLICY CHALLENGES: TODAY AND BEYOND

The years 1989 – 1991 were a watershed in the history of the 20th century. In a series of swift and stunning events, the USSR and its proxy regimes in Eastern Europe collapsed. Grass roots revolts by disaffected youth were seen in both Europe and Asia as evidenced by the ceremonies at the collapse of Berlin Wall, Tiananmen Square, and Myanmar. The ideological struggle between capitalism and communism melted and paved the way for globalization. The world previously polarized by an ideological struggle rapidly morphed into economic blocs. ASEAN, a bulwark against the spread of communism in Southeast Asia, rearranged to include Vietnam, Laos and Cambodia.

In the post Cold War era, two main and often opposing trends emerged. The first was a willingness of the international community, particularly the US to play a mediating role in settling conflicts from Northern Ireland to East Timor. Associated with this trend was the break up of larger countries into smaller nations of Eastern Europe and the Commonwealth of Independent States of the erstwhile USSR. Simultaneously, neighboring states realized the benefits of economic interdependence coalesced into trading blocs. Among the most notable groupings are NAFTA (North American Free Trade Agreement), European Union, and ASEAN (Association of Southeast Asian Nations). India in the early 90's seemed ill suited to cope with the changes in the global environment. It was largely dependent on the former Soviet Union for military equipment and spares. India's economy was highly regulated and centrally controlled and its ties with the US remained limited.

During the late 80's and the 1990's, the end of the Cold War heralded realignment in global relations. India engaged new friends, maintained steadfast contact with old friends, and an ever watchful eye over enemies. India started its journey of economic liberalization, and the Gujral doctrine dampened hegemonic fears among neighbours. India extended its influence into the distant neighborhoods of Southeast Asia and the Middle East. The tenure of Prime Minister Rao witnessed burgeoning economic and political relations. Astute foreign policy laid the cornerstone in the foundation of India's post Cold War foreign policy, and subsequent administrations advanced this agenda.

India established economic and diplomatic relations with Israel and deepened ties with the Arab states. India's economic engagement of ASEAN continued at a steadfast rate throughout the 1990's. Relations with the US gradually thawed and even blossomed. Overall, the pre-Cold War Indo – US ties were held hostage to the larger Cold War agenda and to US-Pakistan relations. The 1980's brought about a rapprochement in Indo – US ties due to the Soviet invasion of Afghanistan, India's desire to open its economy, and clandestine Pakistani acquisition of nuclear weapons. The post Cold War era reduced the confinements of the past, and new administrations in both countries sought to increase ties. The Clinton administration's simple message "it's the economy stupid" allowed both governments to set aside some past disagreements and focus on mutual economic growth. Relations with Russia continued to mature and involved a long standing multidimensional approach involving security, military, and economic links.

Despite the upswing in India's global contacts and the post Cold War era bonhomie, Pakistan remained a sore point due to its obduracy in Kashmir and support of cross border terrorism. The Soviet withdrawal from Afghanistan allowed Pakistan to redirect trained mercenaries towards Kashmir in order to achieve long sought goals. As tensions between India and Pakistan flared over various reasons, President Clinton repeatedly offered unsolicited American services and at one time even asked China to play a role. Indian policy treaded a difficult course of exposing Pakistan's role in cross border terrorism. At the same time it avoided internationalizing the Kashmir issue and invite serious meddling. Internationalization would play into Pakistani hands of devaluing the bilateral Simla Agreement. One notable event borne out of over zealous efforts at peacemaking was the Robin Raphel fiasco. It inadvertently questioned the legitimacy of the Indian Union and threatened burgeoning Indo – US ties. India's diplomats successfully raised objections and prevented further carelessness by the Clinton Administration.

India's engagement of Southeast Asia was dubbed as "Look East Policy." India's economic engagement of ASEAN continued at a steadfast rate throughout the 1990's and reaped dividends in the form of trade agreements, increased contact between people, and the establishment of sub-regional grouping such as BIMSTEC (Bangladesh India Myanmar Sri Lanka Thailand Economic Council) and GMC (Ganga Mekong Cooperative). These groups worked towards free trade agreements, common development of infrastructure, and integration of national economies into the global economy. In addition to an economic dimension, India's engagement was motivated by strategic reasons. China's economic and military interaction would restrict India's role in Southeast Asia. India capitalized on ASEAN's concern about Chinese influence to bolster its position. India's northeast region would serve as a launch pad for economic interaction and revitalize an ailing portion of the country. India's engagement of Myanmar despite significant Chinese influence indicated broad goals of engaging neighbours on economic and strategic terms. Indo –

Myanmar ties formed the first and critical step in India – Southeast Asia ties while improving security in the Northeast region and paving the way for future economic development.

In a stunning move India carried out three nuclear tests on May 11, 1998. As the Clinton administration preached nuclear morality, India retorted with an additional 2 tests on May 13, 1998. India "gate crashed" into the exclusive nuclear club. Despite bravado about a de-nuclearizing India from a non proliferation regime in Washington the world accepted India as a nuclear reality. The usually economically savvy Clinton administration sought to replace incentives with economic sanctions in order to punish India. In retrospect, the economic sanctions overwhelmingly failed. The dialogue between India and the US resulted in a lengthy exchange on mutual security situations. India voluntarily agreed to the principle of the NPT (Non Proliferation Treaty) as a way of calming American apprehensions. Pakistan soon retorted to India's tests. Despite disclosed nuclear capability, a conflagration between India and Pakistan in the spring of 1999 did not escalate to a nuclear exchange. Furthermore, it amply demonstrated the success of Indian policy and marginalized Pakistan for promoting instability. On the other hand, the Kargil imbroglio served as a convenient way for the West to continue the Indo – Pak dyad to encompass nuclear tensions. The region was dubbed the most dangerous place in the world and serve as a vehicle for numerous peace making attempts and a Presidential visit.

The fears of the most dangerous place in the world were confirmed in an unimaginable way on September 2001 as terrorists struck the World Trade Centre and the Pentagon. The Taliban regime in Afghanistan gave sanctuary to Osama bin Laden, while Pakistan obstructed attempts to capture him. After the 9-11 attacks, Pakistan was forced to officially turn against the Taliban and aid US efforts. India was driven by economic and strategic compulsions. It offered significant aid to the US in the initial phase of the War on Terror. According to India, the 9-11 attack sharply focused attention on Pakistan's sponsorship of terror.

Additionally, due to strong economic linkages any downturn in the US economy would adversely impact Indian economic growth and hurt Indian Diaspora in the region. The presence of American military personnel and long term interests in Afghanistan irrevocably changed the security situation for India. Pakistan's overt cross border terrorism would be checked, and the reversal of the Taliban reduced training camps for future jihadis. On the other, Pakistan secured by American interests would resort to adventurism against India without fear of retaliation as evidenced by December 2001 attack on the Indian parliament. In the post 9-11 scenario, India benefited from the removal of the Taliban regime, established diplomatic and economic linkages with Afghanistan, and furthered ties to Central Asian neighbours. India desires a stable Afghanistan that retards the growth of fundamentalist forces and allows India access to the region's trade and energy commodity. The American engagement of Pakistan is a double edged sword, on one hand it limited Pakistan's ability to spread the nuisance of terrorism, but it resulted in military benefits that could be potentially directed against India.

INDIA'S NEW GOVERNMENT AND ITS FOREIGN POLICY OPTIONS

The major determinants of the foreign policy of any nation are its national security interests and its economic interests. Logically, it is these two national interests around which should revolve the various formulations of the country's foreign policy. Foreign policies of nations do not function in a vacuum insulated by delusional moral and ideological obsessions. Foreign policies perforce, have to take into account the prevailing regional and international strategic realities with which a nation has to strike workable equations based on one's own existing power attributes and strategic utility to the key global powers.

India's foreign policies in the last eight years under the previous Bharatiya Janata Party (BJP) led Government can be assessed as successful when measured against the above indicators. The BJP Government's foreign policies did make India "shine" in the international arena, not by delusional rhetoric but by an initial display of power potential by carrying out the nuclear weaponisation in 1998. It was a defining moment. Initial opposition by the United States and others were soon converted into opportunities for strategic partnerships/strategic cooperation with United States, Israel, France, UK, Vietnam and Myanmar. For the first time, even joint naval exercises were held with China. India's then foreign policies were also successful in bringing significant international pressure on Pakistan to change tack.

Foreign policies of any nation need bi-partisan support, as the country's national interests do not change with a change of political power. While the economic determinant could change in terms of nuances with a change of Government, the national security determinant cannot and should not, as the strategic perspectives that go into its formulation have to be long range.

Regrettably, the new Indian Government, led by the Congress Party and through its flip-flop and ill-considered statements has given indications, that it is all set to undo the foreign policy gains of India in the last eight years. The Congress Party's election manifesto, formulated by its present Foreign Minister reflected the Congress Party's traditional dislike of the United States and it also reflected this Party's resentment with the gains made by the BJP Government in terms of evolving a strategic partnership with the United States. In generic terms, India's new Government has three options open in relation to giving shape to its foreign policies, and these are:

1. Non-alignment Foreign Policy.
2. Independent Foreign Policy.
3. India's Inter-dependent Foreign Policy with United States Option.

The ramifications of each are discussed in the succeeding paragraphs.

Non-Alignment as Foreign Policy Precept

Non-Alignment was Nehru's brainchild and the Congress Party's foreign policy fetish thereafter. Non-Alignment also seems to be the obsessive mind-set of the Congress Party's present Foreign Minister and many of his genre in the Indian Foreign Service. However, even in the heyday of Non-Alignment India was never genuinely non-aligned. It had a marked tilt towards the former

Soviet Union, Communist China and the countries of the Communist/Socialist bloc. The key components of India's non-alignment policies were opposition to United States policies in all the strategic sub-systems of the world.

The danger today is that a combination of the Congress Party's attachment of non-alignment combined and seconded by the Communist Parties as leading members of the Congress Coalition Government, and furthered by a Foreign Minister with an obsessive-mindset of non-alignment could veer away India's foreign policies in this direction.

The chief manifestations of this option in terms of India's foreign policy would be:

- United States policies in Greater Middle East, South East Asia and East Asia to be opposed, based more on inclination than substance.
- Enhancement of India's relations with Russia.
- Enhancement of India's relations with China in the pursuance of the "Panch Sheel" Concept-a concept much abused by China against India.
- Devaluation of United States-India evolving strategic partnership.
- Military-to-Military contacts with United States to be downplayed.

Proponents of this foreign policy option, fail to take into account the following ramifications of the above manifestations:

- Non-Alignment, even in the most genuine form was applicable only in a bi-polar world.
- Non-Alignment today exists as " fossilized remains" of Indian's delusional foreign policies.
- India cannot afford politically, strategically or economically to remain at odds with the United States as the "unipolar power".

India's non-alignment years in terms of her foreign policy formulations and attitudes were a national waste both strategically and economically. India's new Congress Government, in the interests of India's national security and economic development should not "inflict" this option on India.

INDIA'S INDEPENDENT FOREIGN POLICY OPTION

The Congress Party keep freely mixing up and using the word "independent" with "non-alignment". The two, in the option of the author are entirely different. "Non-Alignment" was a policy precept of the Third World countries, as relatively powerless countries against the Big Powers.

An "independent foreign policy" precept connotes that a nation has such highly developed national power attributes, that it is not susceptible to political and economic coercion by stronger powers and also that its national power attributes endow on it the strength to chart-out an independent foreign policy without fear of restraint from any quarter.

India today has not reached the 'independent foreign policy' stage as yet due to the following reasons:

- India's half-a-century of mis-governance has thwarted the materalisation of its power potential.
- Nearly half-a-century of non-alignment foreign policies has left India with no genuine friends in the international arena.
- Decades of ineffective national security management has left India with not even regional power capabilities in the Indian sub-continent.

An "independent foreign policy" option in its most genuine and purist form is presently not available as an option to India. Taking "independent stands" on international issues without the "muscle to back-up it up" does not constitute an "independent foreign policy" It is only rhetoric.

India's Inter-Dependent Foreign Policy With United States Option

In a globalised world, inter-dependence transcends national barriers not only in the economic field, but also extends to the strategic and political fields. It has also extended itself to the fields of terrorism and crime-syndicates. The United States is the world's predominant power.

Its predominance extends in all fields from economics, politics, strategic and control of global financial and energy resources. Its likes and dislikes shape the international strategic realities. No amount of efforts to create a " multi-polar world" by China or France, for over a decade now, has borne fruit. Why, in fact, China itself rose to 'super-stardom' by weaving foreign policies inter-dependent with those of USA in the late 1970's and 1980's.

India has no option today but to follow foreign policies of interdependence with the United States, for the following reasons:

- India's economic advancement and consequent rise to regional power status and key global player can only come about with United States strategic and political concurrence.
- India's economic modernisation and strategic mobility upwards can only be ensured by United States military presence in Pakistan and Greater Middle East. The same would constrain India's long range threat from China.
- India's aspirations to become an "Indian Ocean Power" cannot materialise without convergence with United States national security interests.
- India's vast outlay of financial resources for infrastructure and economic development cannot come about without United States direct involvement and goading of international financial institutions.

India for all practical reasons needs the United States, in terms of materialisation of her national aspirations and protection of her national security interests.

Concluding Observations

India's foreign policies cannot be made captive to the delusional non-alignment gladiators or India's Communist Parties who have never been known for their objectivity or to India's minority Indian Muslims vote banks where every issue is viewed in a pan-Islamic context.

In today's global security environment and the international strategic realities likely to persist for the next 50 years, India neither has the luxury nor the time to find new anchors for her foreign policies from the fossilised remains of Nehruvian Non-Alignment or her "presumed power potential" not concretised so far.

In the last eight years the centre-piece of India's foreign policy has been the evolution of a strong political and strategic partnership with the United States. United States and India recognized the mutual convergences and imperatives and have been engaged in establishing a substantive bi-lateral relationship.

India's national security and economic interests dictate that this is India's only foreign policy option available. India's national aspirations can best be met by formulating India's foreign policy inter-dependent with United States national interests and not in opposition to it.

CHALLENGES AHEAD

During the Bush administration, Indo – US ties acquired a security dimension with regular military exercises and limited access to civilian and military technology. Thinkers in both governments sought to make the two countries "natural allies" and often touted that India could play a pivotal role in America's Asia policy in the new century. Despite the rhetoric, there are numerous issues of divergence such as American unilateralism, support of Pakistan's regime that fosters terrorism against India, and future containment of China and Iran. If these points of divergence are not discussed or mutually resolved will unravel ties and threaten to undercut the momentum of Indo – US relations. Furthermore, the US must quietly bury the India – Pakistan dyad, the staple of many public announcements. Any ongoing use of the dyad will seek to accentuate the ridiculous because a reasonable comparison between the countries cannot exist.

Nonetheless, one must note several significant points of convergence such as economic development, balance of power in Asia, stemming of terrorism and policy with regard to Afghanistan. Stability in Afghanistan forms the pivot of India's political, economic and strategic policy in Central Asia. Any constraints on Indian policy in the region will ease the path of fundamentalist influence. Trends such as the resurgent Taliban and marginalization of minority groups are worrisome as it could unravel the progress of the past 3 years. The success of a representative government in Afghanistan and freedom from the Taliban keeps fundamentalist forces at bay in the region and promotes stability in Central Asia. The establishment of intercultural contacts, strong diplomatic interaction, and aid in the form of food and vehicles are meant to not only promote good will and help a troubled neighbour, but also are a stepping stone to mutually lucrative trade corridor extending into the interior of Asia. Iran forms the second pillar of India's engagement in the region. It diversifies India's engagement of the Islamic world and bypasses Pakistan. American action against Iran will affect India's policy in Central Asia, strengthen the factors of instability but also could widen the area of instability from Iraq to Afghanistan and promote Islamic fundamentalism.

The Pakistani government's continued stubbornness poses a strong challenge to India's foreign policy. Pakistan's "invader" mindset is evident from non-compliance with past treaties, support of cross border terrorism, view of historical events and the names of its missiles. It is simplistic to view Pakistan as a monolith. In actuality, Pakistan has a sizeable amount of diversity across ethnic groups, religious sects, and political ideology. Unfortunately, such diversity is not represented in its military dominated government. Moderate factions are often held at bay by the government's backing of fundamentalist forces and its promotion of a paranoid world view to its populous. Suppression both ethnic and political diversity has lead to numerous dissident factions seeking regional autonomy or a change of government. Despite a façade to the contrary, the Pakistani government shows no sign of significant or lasting change regarding Islamic fundamentalism which threatens the region and beyond. American policies based on encouraging Pakistan to restrain zealots, cooperate in capturing Osama bin Laden, and maintain stability in Afghanistan is very limited. Pakistan's incorrigible behavior is the very problem. Pakistan misdirects American aid and furthers the very bothersome habits it is designed to eradicate. In the long term, Pakistan is a moribund nation, and American realization of this reality by preparation of contingency plans to deal with the consequences would provide true security in the region.

India faces challenges on its eastern flank. Nepal's Maoist movement continues to ravage the country despite the involvement of the Nepali army. Borne out of the frustration of a disenfranchised population, it continues to displace government influence. Several truces have been broken, and the onslaughts of Maoist attacks on Nepali forces and on Katmandu continue at an unabated pace.

The insurgency must be tackled with a multi-modal that includes military, social and economic means designed to parch the support for the Maoists. Maoist ties to anti-monarchy forces in Bhutan, and terrorist groups in India's Northeast provide regional enemies with a convenient way to meddle in India's security matters.

Bangladesh's ongoing struggle, thirty years after a hard won independence, to establish a confident national identity blending Bangla nationalism and Islam will consume resources, affect its interactions with neighbours, and cause internal upheaval. The core problem in India – Bangladesh relations is Bangladesh's insecurity over its identity which manifests a paranoid suspicion of a larger and more powerful neighbour. Bangladesh often rivals Pakistan in its stubbornness, and its refusal to economically integrate with India despite mutual benefits.

China continues to play dual twin roles of engaging India while simultaneously backing Pakistan and other smaller neighbours acquire military items. Ties have historically been soured due to 1962 war, support of various Northeast terrorist groups and role in Pakistan's clandestine nuclear program. Prime Minister Vajpayee's visit to engage civilian Chinese leadership may bear fruit with cooperation in technology, tourism, and increased contacts. China's dual strategy towards India can best be seen in the engagement during Prime Minister Vajpayee's state visit and subsequent reports of Chinese army entry into Indian territory. Various factions within the Chinese government have individual interests; some seek to compete with India while others favour cooperation. The current trend in Sino – Indian relations will likely continue with cooperation on an economic front and competition on a strategic front. Southeast Asia has responded to India initiatives and has proposed closer economic and military cooperation. ASEAN realizes its position between India and China and seek to promote ties with both for their benefit. This region may become the hotly contested area between ascendant India and China because of its ethnic mix, historical background, and economic.

Rapid economic growth is fueled by readily available energy. Unsurprisingly energy has become major focus of policy both internal and external. Books written by government officials now mention energy security as a part of national security. India has invested in a multilateral strategy to gain energy. It involved expansion of indigenous energy as well as involvement in foreign projects. India has explored oil and natural gas options in Nigeria, Sudan and Russia. Closer to home, energy deals with Iran, Bhutan, and Myanmar are afoot. Energy related projects such as the pipeline across Pakistan into India and another natural gas pipeline from Bangladesh to India seem promising despite occasional flare ups in tension. In the coming decades, energy policy will form an increasingly important component in India's foreign policy and national security perceptions.

Since Independence, India has struggled to maintain a balanced place in the world as an old civilization and a new nation in a hostile neighborhood. It avoided Cold War entanglements as much as possible while plotting an independent course. It championed the cause of developing nations. India's foreign policy rose to the challenge posed by the end of the Cold War.

Though the initial outlook in the early 1990's seemed bleak, the post-Cold War era presented a unique opportunity to engage countries based on strategic and economic grounds. Overall, the first decade of the post Cold War era was a difficult time as foreign policy often tilted to compensate for previous leanings. Overtime, India's policy has matured into a balanced engagement of the major powers, and strategically important regions. India must continue to engage while avoiding entanglements.

Its alliances must be limited by mutual goals, and not be forced to serve as a wedge in larger rivalries. Foreign policy must tread a focused path between advancing long term goals and agile enough to respond to abrupt changes. In the coming decade, India's foreign policy will aid in choosing allies, forming partnerships based on mutual interests, and in fending off old and new enemies. The issues of international terrorism, Islamic fundamentalism, competition for a sphere of influence and acquisition of energy will dominate India's policy in the foreseeable future. India's policy should be grounded in present concerns as well as historical dialectics; a patchwork combining the legacy of an ancient civilization, security imperatives of the Raj and its importance as a cultural and commercial crossroad.

INDIA'S FOREIGN POLICY CHALLENGES 2005

India's foreign policies, fortunately, have enjoyed bipartisan political support domestically, markedly from the 1990s onwards. The year 2004 witnessed a change of political complexion of the Government in India raising uncertainties in international quarters that under a Congress-led Government foreign policies may revert back to the Nehruvian mould. Initial pronouncements by the new Government and especially its new foreign minister created some confusion. However, international realities and global security environment soon forced the new Government to prudently stick to the earlier general direction.

India's foreign policies first significant change in direction, attendant with change in India's economic policies took place under the stewardship of a Congress Prime Minister from South India and not belonging to the Nehru-Gandhi dynasty, namely Prime Minister Narasimha Rao, who recently passed away. He was the initiator of India's 'New Look' foreign policies.

Foreign policies of any nation do not function in a vacuum. They are a product of the prevailing international environment and the country's indices in terms of its geo-strategic location, economic health, military strength and domestic stability. Hence PM Narasimha Rao's 'New Look' foreign policies arose from the prevailing international environment at the end of the Cold War, the disintegration of the former Soviet Union and its global countervailing power and the need for India to detach its foreign policies from domestic minority vote bank considerations and also to focus on neglected regions. Hence the thrust for a strategic partnership with Israel in West Asia and the 'Look East" foreign policy. So also was the quest for a substantive relationship with the United States. This was not to the liking of many of the Congress Party hierarchy.

The latter half of the 1990s till 2004 witnessed a BJP Government in power. Its tenure coincided with the post-Cold War era, the major rise of United States unilateralism and the new American policies of pre-emption and military intervention in global affairs without restraint.

The Vajpayee Government of the BJP continued with the overall general direction of foreign policies of the Narasimha Rao Government. However greater intensity was accorded to the build-up of US-India strategic cooperation, normalising and enlarging cooperation with China, besides Vajapayee's personal commitment to bring a military adventurist and terrorism proxy-war nation like Pakistan to the dialogue table.

India's Foreign Policies-Imperatives for a Change of Direction/ Nuances: Constancy of operational factors/considerations are not the hallmark of the international situation. It is a rapidly changing world, where increasingly the global security environment undergoes changes rapidly and new equations are struck and new doctrines postulated by United States unilateralism, at times in immoral contradiction of its established and declaratory policies e.g. Compromising on counter-terrorism against Islamic Jehad and condoning Pakistan's WMD proliferation.

While the turn of the millennium augured well for the general direction of Indian foreign policies under two separate political dispensations with an over-emphasis on a US-India strategic partnership, the last few years of the 21st Century indicated otherwise.

The last few years of the 21st Century in terms of international/ political developments impacting on India's foreign policies presents the following broad picture:

- United States with its tactical obsession with Pakistan has placed the emerging USA-India strategic partnership on the back-burner. India is no longer a priority for USA.
- Russia at long last has realized that it is no longer a "natural ally of the West". The post-Cold War knee-jerk reaction of forging a strategic alliance with China has not brought the

desired fruits. Russia may look for resurgence on its own strengths.

- China despite a phenomenal rise in trade with India and a flurry of visits by senior Chinese leaders to India has yet to give up its strategic nexus with Pakistan. China continues with the military build-up of Pakistan and establishing the infrastructure of a Chinese military presence in Pakistan.
- The Indian sub-continent or so called South Asia, presents a dismal security environment. Pakistan strategically buoyed by American political, economic and military aid continues with its illusions of strategic parity with India and has not displayed any indicators of political maturity or conflict resolution. Turmoil and conflict continues in Nepal and Sri Lanka. Bangladesh under the present political dispensation is anti-Indian and emerging as an alternative base for Pakistan's proxy war against India.

The indicators above present significant challenges for India's foreign policies in 2005 as they generate imperatives calling for a change in direction/nuances of India's existing foreign policies thrusts. The thrust of this chapter is to present a perspective analysis of India's foreign policy challenges for 2005.

INDIA IN ASIA

Before India may look towards acquiring global power status, it will have to address the regional perspectives of its foreign policy. As Asia consists of several regions, India's foreign policy is formulated according to the engagement with each region. South Asia, India's immediate neighbourhood, is yet dealing with several political and economic issues. Many of the states, such as Pakistan and Nepal, have recently adopted democracy and the international community will look towards India to help promote it in the region. The future of the South Asian Association for Regional Cooperation (SAARC) seems increasingly uncertain and India will have to employ more foreign policy resources into the success of this multilateral forum so that it may continue to engage its South Asian neighbours. The challenge for India in engaging South Asia is the general suspicion towards it from other South Asian countries. India, is three times larger, in terms of economy, population and land mass, than the other South Asian countries, and is often accused to harbour hegemonic ambitions in the region by its neighbours.

As such, many of its initiatives and policies within the region are not well received. India may have to be more innovative in its foreign policy in South Asia and exercise its economic diplomacy and soft power to engage these countries. This has been made more difficult by two critical factors. Firstly, India-Pakistan ties remain shaky even though they have improved in the last five years. Any initiative India takes towards South Asia will include Pakistan and New Delhi may yet be reluctant to engage Islamabad in a closer partnership as it still considers the latter as its security threat. In addition, China's involvement within South Asia hinders India's ability to engage the region. China, an observer country in SAARC, is a close ally of Pakistan and has been accused consistently of aiding Islamabad in their conflicts with India. China has also begun to engage other South Asian countries, such as Bangladesh and Sri Lanka, on energy cooperation and economic development among other things. These factors will force India to revise its foreign policy in South Asia as it strives to arrest China's increasing influence in the region.

In 1991, then Indian Prime Minister Narasimha Rao launched the Look East Policy, which has arguably become India's most articulate foreign policy. Initially formulated to increase India's engagement with the South East Asian countries and the ASEAN organization, the Look East Policy now provides the direction for India's foreign policy towards East Asia and Australia and New Zealand. With the initial thrust of the Look East Policy focusing on economic diplomacy, India has now expanded its engagement with these countries to include security and political cooperation.

The Look East Policy has been considerably successful from India's perspective but New Delhi will have to develop this policy thought further to reflect its changing needs as India continues to grow in influence within East and Southeast Asia. Once again, China's political, security and economic clout in these regions have to be factored into India's foreign policy here. Both India and

China will benefit from cooperation with each other in these areas so they are unlikely to be embroiled in an outright conflict here.

Nevertheless, both countries will continue to compete for markets, resources and a strong security presence here. The main points of contention will be India's desire to exercise naval domination in the Indian Ocean over China, to capture key energy sources and secure important energy routes, to build a reliable security partnership with the region and lastly, to be a part of the evolving East Asian Economic Community, which China may try to hinder as it did in objecting India's membership of the East Asian Summit. A lot will also depend on the role US plays in these regions, notably South East Asia. Japan has significant influence in East Asia but will have to step-up its presence in South East Asia. With greater US and Japan presence in South East Asia, India will not have to focus its foreign policy aims on China in this region and can expand its own role and engagement here. Another consideration for India in South East Asia is that of Myanmar. New Delhi has been under increasing international strain to promote democracy in Myanmar and to help pressure the junta to end military rule in this country.

India's foreign policy in other parts of the world will be designed to complement its global ascendancy. In Africa, India will continue to leverage on the economic development aid it provides to these countries to gain access into key oil and gas sources. India will also continue to develop its partnership with South Africa as they look to intensify their economic cooperation. In Latin America as well, India will look into sourcing key resources from the region as it seeks to develop economic ties with Brazil. India has realized that if it wishes to expand its global influence, then it must continue to diversify its engagement in the international sphere. This realization will propel India to deepen and widen its engagement with developing countries in other regions.

As discussed, India's main foreign policy objective is to achieve global power status. It will however, depend greatly on its relationship with the US, and the other five nodes of power, to attain this. That is why India's foreign policy in the 21st century will be developed with the US being its focal point. Besides the US, two other determinants that constantly appear in India's foreign policy considerations are China and energy security. China's rise poses challenges to India's ascendancy and so hinders it achieving its foreign policy objectives. Although it seems unlikely that this rivalry will lead to a direct conflict, especially since they benefit from mutual cooperation, they will continue to compete in various parts of the world. Energy security is another area, which clearly influences India's foreign policy due to the importance of energy fuel to India's economic growth. As such, it may choose to 'eepen its engagement with oil and gas rich countries to diversify its sources of fuel. Regardless, it can be seen that India's foreign policy in the 21st century will depend very much on its engagement with the US and China and its ability to secure key energy sources. Perhaps the greatest feature of the manner in which India's foreign policy has evolved in the 21st century is a clear indication of sensible decision-making over idealism thinking. As long as India continues to formulate a pragmatic foreign policy, it is likely to attain its global power status and make its mark on the 21st century.

INDIA'S CHALLENGE IN RELATIONS WITH CHINA-ENLARGEMENT WITH VIGILANCE

China's policies towards India changed significantly after India's nuclear weapons tests in 1998. China after its initial hysterical reactions on India's nuclear weaponisation settled down to accept the new strategic reality on its Southern frontiers.

China's new approaches towards India manifested itself in the following ways:

- China ensuring peace and tranquility on the Sino-Indian frontiers.
- China-India economic cooperation and two way trade registering a phenomenal growth which is likely to tough US $10 billion.
- Increased China-India military-to-military contacts.

All of the above augurs well for Sino-Indian relations, but at the same time Indian cannot ignore the following Chinese moves:

- China's slow movement on the boundary dispute dialogue.
- China's continued military build-up of Pakistan.
- China's strategic military cooperation in South Asia with Pakistan and Bangladesh, both adversarial with India.
- China's development of naval infrastructure on India's flanks-Gwadur (Pakistan) and Chittagong (Bangladesh).

China therefore prevents a significant foreign policy challenge to India in 2005. India's foreign policy planners need to aim at:

- Enlargement of Sino-Indian relations.
- Attempt dilution of Sino-Pakistan strategic nexus by imaginative diplomatic maneuvers.
- Emphasising the strategic realties on China of the choices of cooperating with a rising major power like India as opposed to building up a regional spoiler state in the form of a pygmy state like Pakistan.

Concurrent with India's attempts to enlarge and enhance its relationship with China, India needs its utmost to exercise vigilance and detailed scrutiny of China's strategic moves in South Asia, till such time China shows definite signals of change of priorities in its South Asian policies.

India and the European Community and the Potential for Multi-polarity: The European Community with specific reference to France and Germany offers the potential for working towards a more multi-polar world. The European Community with the rising value of the "Euro" and its attraction as an alternative to the US dollar in terms of global nesting of financial reserves and trading leads to the prospects of the emergence of an alternative "Euro Trading Area" to the Dollar.

The rising economic strength of the Euro coupled with the political independence of countries like France and Germany offers an attractive foreign policy challenge to India. India also enjoys the luxury of being a lucrative market for European defence equipment sales.

A selective use of this option by India could help Indian foreign policy planners to elicit favourable political responses for India's national security and economic interests.

EAST ASIA AND SOUTH PACIFIC CHALLENGES

The challenge here is that the major countries located in this region i.e. Japan, South Korea and Australia are strong United States allies linked to USA with substantive defence ties. Hence their attitudes towards India will be determined by existing USA attitudes towards India. However of late it seems that Japan while attaching value to the Japan-US security linkages is embarking on a more independent political course. Under the Vajpayee Govt. high-level exchanges have taken place from both sides. India and Japan have also agreed to work together for demanding a UN Security Council Permanent Membership with full veto powers.

Japan has revived interest in significant investments in India's infrastructure and enough convergences exist in the strategic area also. India's foreign policy challenge in 2005 should be to vigorously pursue Japan towards a strategic partnership with India. South Asia Foreign Policies Should Ignore Pakistan and Dwell on the Rest of the SAARC Countries: In the last five years, India's foreign policies in South Asia, under American prodding or pressure has led to the following:

- Legitimising Pakistan's military dictatorship by inviting Musharraf for the Agra summit.
- Equating Pakistan with India by engaging in unconditional talks with a terrorist and proxy war state and an implacable foe of India.
- Seeking peace with a country whose very existence which has been framed by the Pakistan Army and its Generals as a "Warrior State" not amenable to peace in South Asia.
- Misreading Pakistani masses yearning for peace with India as the political aspiration of the Pakistani military dictatorship.

India should long ago have dispensed with its Pakistan-centric South Asian foreign policies. It is high time that India's foreign policy planners ignore Pakistan totally from their strategic calculus for South Asia. India should concentrate in a focused manner to improve and enhance its relationships with Nepal, Bhutan, Bangladesh, Sri Lanka and the Maldives. The political stability of these countries is more critical for a South Asian stable security environment than pandering to an inflated egoist state like the militarized Pakistan.

India if it has to exercise political magnanimity in South Asia, it should be towards these countries and not Pakistan as American interlocutors suggest. Pakistan even under a combination of a rabid Mullah-cum-Pakistan Army dictatorship cannot pose more military threats to India than it has done so far. Pakistan should be left in the American lap, a situation relished by both. Let USA take care of Pakistan's stability and India should concentrate on the rest of South Asia.

FUNDAMENTALS OF INDIA'S FOREIGN POLICY AND THE NUCLEAR OPTION

India's foreign policy chews over the spirit of the Freedom Movement and has been greatly shaped by Nehru as is illustrated by the fact that he not only was India's first prime minister but also managed India's foreign affairs. The pillars of India's foreign policy are peaceful coexistence, non- alignment and conflict resolution through negotiation, mediation and conciliation. The problem was that the emerging post-war bipolar world order had little if no respect for these ideals.

The Cold War did not remain cold because the United States and the Soviet Union believed in peaceful coexistence but rather in nuclear deterrence. For nations non- aligned with either of the two world powers this meant that they could not enjoy the benefit of being under a "nuclear umbrella". Despite these circumstances Nehru and his closest advisor, Defence Minister V.K. Krishna Menon, opposed a nuclear weapon program. Nehru was however in favour of developing a civilian nuclear program because he believed that nuclear technology would provide India with the "the ability to leapfrog many technologies" and thus accelerate economic development. India's civilian nuclear program will be discussed under 1.3. A civilian nuclear program can also be utilized for military purposes and Nehru was well aware of that. Thus, while rejecting a nuclear weapon program he nevertheless did not foreclose the "option" strategy.

NUCLEAR PROLIFERATION POLICIES DURING THE COLD WAR

In the South Asian context, a conflictual bipolar security complex, India and Pakistan's transformational process of emerging as opaque nuclear powers was an example of different motivations, aspirations and ambitions for obtaining nuclear status. While the dominance of *realpolitik* trends over states' nuclear decision-making process is not an entirely surprising phenomena, the evolution of India's approach to the nuclear option is interesting from philosophical and strategic viewpoints. The genesis of the Indian nuclear policy from a categorical opposition to nuclear weapons in the Nehru era to Pokhran I, India's first so-called Peaceful Nuclear Explosion (PNE) in 1974, signified a discontinuity in New Delhi's post-1947 strategic thinking. What caused this discontinuity? What factor(s) led the country of Mohandas Gandhi, who once labelled nuclear weapons as 'diabolic', to obtaining potential nuclear power status under Indira Gandhi? Do the same factors suffice in explaining Pakistan's motives for developing its own nuclear capabilities in the mid-1980s? While some political scientists emphasised national security considerations in locating the roots of India and Pakistan proliferation policy, others have used an alternative theoretical approach with a greater level of structural balance between domestic, military security and symbolic motives. The latter multi-causal approach, summarised by Scott D. Sagan, is particularly useful in providing an inclusive analysis of nuclear proliferation causes. In this context and through the application of Sagan's explanatory models, the essay attempts to analyse the layers in India and Pakistan's 'nuclear thinking' leading to the development of military nuclear technology. The alternative multi-causal explanation constitutes a practically efficient theoretical framework for the comprehensive understanding of states' hybrid logic for nuclear proliferation.

Opposing the neorealist mono-causal security-oriented analysis (i.e. "the security model"), Sagan's approach considers the domestic and norms aspects as effective factors in triggering military nuclear proliferation, thus offering two additional explanations: "the domestic politics model" and "the norms model." According to

Sagan, security model states (either weak or strong) perceive nuclear weapons as an enormously powerful means of deterrence to secure their national security in an anarchic international system, if their regional or trans-regional rival(s) acquire nuclear capability. Strong resourceful states develop their own bomb, while weak states, incapable of proliferation, are obliged to join a balancing alliance with a nuclear power to maintain their security and sovereignty with the promise of nuclear retaliation. In contrast, the domestic politics model reflects the influence of three main domestic actors on governments' nuclear proliferation policies: first, states' nuclear energy establishments (consisting of scientific institutions and civil companies); second, the military elites (especially in the Air Force branch) as domestic bureaucratic actors; and third, politicians who tend to profit from the nuclear weapons discourse for political parties or individual standing regarding pro-proliferation public opinion. Therefore, these pro-proliferation actors gain additional influence if nuclear weapons are a positive symbol in states' domestic debates – thus the states proliferate in accordance with the influence of one or more of the aforementioned actors. Finally, in the norms model, states' nuclear policies are pro-proliferation due to 'nuclear symbolism' and the 'nuclear myth': states observe military organisation and advanced weaponry as essential elements in their image as modern and sovereign states. The 'nuclear myth', or symbolic implications of nuclear proliferation (e.g. technological advancement, military might, projection of grandeur, etc), are perceived as a means of forming states' modern identity and enhancing their international prestige. While there seems to be an analytical overlap and theoretical interference between the domestic and symbolic models, Sagan's three models offer an efficient toolbox for examining the deciding factors in India and Pakistan's nuclear policies.

The security-model analysis of Indian nuclear policy prior to Pokhran I can be conducted by analysing India's threat perception at the regional and trans-regional levels. The trans-regional level analysis confirms the gravity of Sino-centrism in India's trans-regional threat perception sphere, and the validity of Sagan's security-model explanation. The dynamics of post-1962 Sino-Indian bilateral relations is the fundamental factor in India's horizontal proliferation policy in the security model. While the Sino-Indian protracted conflict began in 1953 over territorial claims, the 1962 Sino-Indian war and its disastrous consequences for the non-aligned India moved the Chinese threat factor from the periphery of New Delhi's threat perception circle to its centre, triggering incremental yet significant changes in Indian defence policy and military strategy. The subsequent Indian military reorientation towards re-equipment and operational reinforcement (e.g. the creation of ten mountain divisions designed for warfare in the Himalayas and increasing the Army's manpower ceiling to 825,000) confirms the demise of Nehru's *moralpolitik*-type policies regarding China. However, the fundamental shift in India's nuclear weapons position occurred when Beijing shocked New Delhi with the detonation of its first nuclear device in October 1964. New Delhi's subsequent reaction to China's nuclear capability demonstrated a paradigm shift in India's previously Nehruvian anti-proliferation policy towards what then Prime Minister Lal Bahadur Shastri reluctantly phrased as India considering "nuclear explosion for peaceful purposes". Compatible with the security-model's two policy scenarios, India's inability to develop its own nuclear weapons forced New Delhi to secure nuclear deterrence by joining a balancing alliance with a nuclear power. Accordingly, when India's request to the United States, the Soviet Union and the United Kingdom for nuclear guarantee was refused, India's only option for deterring a nuclear China and maintaining its national security was to obtain horizontal proliferation on its own, leading to the 1974 PNE.

Similarly, the regional-level analysis indicates the significance of nuclear weapons in India's quest for regional hegemony and security in the South Asian region, although against the much less significant threat of Pakistan. A quick glance at pro-Indian political scientists' analysis of the motivation of India's quest for regional security through nuclear weapons reveals New Delhi's mindset regarding Pakistani conventional threat as well as India's strategic policy manoeuvre to achieve several objectives at once. In the bipolar South Asian security complex, Pakistan was (and is) India's major regional security and strategic concern. In spite of its conventional inferiority to India, Pakistan attacked its greater and more militarily powerful neighbour in 1948, 1965 and 1971. While India's decisive military victory in the 1971 war, and the subsequent disintegration of Pakistan through the independence of Bangladesh, considerably weakened Pakistan, it managed to retain most of its military infrastructures. The series of Indo-Pakistani military conflicts convinced Indian strategists that Pakistan could use the period of Indian domestic political instability to launch other military attacks on India. In the light of alarming Sino-Pakistani cordial relations, and the presumption of Pakistani will to attack India, India's nuclear proliferation became instrumental in maintaining Indian regional security as well as establishing Indian regional hegemony through deterring Pakistan from future attacks. As Saira Khan formulates, the most efficient war-avoidance strategy for India in such conflictual regional settings was 'deterrence by possession of nuclear weapons.'

Similar to the Indian behavioural pattern for proliferation, but in contrast to India's multi-layered threat perception, the application of the security-model framework on Pakistan's nuclear policy produces a mono-causal explanation: Pakistan's nuclear proliferation was a linear reactionary policy to India's 1974 nuclear detonation. In addition to Indo-Pakistani territorial, ideological and ethnic elements of conflict that have formed the essentials of the South Asian security complex since 1947, the 1971 war and dismemberment of Pakistan reinforced Indo-centrism in Pakistan's threat perception. The war crippled Pakistan's economy and displayed the perceived unreliability of Pakistan's allies (i.e. the United States and China) in the time of crisis. Realising its conventional military inferiority to India, in 1972 President Zulfiquar Ali Bhutto initiated a nuclear policy in pursuit of nuclear weapons. Islamabad's nuclear program, however, gained a critical boost by India's 1974 PNE. Closely resembling the pattern of India's reaction to the 1964 Chinese nuclear test, Pakistan's nuclear policy was decisively directed towards inevitable nuclear proliferation after India's 1974 PNE. Against India's combined conventional military superiority and nuclear weapons capability, Pakistan had to obtain its own nuclear weapons as soon as possible to provide deterrence against the gravest threat to its national security. In this context, with Islamabad's failure to obtain security guarantees from the nuclear powers against a nuclear India, Pakistan had no other option other than to embark on its own nuclear proliferation program.

Applying the domestic-model of analysis on the Indian case clearly exhibits the decisive influence of two of the three domestic actors outlined by the model on India's nuclear decision for horizontal proliferation: nuclear energy establishments (consisting of pro-proliferation scientists and defence laboratories) and politicians eager to enhance their respective parties or/and individual standing in public opinion. Due to the pattern of the civil-military relationship in India where the former utterly dominates the latter, military elites as bureaucratic domestic actors had practically no influence over New Delhi's process of nuclear decision-making.

After the Chinese 1964 nuclear test, Homi Bhabba, the head of India's Atomic Energy Commission (AEC), tenaciously lobbied for the allocation of required resources for developing nuclear weapons. Eventually, the AEC leadership's lobbying for proliferation along with pro-nuclear Congress party pressure on the government forced the reluctant Shastri to order the initiation of a classified project to develop technical ability to design and detonate a PNE within a certain timeframe. In spite of Bhabba's successor, Vikram Sarabhai's fierce opposition to any form of nuclear proliferation, the AEC developed an alliance with defence laboratories for lobbying the new Prime Minister Indira Gandhi.

In a meaningful coincidence, the dynamics of Indian domestic politics in the early 1970s were defined in terms of economic recession, large-scale riots in various regions and the internal conflict in the ruling Congress party, thus an all-time low domestic support for Gandhi's government. In such dire circumstances, with the Prime Minister acknowledging that a theatrical nuclear explosion could have been a decisive 'political ace' for increasing her standing in public opinion, Gandhi's approval of 1974 PNE is hardly surprising.

In a later interview, in spite of her initial denial, Gandhi admitted that the PNE "would have been useful for election". As the result, immediately after the detonation, public support for

Gandhi's government and the ruling Congress party increased by one-third, both being "restored to the nation's confidence." Considering the pre-PNE Indian domestic politics dynamics, the influence of AEC, the Prime Minister and the ruling party on nuclear proliferation is evident.

Domestic-model Framework

In contrast, the application of the domestic-model framework on the Pakistani case constitutes the presence of non-political domestic dynamics and a higher level of military influence on the process of Pakistan's pursuit of nuclear weapons. As mentioned earlier, a year after the 1971 war and two years before Pokhran I, Pakistan's former leader Bhutto instructed the country's top scientists to concentrate on the development of nuclear weapons.

Yet, such policies could not be pursued without the involvement of the military institution in the process. Decades of military rule has promoted the Pakistani military as the strongest bureaucratic institution in the country, setting the pattern of the country's civil-military relationship in favour of military control. However, in spite of the military's vast influence in Pakistan's polity, nuclear decisions were made within a coordinated policy framework consisting of Prime Minister Bhutto, the chiefs of the armed forces, the Foreign Minister and the chief of joint services headquarters.

The pro-bomb direction of Pakistani organic nuclear decision-making machinery was maintained even after the fall of Bhutto in 1977. The policy momentum and continuity in the country's pursuit for nuclear weapons in the post-Bhutto era confirms the absence of a domestic politics perspective in favour of the strong presence of a national security perspective: all Pakistani political leaders with different attitudes and policy perspectives maintained the essentials of Bhutto's nuclear policy. As for the nuclear establishment agency's influence, however, a division in the scholarly literature is detectable: while Kapur introduces I. H. Usmani, chairman of Pakistan Atomic Energy Commission (PAEC) as the most important figure in Pakistan's nuclear decision-making during 1970s, Khan maintains that the scientific institutions' influence was largely barred by the institutionalised military, limiting their range of influence to the lobbying of politicians and military elites in favour of proliferation. Yet, in spite of Kapur's exaggerated emphasis on Usmani's influence, the dominance of the security discourse over Pakistan's nuclear policy process is to such a degree that the domestic model's dynamics echoes the trends of the security model.

Finally, analysis of India's Cold War period nuclear proliferation policy signifies the link between India's quest for obtaining international prestige as a mean of gaining 'great power' status and its pursuit of the absolute weapon. From India's perspective, a direct link between nuclear proliferation and international prestige existed: countries in possession of nuclear weapons enhanced their standing in the international system's power pyramid. Nuclear states, developed or underdeveloped, were (and continue to do so) taken seriously by other members of the international community because of the practical implications of possessing the ultimate weapon.

India's perspective regarding nuclear symbolism was formed by observing the impact of China's 1964 nuclear explosion on Beijing's power status and international recognition of Chinese power which followed. In addition, China obtained its seat in the United Nations which had previously been denied. The United States' recognition of China's power demonstrated to India the symbolic importance of nuclear weapons in establishing a state's prestige. Remembering the existence of rivalry between the two states, the Chinese model of enhancing prestige propelled India to embark on a quest for horizontal nuclear proliferation to enhance its prestige, not only in the international context, but in regard to its territorial quarrel with China.

In contrast to India, and in spite of the 'Islamic bomb' rhetoric, Pakistan's nuclear proliferation program did not focus on enhancing the country's international prestige nor did it perceive nuclear weapons as a means of promoting a sense of Islamic nationalism. Reviewing the views of Pakistani scholars, strategists and officials regarding the country's motivations for nuclear proliferation clarifies the symbolic-model inefficiency for explaining the rubric of Pakistani proliferation policy. In an interview with Khan, former Pakistani Foreign Minister Agha Shahi rejected the existence of any considerations of symbolic type in Pakistan's military nuclear program.

Similarly, the strategist Ross Masud, the Chairman and Director General of the Islamabad's Institute of Strategic Studies confirmed Shahi's view that the projection of Pakistani grandeur by nuclear weapons "has never been a factor in Pakistan's decision-makers' minds", contributing any enhancement in Pakistani prestige to an unintended "spillover effect". In this context, Pakistan's nuclear policy was fundamentally less concerned about the notion of prestige enhancement than national security. However, as mentioned by Masud, while the Pakistani horizontal nuclear proliferation could produce the prestige dimension, such an outcome could not be regarded as the cause of proliferation but as its secondary consequence.

In addition, the much referred notion of the 'Islamic bomb' was in fact more of a rhetorical strategy to attract financial support from wealthy Arab states than a symbol of the Muslim states' international prestige. Therefore, the application of a symbolic-model framework on Pakistan's proliferation policy does not demonstrate the symbolic motive as a primary factor in the country's nuclear weapons development.

After outlining the general theoretical frameworks and their policy implication, the essay discussed India and Pakistan's motivations for horizontal nuclear proliferation according to the security model, the domestic politics model and the symbolic model, respectively. Analysing India's motivations through the security-model framework introduces nuclear China as primary incentive for India's nuclear proliferation and India's thrive for regional hegemony in the South Asia through deterring Pakistan as the secondary motivation. In contrast, the same model shows that Pakistan's sole concern for deterring India as its primary motivation for nuclear proliferation. In the domestic level, while India's nuclear policy was heavily influenced by leaders' political motivations and nuclear energy establishments lobbying – Pakistan's proliferation policy, witnessing a high level of military influence, lacked a domestic politics perspective and was mostly concerned with security perspective. Finally, while the application of symbolic model on India's nuclear policy confirms the significance of nuclear symbolism in India's quest for international prestige through nuclear proliferation, it demonstrates prestige angle as secondary to security-centric Pakistani proliferation policy.

INDIA'S DRAFT NUCLEAR DOCTRINE

In April 1998, the Indian government had constituted a Task Force to recommend the establishment of a National Security Council (NSC). The Task Force submitted its report in June 1998 and, in November 1998, the government constituted a three-tier NSC with a full time National Security Advisor and a National Security Advisory Board (NSAB). Although the first task that was planned to be originally entrusted to the NSAB was to conduct a strategic defence review, because of post-Pokhran II compulsions, the NSAB was asked to first formulate India's nuclear doctrine. The NSAB submitted a draft nuclear doctrine paper to the government that was released to the public for wider debate on August 17, 1999. The key features of the proposed nuclear doctrine are reproduced below:

India shall pursue a doctrine of credible minimum deterrence. In this policy of 'retaliation only', the survivability of our arsenal is critical. This is a dynamic concept related to our strategic environment, technological imperatives and the needs of national security. The actual size, components, deployment and employment of nuclear forces will be decided in the light of these factors. India's peacetime posture aims at convincing any potential aggressor that:

- Any threat of use of nuclear weapons against India shall invoke measures to counter the threat; and
- Any nuclear attack on India and its forces shall result in punitive retaliation with nuclear weapons to inflict damage unacceptable to the aggressor.

The fundamental purpose of Indian nuclear weapons is to deter the use and threat of use of nuclear weapons by any state or entity against India and its forces. India will not be the first to initiate a nuclear strike but will respond with punitive retaliation should deterrence fail. India will not resort to the use or threat of use of nuclear weapons against states that do not possess nuclear weapons, or are not aligned with nuclear weapons powers.

The draft nuclear doctrine, while generally following the policy guidelines enunciated by the Prime Minister in Parliament, fleshed out his pronouncements and "provides a broad framework for the development, deployment and employment of India's nuclear forces." The draft paper proposes that India should establish a credible, minimum nuclear deterrent capability comprising sufficient, survivable and operationally ready nuclear forces based on the principle of no first use of nuclear weapons. It emphasises that the level of India's nuclear capability should be consistent with maximum credibility, survivability, effectiveness, safety and security. It provides for the establishment of effective intelligence and early warning systems. It recommends that India's nuclear forces be based on a triad of strategic bombers, land-based ballistic missiles and submarine launched ballistic missiles (SLBMs). Though a sea-based nuclear capability will take many decades to develop, the requirement of SLBMs is considered inescapable due to their relatively lower vulnerability. Nuclear forces that need to survive a first strike have no option but to ensure that at least 50 to 60 per cent of the arsenal is made comparatively invulnerable by being maintained as SLBMs. The draft paper proposes that India's nuclear strike capability be configured to inflict punitive retaliation the consequences of which would be unacceptable to a potential adversary who will therefore be deterred from doing the unthinkable. The doctrine highlights the cardinal supremacy of civilian control over India's nuclear weapons and proposes that the final authority for the release of nuclear weapons must vest with the Prime Minister or his designated successor(s).

The proposed doctrine also rejects the concept of nuclear warfighting and does not, hence, consider it necessary for India to match its nuclear warheads and delivery systems with those of its potential nuclear adversaries. A small number of survivable nuclear warheads and delivery systems that can inflict damage which would be unacceptable to the adversary are considered adequate for the purposes of deterrence. Although the paper has left some ambiguity by not clearly rejecting the need for tactical or battlefield nuclear weapons in India's context, the tenor of the paper and its emphasis on a retaliatory policy appear to rule out any thinking towards tactical nuclear weapons. However, the real distinguishing feature of India's nuclear doctrine is that it is "... anchored in India's continued commitment to global, verifiable and non-discriminating nuclear disarmament..." that has been described as India's national security objective. The use of nuclear weapons is considered "the gravest threat to humanity and to peace and stability in the international system." The doctrine paper clearly points out India's desire to see the world completely rid of nuclear weapons.

As expected, the draft doctrine initiated a major debate in the country about its nuclear policies. Amitabh Mattoo called it "an unapologetic realpolitik articulation of the principal raison d'être of India's nuclear weapons and the requirements needed to lend credibility to the country's deterrent posture." While agreeing with the thrust of India's nuclear policy, he wrote that India's primary quest appeared to be to acquire the strategic autonomy necessary for making independent decisions in an often unfriendly world and to pursue economic and political development without fear of external threats. R. Prasannan called the draft doctrine a wish list attached to the collective speeches of the Prime Minister and his Cabinet colleagues. Bharat Wariavwalla criticised the draft doctrine on the grounds that the definition of minimum deterrence would be very different vis a vis China and Pakistan and, hence, the term is much too loose to pass off as doctrine.

Many analysts and even foreign governments have sought to raise doubts about India's draft nuclear doctrine. It did not help matters that the doctrine was unveiled the week after the Indian Air Force had shot down a Pakistani Atlantique reconnaissance aircraft that had intruded into Indian territory. The US government rejected the Indian desire to develop a nuclear arsenal." The Indian tests also spurred fears of a new Middle East arms race. However, not all Western powers denounced India's attempts to establish a credible weaponised nuclear deterrent. France welcomed the release of India's draft nuclear doctrine as a "logical and indeed wanted step". The most surprising criticism of the draft doctrine is that it conjures up dark visions of a nuclear arms race in Southern Asia. If all nuclear weapons states were to follow a no first use policy, it would be logical to assume that there would gradually be a net reduction in the size of nuclear arsenals - an arms race in reverse! Jasjit Singh offers the following explanation:

The concerns about a potential arms race reflect a perception arising out of the prism of Cold War mind-sets where first strike (and even "launch on warning") was the order of the day. This necessitated large arsenals and potentially pre-emptive strikes with nuclear weapons. The result was the peak of 67,000 nuclear warheads. But China did not follow the same route and relied on minimum deterrence concept with a no first use commitment. There is no evidence that China's nuclear posture led to any arms race. Even in future, China's nuclear arsenal is likely to be dictated by the size of US/Russian arsenals and issues like ballistic missile defences etc. rather than the defensive doctrine of India.

The worst criticism of the draft doctrine has been that opting for a triad of nuclear forces is not indicative of a minimalist posture but of a maximalist one, particularly as sea-based nuclear weapons have been envisaged to form part of the nuclear force. This criticism fails to take into account the fact that the credibility of a nuclear deterrent that is limited to retaliatory strikes only hinges around the ability of the nuclear force to survive a first strike in sufficient numbers to inflict unacceptable punishment in retaliation. Since submarines offer the best survival potential, India has to rely on a small number of SLBMs for credible deterrence. Raja Menon has also criticised the proposed doctrine: "...There is a serious dysfunction between 'minimum deterrence' and a tri-Service arsenal. The two cannot go together, and is (sic) akin to yoking a horse and camel together." However, surprisingly, he finds no use for aircraft-delivered nuclear bombs and states that "to even consider the role of the army in nuclear deterrence, minimum at that, is truly distressing." His hypothesis is that an arsenal for minimum deterrence requires only second-strike weapons, which can only be based on SSBNs.

Some critics have averred that the nuclear threats have not been enunciated and that the draft document does not define the nuclear force levels that India considers "minimum". Others have protested that the costs of India's nuclear deterrent have not been spelt out. The critics of the draft document forget that doctrine defines only a set of beliefs and guidelines on which policy and strategy is based. In the Preamble of the draft paper it is clearly stated in Para 1.6 that "this document outlines the broad principles for the development, deployment and employment of India's nuclear forces." Details regarding the targeting philosophy, nuclear force structures and the finer nuances of command and control cannot be expected to appear in a paper on nuclear doctrine.

The exception in the draft doctrine that India's non-use of nuclear weapons policy against countries that are not nuclear weapons states does not apply if they are militarily aligned with nuclear weapons states, has also been criticised. This exception would include non-nuclear members of NATO and the military allies of the US such as Japan. Rajesh Rajagopalan explains the reasons behind such exceptions: Two reasons could be suggested for this exception, one practical and the other strategic. The practical reason is that the Negative Security Assurance (NSA) of various nuclear weapons states, around which this non-use policy is based, makes similar exceptions. In fact, the exceptions there are broader and the NSA does not apply to countries that have refused to sign the NPT or are suspected of nuclear weapons ambitions...

The strategic reason... (is that) a good number of non-nuclear countries still host the nuclear arms of nuclear weapons states and share in the command and control infrastructure of nuclear powers. Theoretically, a nuclear attack on India could be mounted by the nuclear forces hosted in third countries. Excluding these countries would mean that no retaliation could be mounted on the bases from where such attacks are launched...

Rajesh Rajagopalan points out that 'minimum deterrence' is mistakenly characterised as doctrine whereas it actually refers to the nuclear force structure. He states that the Indian doctrine is one of 'assured retaliation' and this is to be given effect by a minimalist nuclear force as "an assured retaliation posture is premised on the belief that no one will start a nuclear war if they are assured of a nuclear retaliation, even if it is a weak retaliation. In other words, for an Indian nuclear deterrent to work effectively against China or Pakistan, it is not necessary to threaten them with complete destruction: even retaliating with a few nuclear warheads will create unacceptable costs to both." While the interpretation is no doubt technically correct, it is also true that a policy of assured retaliation, combined with a small nuclear force built on the principle of sufficiency, could overall be characterised as minimum deterrence. However, it is a finely nuanced distinction that must be noted.

Pakistani government spokesmen and scholars have been particularly critical of India's no first use doctrine on the grounds that it is only a declaratory policy and can be easily changed when the need arises. They have failed to take note of the fact that a country's nuclear force structure, command and control system, alert status and its deployment posture are based on its nuclear doctrine. First use doctrines require hair trigger alerts, launch-on-warning and launch-through-attack strategies and elaborate surveillance, early warning and intelligence systems with nuclear warheads loaded on launchers and ready to fire. Nuclear armed aircraft would need to be ready on runway alert, if not constantly airborne as in the case of the erstwhile US Strategic Air Command. India cannot ever resort to any of these measures without Pakistan learning about them almost immediately. What the Pakistanis also forget, or deliberately ignore, is that India has offered to negotiate a mutual no first use treaty with Pakistan that would be binding and verifiable. India's track record of adherence to international treaties has been exemplary. Unfortunately, the same cannot be said of India's neighbours who have violated numerous treaties with impunity, including the NPT and the MTCR.

The charge that India's nuclear doctrine would initiate an arms race in the Southern Asian region is specious and unjustified. China's gradual moves towards a nuclear triad over a period of three and a half decades have not forced India to play "catch up". Even now India does not feel it necessary to match China's 400-plus nuclear warheads, or to follow China and develop multiple independently targetable re-entry vehicles (MIRVs). India has decided to base its deterrent on a small force of survivable nuclear warheads and delivery systems for a retaliatory strike that can inflict punitive damage on a handful of value targets.

There is no reason why Pakistan should feel compelled to match India's nuclear warheads and missiles, particularly as it has opted for a first strike doctrine and does not have to worry about the survival of its nuclear forces. With a first use doctrine, even for deterring conventional war Pakistan does not need to match India warhead for warhead and missile for missile. Kenneth Waltz has argued that the distinction between nuclear forces designed for war fighting, that need to be compared with one another, and those designed to deter the use of nuclear weapons, must be clearly understood. Forces designed for deterrence need not match the adversary's nuclear forces as long as they can do unacceptable damage to the adversary with unacceptable damage sensibly defined. Putting it most appropriately, he has said that "more is not better, if less is enough." Hence, those who are raising the bogey of a nuclear arms race in Southern Asia need to review their alarmist views.

It emerges quite clearly that most of the criticism of the proposed nuclear doctrine stems not from any genuine disagreement with India's no first use doctrine and its professed need to establish a credible minimum nuclear deterrent, but from the desire of many Western countries that India should "cap, reduce and eliminate" its nuclear capability and sign the NPT and the CTBT as a non-nuclear weapons state. Since India's nuclear tests and its declaration of the weaponisation of its nuclear deterrent were based on substantial national security interests, the cap, reduce, eliminate mantra is unlikely to now get anywhere.

8

Foreign Policy, Diplomacy and National Consensus

The foreign policy of a country is geared towards protection and promotion of vital national interests through negotiations and diplomacy. Outbreak of conflict or war is, therefore, called the vanishing point of diplomacy.

For negotiation and diplomacy to succeed there is need, among others, for a degree of consensus involving the government, the opposition and the civil society on the critical issues of foreign policy; a bipartisan foreign policy which has the approval of the parliament. Unless one is able to present a united front to the outside world on critical issues vitally affecting the nation despite political differences, which are natural in a democratic polity, one cannot be in a position to negotiate with strength. This has to be backed by a credible professional defence force, a strong economy and democratic good governance — to cite a few of the elements.

In Bangladesh we were looking forward to new era of democratic good governance, free from the confrontational politics of the past, including an effective parliament with active participation of the opposition based on lessons learnt from 1/11 and the failures of the democratic political process since independence. Unfortunately, we continue to be a divided and polarised nation along party lines, with hardly any consensus on vital issues of foreign and domestic policies. This has seriously affected our negotiating capacity with the foreign countries.

This growing divide has to be reversed without delay by achieving a modicum of consensus on vital national issues between the government and the opposition. I would, therefore, suggest that the prime minister and the leader of the opposition should meet and come to an understanding on all critical issues, including paving the way for return of the opposition to the parliament. This should be followed by a constructive foreign policy debate in the parliament with a view to achieving a bipartisan foreign policy for Bangladesh – something which has eluded us since independence. This will empower the government to negotiate with foreign countries.

However, our hope for achieving the consensus has received a serious setback with the widening public rift between the government and the opposition over the refusal of the leader of the opposition to participate in the anti-poverty rally and the prime minister's unexpectedly strong reaction. This has complicated the existing strained relationship between the government and the opposition, and with it the prospect of national unity and consensus on vital issues including issues of foreign policy. Notwithstanding this, we need to persist with our efforts to heal the rift for the sake of preserving and strengthening our democracy and independence.

Reverting to the issue of our foreign policy and diplomacy I will first touch on the burning issue of the maritime boundary with India and Myanmar. On this issue, I am sure that our policy makers have weighed carefully all the implications before deciding to take the dispute to the International Tribunal for a verdict. I am not an international lawyer, and as a diplomat I would prefer to give negotiations preference over a legalistic approach.

Even without getting into the merit or demerit of the decision to take the matter to the Arbitration Tribunal, I feel that we should have first lodged our claim with the UN on our maritime boundary. For us it is vital to file our claims, particularly to 200 nautical miles of Exclusive Economic Zone in accordance with the UN Convention on the Law of Sea (UNCLOS). We need not wait until July 27, 2011 to do so as India and Myanmar have already filed their claims. Our case involving delimitation of boundaries and energy exploration would be strengthened.

The dispute with India and Myanmar as to whether the principle of equity as claimed by Bangladesh or principle of equidistance as demanded by India and Myanmar should be followed for demarcation of the maritime boundary is something which will have to be settled after we have filed our claim with the UN. Otherwise, it would be like putting the cart before the horse. Moreover, arbitration could take anywhere between 4 to 5 years and the outcome cannot be guaranteed. Arbitration may uphold our claim fully or even partially; then comes the vexing question of enforcement of the decision. If India or Myanmar, or both, drag their feet on the implementation of the Tribunal's decision a more serious challenge to Bangladesh's diplomacy will be posed as international law has no enforcing authority.

We have a number of outstanding problems to be solved with both Indian and Myanmar, though the issues with India are longstanding and of critical nature. They include Tipaimukh, the maritime boundary, border incidents, transit, trade imbalance and a number of other issues. There is escalation of tension with Myanmar, with not only the dispute over the maritime boundary but also border demarcations, construction of barbed fence and the longstanding Rohingya problem. I believe that bilateral negotiations with a comprehensive and interrelated approach offer the best option for resolving the outstanding problems with both India and Myanmar — and the time to act is now.

Bangladesh diplomacy should be geared to take full advantage of the opportunity which will be opened to us during the forthcoming visit of Bangladesh Prime Minister Sheikh Hasina to India. One may expect that all crucial and thorny unresolved issues will be discussed at the highest political level between the two countries to find mutually acceptable solutions if there is sincere political will, which has been the vital missing element so far. There should be no dearth of political will to resolve the outstanding issues this time given the excellent personal rapport between Prime Minister Sheikh Hasina and the Indian leadership, including Prime Minister Manmohan Singh and Sonia Gandi. The dispute over maritime boundary should be taken up for resolution along with all other bilateral issues. An outcome based on mutuality of interests and a win-win situation for both parties would pave the way for opening a new chapter of friendly relationship between the two countries.

If there is meaningful breakthrough with Delhi, it will have a positive impact on our bilateral relations with Myanmar. I would suggest that this should be followed by visit of Prime Minister Sheikh Hasina to China and Myanmar.

Negotiation and diplomacy would seem to be in our best national interest; let us give this a chance to succeed, provided we are united and clear in what we want to achieve through negotiation and diplomacy. "Let us never negotiate out of fear. But let us never fear to negotiate." In the ultimate analysis history and experience have demonstrated that there is no durable military solution to any conflict, be it for the big or a relatively smaller country.

PUBLIC DIPLOMACY

In international relations, public diplomacy or people's diplomacy, broadly speaking, is the communication with foreign publics to establish a dialogue designed to inform and influence. There is no one definition of Public Diplomacy, and may be easier described than easily defined as definitions have changed and continue to change over time. It is practiced through a variety of instruments and methods ranging from personal contact and media interviews to the Internet and educational exchanges.

Background and Definitions

Nicholas J. Cull of the USC Center on Public Diplomacy, wrote in his essay "'Public Diplomacy' Before Gullion: The Evolution of a Phrase:

"The earliest use of the phrase "public diplomacy" to surface is actually not American at all but in a leader piece from The Times in January 1856. It is used merely as a synonym for civility in a piece criticizing the posturing of President Franklin Pierce. The modern meaning of the term "public diplomacy" was coined in 1965 by Edmund Gullion, dean of the Fletcher School of Law and Diplomacy at Tufts University and a distinguished retired foreign service officer, when he established an Edward R. Murrow Center of Public Diplomacy

The brochure for the new center provided a description of the concept: "Public diplomacy... deals with the influence of public attitudes on the formation and execution of foreign policies. It encompasses dimensions of international relations beyond traditional diplomacy; the cultivation by governments of public opinion in other countries; the interaction of private groups and interests in one country with another; the reporting of foreign affairs and its impact on policy; communication between those whose job is communication, as diplomats and foreign correspondents; and the process of intercultural communications."

Over time, the concept and definition has evolved by various practitioners. Other definitions and descriptions include:

The most important roles public diplomacy will have to play for the United States in the current international environment will be less grand-strategic and more operational than during the Cold War. Support of national policy in military contingencies is one such role, and probably the most important. - Carnes Lord (former Deputy Director USIA), Professor of Statecraft and Civilization, October 1998

Public diplomacy - effectively communicating with publics around the globe - to understand, value and even emulate America's vision and ideas; historically one of America's most effective weapons of outreach, persuasion and policy. - Jill A. Schuker (former Senior Director for Public Affairs at the National Security Council) July 2004

Public diplomacy may be defined, simply, as the conduct of international relations by governments through public communications media and through dealings with a wide range of nongovernmental entities (political parties, corporations, trade associations, labour unions, educational institutions, religious organizations, ethnic groups, and so on including influential individuals) for the purpose of influencing the politics and actions of other governments. - Alan K. Henrikson, Professor of Diplomatic History, April 2005.

Public diplomacy that traditionally represents actions of governments to influence overseas publics within the foreign policy process has expanded today - by accident and design - beyond the realm of governments to include the media, multinational corporations, NGO's and faith-based organizations as active participants in the field. Crocker Snow Jr., Acting Director Edward R. Murrow Center, May 2005.

"PUBLIC DIPLOMACY refers to government-sponsored programs intended to inform or influence public opinion in other countries; its chief instruments are publications, motion pictures, cultural exchanges, radio and television." (U.S. Department of State, Dictionary of International Relations Terms, 1987, p. 85)

The United States Information Agency (USIA), which was the main government agency in charge of Public Diplomacy until it merged with the Department of State in 1999, described it as: Public diplomacy seeks to promote the national interest and the national security of the United States through understanding, informing, and influencing foreign publics and broadening dialogue between American citizens and institutions and their counterparts abroad.

For The Planning Group for Integration of USIA into the Dept. of State (June 20, 1997), public diplomacy is defined as follows: "Public Diplomacy seeks to promote the national interest of the United States through understanding, informing and influencing foreign audiences."

According to Hans N. Tuch, author of Communicating With the World (St. Martin's Press, NY, 1990), public diplomacy is defined as: "Official government efforts to shape the communications environment overseas in which American foreign policy is played out, in order to reduce the degree to which misperceptions and misunderstandings complicate relations between the U.S. and other nations."

Standard diplomacy might be described as the ways in which government leaders communicate with each other at the highest levels, the elite diplomacy we are all familiar with. Public diplomacy, by contrast focuses on the ways in which a country (or multi-lateral organization such as the United Nations) communicates with citizens in other societies. A country may be acting deliberately or inadvertently, and through both official and private individuals and institutions. Effective public diplomacy starts from the premise that dialogue, rather than a sales pitch, is often central to achieving the goals of foreign policy: public diplomacy must be seen as a two-way street. Furthermore, public diplomacy activities often present many differing views as represented by private American individuals and organizations in addition to official U.S. Government views. Traditional diplomacy actively engages one government with another government. In traditional diplomacy, U.S. Embassy officials represent the U.S. Government in a host country primarily by maintaining relations and conducting official USG business with the officials of the host government whereas public diplomacy primarily engages many diverse non-government elements of a society.

Film, television, music, sports, video games and other social/cultural activities are seen by public diplomacy advocates as enormously important avenues for otherwise diverse citizens to understand each other and integral to the international cultural understanding, which they state is a key goal of modern public diplomacy strategy. It involves not only shaping the message(s) that a country wishes to present abroad, but also analyzing and understanding the ways that the message is interpreted by diverse societies and developing the tools of listening and conversation as well as the tools of persuasion.

One of the most successful initiatives which embodies the principles of effective public diplomacy is the creation by international treaty in the 1950s of the European Coal and Steel Community which later became the European Union. Its original purpose after World War II was to tie the economies of Europe together so much that war would be impossible. Supporters of European integration see it as having achieved both this goal and the extra benefit of catalysing greater international understanding as European countries did more business together and the ties among member states' citizens increased. Opponents of European integration are leery of a loss of national sovereignty and greater centralization of power.

Public diplomacy has been an essential element of American foreign policy for decades. It was an important tool in influencing public opinion during the Cold War with the former Soviet Union.

Since the attacks of September 11, 2001, the term has come back into vogue as the United States government works to improve their reputation abroad, particularly in the Middle East and among those in the Islamic world. Numerous panels, including those sponsored by the Council on Foreign Relations, have evaluated American efforts in public diplomacy since 9/11 and have written reports recommending that the United States take various actions to improve the effectiveness of their public diplomacy.

The United States Advisory Commission on Public Diplomacy was established in the late 1940s to evaluate American public diplomacy effort. The Commission is a seven member bipartisan board whose members are nominated by the President and confirmed by the United States Senate. William Hybl is the current chair, and other members include former Ambassadors Lyndon Olson and Penne Percy Korth Peacock, as well as Jay Snyder, John E. Osborn and Lezlee Westine. In 2008, the Commission issued a report entitled "Getting the People Part RIght" that was largely critical of the State Department's personnel policies and practices in hiring, training and promoting public affairs and public diplomacy officers. The report attracted significant attention, and was the subject of a Senate hearing.

This traditional concept is expanded on with the idea of adopting what is called "population-centric foreign affairs" within which foreign populations assume a central component of foreign policy. Since people, not just states, are of global importance in a world where technology and migration increasingly face everyone, an entire new door of policy is opened.

Methods

There are many methods and instruments that are used in Public Diplomacy. Nicholas Cull divides the practice into five elements: listening, advocacy, cultural diplomacy, exchange diplomacy and international broadcasting (IB).

Methods such as personal contact, broadcasters such as the Voice of America, Radio Free Europe and Radio Liberty exchange programs such as Fulbright and the International Visitor Leadership program, American arts and performances in foreign countries, and the use of the Internet are all instruments used for practicing Public Diplomacy depending on the audience to be communicated with and the message to be conveyed.

NATIONAL POLICY

The National Policy was a Canadian economic program introduced by John A. Macdonald's Conservative Party in 1876 and put into action in 1879. It called for high tariffs on imported manufactured items to protect the manufacturing industry. Macdonald campaigned on the policy in the 1878 election, and defeated the Liberal Party, which supported free trade.

Usage

The term *National Policy* originally referred to a proposed raise in tariffs by the Macdonald-led Conservatives ("Tories") during the 1878 election campaign. Over time the term became a associated with the entire Tory platform for developing the economy, especially increased immigration to Western Canada, and the development of the Canadian Pacific Railway's transcontinental line.

Manufacturers

Macdonald hoped that by creating a strong manufacturing base in Canada, the nation would become more secure and less reliant on the United States. He was also closely linked to the Montreal and Toronto business interests that would benefit from such a policy, and they played an important role in keeping the Tories in office until 1896. Despite a brief experiment with free trade in the Canadian-American Reciprocity Treaty before Confederation, the Americans were intent on pursuing a strongly protectionist policy, with tariffs higher than Canada imposed under the National Policy.

With such high American tariffs, Canadian firms could not compete in the United States, but American firms could enter Canada. Canadian producers were particularly hurt by US producers dumping surplus goods in Canada, so as not to lower prices in the United States. tariffs were put on goods coming into Canada. These tariffs would make American goods more expensive.

The policy was introduced in the budget on March 14, 1879, and it created high tariffs on the import of most manufacturing goods. At the same time, the tariffs on raw materials were lowered also to help manufacturers. The tariff was not as high as that in the United States, however. The Canadian government was dependent upon revenue from customs - an income tax had not yet been introduced, largely because it was feared that would hurt immigration at a time when Canada was having trouble attracting immigrants. Too high a tariff would have cut off almost all imports, thus depriving the government of revenue.

The policy quickly became one of the most central aspects of Canadian politics, and it played an important role in keeping the Tories in power until 1896, when Wilfrid Laurier and the Liberals campaigned on a promise to keep the National Policy in place. While many Liberals still supported free trade, the National Policy was too popular in Ontario and Quebec to end. When the Liberals campaigned on free trade in the 1911 election, they lost the election.

Unpopular in West

While the policy was popular in central Canada, it was extremely unpopular in western Canada. This opposition to the National Policy played an important role in the rise of the Progressive Party of Canada in the 1920s. Its platform was entitled the "New National Policy", and it advocated free trade.

Dismantled by Liberals

The National Policy was slowly dismantled under the many years of Liberal rule under William Lyon Mackenzie King and Louis St. Laurent. At the same time, the United States was lowering its tariffs. Economic integration surged during World War II, and in 1965 the automobile industry in the two nations became fully integrated. Complete free trade was not achieved until 1988 with the Canadian-American Free Trade Agreement brought in by Brian Mulroney's Progressive Conservative government.

Assessment

The assessment of the National Policy is mixed. In general, economists argue that it increased prices and lowered Canada's efficiency and ability to compete in the world. By not becoming merged into the larger, more efficient American economy, Canada built too many monopolistic firms, and too many small inefficient factories with high prices for consumers. The overall impact was not large because the policy applied only to the manufacturing sector, which played a relatively small role, compared to agriculture, fishing, transportation, mining, lumbering and services, which were not affected by the National Policy. Historians tend to see the policy in a more positive light, viewing it as a necessary expense to create a unified nation independent of the United States. In the years right after the policy was introduced, Canada experienced the same type of economic boom that many other nations experienced, as well as the construction of a manufacturing base and the development of the nation, which is generally what the Tories and economic nationalists use to justify the policy. However, Canada also suffered a net population ouflow, as more people emigrated out of Canada (usually for the United States), than arrived as immigrants.

Eden and Molot (1993) argue that there have been three national policies in Canada: the "National Policy" of defensive expansionism, 1867–1940; compensatory liberalism, 1941–81; and market liberalism, starting in 1982. The defensive expansion phase relied on the tariff, railway construction, and land settlement to build the country. The second national policy combined a commitment to the GATT system, Keynesian macroeconomic policies, and the construction of a domestic social welfare net. Current national policy relies on Canada-US free trade and NAFTA free trade, market-based policies, and fiscal restraint. They argue for a fourth policy called "strategic integration." It would consist of free trade, both external and internal; the building of a national telecommunications infrastructure based on the development and diffusion of information technologies; and human capital development.

GLOBAL POWER BALANCE 2020: PERSPECTIVES

The global power balance has been in a churning state ever since the turn of the millennium. The disintegration of the Soviet

Union enabled the United States global strategic predominance to be unrivalled and unquestioned. Concerned by United States unilateralism. , Russia and China as the two nations most strategically affected set in motion two significant initiatives to offset the US predominance.

Russia under the dynamic leadership of President Putin set Russia on a course of strategic and military resurgence. This was facilitated by rising Russian oil revenues. China with significant economic resources at its disposal embarked on a strategic build-up of its strategic assets and military upgradation. The United States decade-old strategic global predominance was now to be under challenge by Russia and China. This strategic challenge by these two nations became further accentuated as a result of United States getting inextricably tied down militarily in Afghanistan and Iraq.

The current global economic turbulence has prompted many strategic analysts to re-examine the short-term global balance of power perspectives with 2020 taken as a more identifiable time frame. Some would like to believe that the current economic melt-down could affect the global power balance and the inter-se strategic equations between USA, Russia and China. They would like to suggest that the United States as the strongest economy in the world could weather the storms, but Russia and China, and especially Russia's resurgence and its strategic challenge to the United States could be diluted.

This Author would like to maintain that the economic meltdown today is globalised in its dimensions and would therefore affect USA, Russia and China without any exception. However, Russia and China's strategic programs directed at altering the global power balance would not be diluted. This besides other reasons, is valid, because Russia and China are not involved in any costly strategic distractions like the United States in Iraq and Afghanistan, requiring a significant outlay of financial resources.

Otherwise too, it is conceded by many economists that economies of the world surface more strongly after economic depressions. Strategically, the historical evidence cannot be ignored that the Second World War took place within a decade of the Great Depression in which the United States was the most vitally affected.

Therefore, in strategic analysis such economic depressions may act as "speed breakers" but definitely do not bring global strategic power rivalries to a "dead end".

With the above as an introductory background, this Paper attempts to analyse "Global Power Balance 2020: Perspectives" under the following heads:

- Global Power Balance 2020 Will be Bi-polar in Nature
- Multi-polarity is a Political and Strategic Myth
- United States Would Have Strategic Edge Over Russia in a Bi-polar World
- A New Cold War is Inevitable.

Global Power Balance 2020 Will be Bi-polar in Nature

Assertions of this Author in this direction stand examined in fair detail in earlier SAAG Papers and particularly those dealing with Russia's resurgence. This Author firmly believes that the global power balance in 2020 would be bi-polar in nature with the United States and Russia as the two poles.

Russia is being dismissively discussed in US and Western think-tanks and Russia's resurgence is de-emphasised and devaluated. This dismissive attitude is not born out of realistic strategic analysis but wishful thinking that Russia does not emerge as a strategic challenge to United States global predominance.

The moot question that needs to be considered is that who amongst Russia and China is more strategically potent to challenge United States global predominance?

Even on current analysis the following strategic realities suggest that Russia is the foremost candidate to challenge USA and not China (1) Russia's existing strategic nuclear weapons arsenal outnumbers the United States whereas China's nuclear arsenal at about 400 warheads is a remote comparison (2) Russia's existing power projection capabilities extend far beyond its immediate neighbourhood, in all dimensions – land, sea and air. China's power projection is limited to her periphery and limited to ground forces dimensions only (3) Russia is an "energy self-independent" state and this is an essential pre-requisite of national power. Japan and Germany lost the Second World War because they were not "energy self-reliant" (4) Russia has existing strategic partnerships with many countries across the globe. China has no "natural allies" to boost her strategic power (5) Russia's resurgence has been welcomed in many regions and more importantly in the Middle East. China is not viewed as a credible strategic challenger to the United States.

More importantly Russia has been a practitioner of global power politics in the bi-polar environment of the Cold War and successfully provided countervailing power to the United States for 45 years. Further, it needs to be noted that Russia was not defeated by the United States in the Cold War; it was Russia that defeated itself. Russia's current strategic and political resurgence is precisely aimed in this direction once again, namely, to reclaim her former superpower status. It has won recognition in Europe, Middle East, Central Asia and South East Asia too.

Reading between the lines one gets a sneaking feeling that the United States may prefer China as a manageable strategic rival rather than Russia. But the strategic realities indicate that the United States would in 2020 have to accept a bi-polar world with Russia as the second pole.

Multi-polarity is a Political and Strategic Myth

Multi-polarity as a desirable state in the global power balance was forcefully enunciated by China to begin with in the immediate period following the demise of the Soviet Union.

To begin with, in the early 1990s, China advocated a multi-polar world incorporating China, India, Iran and Syria with Pakistan added. Later inducements were to include France and Germany. This enunciation never took off though being repeated periodically.

So the initial Chinese model of multi-polarity comprised Asian nations with no strong strategic linkages with USA as the unipolar power. China then as the only nuclear weapons state in this grouping may have been led to believe that it would emerge as the natural leader of its proposed multi-polar grouping.

Russia today also talks of multi-polarity but one suspects that it is more for political reasons in favour of China than any strategic conviction. Russia would strategically prefer a bi-polar world at the global level and without frowning on multi-polarity at the regional level.

China, Japan and India even with the full development of their strategic strengths cannot hope to equal the strategic potential of being super-powers in the classical sense of definition of the term. They can sit on the global powers high table as associate global players, but not as "super powers". China, Japan and India therefore are incapable of emerging as multiple poles to bring about a multi-polar world. Only the United States and Russia qualify to be superpowers. Available indicators suggest that the United States and Russia would be the two super-powers in 2020 and no scope exists for any of the other global players intruding into that league.

THE ELUSIVE DOMESTIC FOREIGN POLICY CONSENSUS

The very existence of a credible foreign policy establishment presupposes a degree of agreement within the elite on the core objectives of external engagement and a grand strategy to achieve them. I would argue that there never was such a consensus in modern India on the ends and means of its foreign policy. The author would suggest that this is one of the principal reasons for the absence of a permanent establishment that can mediate between decision makers, experts and the public at large. To be sure, there is the widespread belief within India and those outside who study its external relations that there was once a golden age of 'Nehruvian consensus' on foreign policy. That assertion might say something about the contemporary political contestations but reveals little about India's foreign policy history. As a charismatic and domineering political figure, Jawaharlal Nehru did have his way on defining the foreign policy of India in the early years of the Republic. That does not in any way imply there was a national consensus. During 1959 62, Nehru found himself utterly isolated when matters turned difficult with China, large sections of his own party and public opinion turned hostile, and bureaucratic structures came under stress.

A dispassionate look at India's foreign policy record might suggest that there was no national consensus either before or after independence. Throughout the 20th century, the Indian political elite was at odds with itself on characterising the nature of external environment, setting a list of priorities, understanding the shifting dynamic among the great powers, defining a hierarchy of external threats, and identifying friends and enemies. The differences on how to address the grievances of the Muslims in the subcontinent and their relationship with the larger Islamic community have always been profound and continue to hobble India. Some writers have argued that the worldview of the Indian National Congress and the Muslim League were fundamentally divergent. Indian attitudes to the developments in the Middle East at the turn of the 20th century and the wisdom of the *Khilafat* movement.

The massive expansion of the Indian armed forces to serve the British in the two world wars generated profound divisions within the Indian national movement about the appropriateness of their use abroad. So did the creation of the Indian National Army by Subhas Chandra Bose and his alignment with Japanese fascism in the Second World War. There were a range of other issues that were controversial, including the broader question of India's attitude to great power relations.

These are just a few illustrative differences. The absence of a consensus within the national movement on these issues had a huge impact on the nature of the post-Partition territorial arrangements, the dynamics of war and peace in the subcontinent, and India's relationship with the Great Powers.

In the post-independence period, many of India's diplomatic initiatives and ideas that were later seen as representing the very essence of India's foreign policy did not come through a pre-existing national consensus. They were products of the existence of a strong leader like Nehru and his very definitive world view. In the 1950s the Indian communists, who later became a great champion of 'Nehruvian' consensus, rejected the principle of 'nonalignment' as 'immoral' neutrality between 'good' and 'evil'.

For them, Nehru was a 'running dog' of imperialists. It would take them three full decades before recognising the 'anti-imperialist' content of India's nonalignment. The conservatives in the Congress Party, many socialists, and the Hindu nationalists, on the other hand, saw nonalignment as part of Nehru's appeasement of international communism.

Nehru's decisions to take the Kashmir question to the United Nations Security Council, join the British Commonwealth, reticence on the Soviet intervention in Hungary, and the emphasis on nuclear arms control rather than decolonisation at the first summit of the non-aligned movement were among the many controversies that led to deep national divisions on foreign policy during the Nehru years. Nothing, however, reveals the sharpness of those divisions and exposes the current myth that Nehru's policy was more 'anti-imperialist' than the controversies over his policy towards China. The vigorous national contestations of Nehru's positions on the two core territorial issues of independent India – the Kashmir dispute with Pakistan and the boundary dispute with China – makes one wonder what the 'Nehruvian consensus' was all about. My objective here is not to go into the merits or demerits of Nehru's world view or his stewardship of India's foreign policy. It is to simply note the profound differences within India in the early years of its interaction with the world and its management of relations with its neighbours.

Nehru's successors too had to constantly innovate on the diplomatic front and risk domestic opposition; they did not have the luxury of a pre-existing national consensus on foreign policy to guide them at any of their many critical moments. Indira Gandhi's reluctance to criticise Moscow for snuffing out the Prague Spring in 1968 resulted in the resignation of a cabinet minister, Ashok Mehta. Her decision to sign a security treaty with the Soviet Union in 1971 was derided by many centrist scholars in India as a departure from a 'strict' interpretation of nonalignment.

The treaty was not the product of public discourse, scholarly input, and rigorous political scrutiny. It was a foreign policy coup, a brilliant one at that, presented to the nation as a *fait accompli* at a crucial moment in the effort to liberate East Pakistan. Until as late as the 1977 general elections, the Janata Party, which brought together the entire opposition to Indira Gandhi, was suspicious of the 'secret provisions' in the Indo-Soviet treaty and promised to restore what it called 'genuine nonalignment'.

Mrs Gandhi's decision to test a nuclear device in 1974, Foreign Minister Atal Bihari Vajpayee's outreach to Israel during 1977, his visit to China in 1978, Rajiv Gandhi's reversal of India's positions on the border dispute with China (1988), Inder Kumar Gujral's good neighbourly policy (1996-98), Prime Minister Vajpayee's nuclear tests in 1998, and Prime Minister Manmohan Singh's civil nuclear initiative with the United States in 2005 were all foreign policy issues that deeply divided the political classes in India. None of those decisions emerged out of debates within the foreign policy community or stayed within the boundaries of a presumed mainstream national discourse on foreign policy. In most of these cases, broad based support for these decisions emerged only over an extended period of time. As argued by K. Subrahmanyam, "Indian foreign policy was always a leadership function and more often than not did not command a consensus. Nonalignment as a strategy (to be distinguished from nonalignment as an ideology with which Nehru had hardly anything to do), development of close relations with the Union of Soviet Socialist Republics, nuclear tests, strategic weapons programme, economic liberalisation and globalization and the strategy of the balance of power were all initiatives of leaders – Nehru, Indira, Rajiv, Narashima Rao, Vajpayee and now Dr. Singh. Such initiatives, when they prove successful, become established national policies."

THE INTERNATIONAL RELATIONS COMMUNITY'S CONFORMIST TRAP

The absence of an enduring domestic consensus on independent India's foreign policy was not surprising given the extraordinary diversity of the nation and the multiple intellectual strands that went into the making of its national movement. India's consciousness of international affairs and the relevance for its own independence began to grow rapidly after the First World War. But the breadth and depth of the interest, however, would remain limited. Only a few among the leaders of the national movement took consistent interest in international affairs and reflected on how India should react or take advantage of them. This trend line inevitably extended itself into the post-independence period, when Nehru had virtually a free hand in shaping new India's foreign policy. During the early years of independence, there were enough towering personalities with strong views within and outside the government who would question and criticise Nehru's approach to the world. It was inevitable though that debates on foreign policy would eventually conform to the broader political fault lines within the nation. As communists, socialists, conservatives, and a variety of regional formations unveiled their own separate attacks on Nehru's foreign policy, the discourse resonated among their supporters and sympathisers among the intellectual classes, the media and the academia. These criticisms were not always consequential in political terms, given the Congress party's dominance of the political system. They nevertheless provided an intellectual atmosphere in the 1950s that was open and vibrant.

The 1950s saw the attempt to structure a loose but foreign policy establishment that sought to bring together public intellectuals, bureaucrats, professionals, businessmen, scholars and journalists under the rubric of the Indian Council of World Affairs in New Delhi. Nehru took an active interest in promoting what we might now call a civil society initiative. The Institute of Current World Affairs (ICWA) was soon complemented by the establishment of a School of International Studies across the road. The school that was eventually merged into the Jawaharlal Nehru University in New Delhi would become the main source of international scholarship over the next few decades.

In the mid-1960s, the Institute of Defence Studies and Analyses (IDSA), designed as an autonomous institution funded by the Ministry of Defence was co-located with the ICWA and the School of International Studies.

New Delhi's India International Centre and its 'Saturday Club' provided a forum for the movers and shakers of the 'system' to thrash out a range of issues, including national security and foreign policy. Together they offered a nucleus around which a strong and influential community of international relations professionals might have been built. The discourse on international affairs was not limited to Delhi, Calcutta, Bombay, Madras, Allahabad, Jaipur were all important centres of research and publication activity. The major national newspapers published across the nation took great interest in world affairs. The Indian elite was plugged into the international relations community around the world, published in international journals, and hosted research scholars from abroad. Given New Delhi's relative openness to both the East and West during the Nehru years, India became the biggest arena for competing ideological propaganda unleashed by Washington and Moscow. Whether it was effective or not, it added to the extraordinary dynamism of India's intellectual debate during the 1950s and 1960s.

India's public square began to lose some of its vitality and diversity from the late 1960s and down went the project of building a credible international relations community. As Indira Gandhi drifted towards left wing populism at home, moved closer towards the Soviet Union, and sharpened the rhetoric of third worldism, the domestic political discourse on foreign policy began to acquire a monochromatic hue. The biggest victim of this has been academia, especially its humanities divisions. The international relations community, given the close proximity of its subject to the conduct of national diplomacy, suffered even more. The hegemony of the pseudo-left radicalism over the media and the academia actively promoted by the Congress Party in the 1970s snuffed out much of intellectual dissent, both liberal and conservative. The centralisation of the academia in the 1970s disempowered the older centres of foreign policy discourse in the regions. Once 'politically correct' priorities were identified, resources from the central government flew to such approved destinations as Soviet studies, resulting in the utter neglect of American and Chinese studies. The deep suspicion of the United States that took root in the 1970s steadily strangulated the channels of discourse between the Indian international relations community and its counterparts in the West. As India turned its back on Asia in preference for the non-aligned stage, the academic and other contacts in Asia too dried up. The difficult relations with China and Pakistan also meant that the studies of India's neighbourhood got steadily eroded across the nation.

This sweeping damage to the community was compounded by a powerful new imperative of conformism that paralysed international studies and much of the humanities research across the nation. The only source of funding for research, conferences and travel were centralised government institutions, the University Grants Commission and the Indian Council of Social Science Research.

Although there was space for independent research and critical studies of Indian foreign policy, there was no incentive in the academia or the media for such an approach. Criticism or original ideas largely came from political forces and journals on the margins rather than mainstream academic institutions. It is not that either Indira Gandhi or Rajiv Gandhi preferred a disempowered international relations community. In her second term, Mrs Gandhi was looking to break out of the ideological rigidities of the 1970s that were constraining Indian diplomacy. Rajiv Gandhi chose to depart from every presumed canon of the famed 'Nehruvian' consensus – on India's relations with the United States, China, Pakistan and Israel as well as on nuclear weapons policy, to name a few. Neither the contemporary media accounts nor the later academic analyses have fully explored the bold foreign policy innovations under Rajiv Gandhi. When the Congress governments in the 1980s were looking for new ideas on foreign policy in order to end India's growing marginalisation, the conformist academic and media communities were of no great help. They were good as cheerleaders for their preferred political leaders; but not as generators of new ideas or new stratagems for the conduct of foreign policy.

The one exception to the deadening conformism of the 1970s and the 1980s was the IDSA. (Disclosure: the author was on the IDSA staff from 1983-92) In one of the paradoxes of the Indian international relations story, the one bureaucrat who drifted into international relations research and stayed with it, Subrahmanyam was prepared to defy the presumed limits on the foreign policy discourse. As a consequence, the IDSA, under his leadership, was able to launch a national debate on nuclear policy at a time when the subject seemed so forbidding. For the next few decades, the IDSA would be at the forefront of the nuclear discourse in India.

Under the leadership of Subrahmanyam, the IDSA also focused the elite's attention onto the security politics of the Indian Ocean after the British withdrawal from the East of Suez, and made the case for an interest-based foreign policy, but also as a tool to mobilise pressure on the politicians and bureaucrats deciding foreign and national security affairs.

In the 1980s, the IDSA was home to feverish activity by a small group led by Subrahmanyam that tried to simulate the activity of a full-blown foreign policy establishment. Writing foreign policy speeches for political leaders from the government and the opposition, developing public advocacy, running open media campaigns against certain decisions of the government, sending policy briefs on emerging issues to the highest levels of government, rationalising the government's diplomatic decisions, explaining Indian policies to international audiences, drawing in serving bureaucrats and soldiers to spend time researching at the IDSA, deputing IDSA staff to the Foreign Office and the news agencies, and bombarding the media with articles and features were some of the IDSA's many activities. There was no way that the intensity and depth of this campaign could be sustained by any organisation. The IDSA under Subrahmanyam, however, demonstrated the possibilities of constructing a permanent foreign policy establishment that did not owe its loyalty to any particular party or leader, was not tied down to one particular department or ministry in the government, was neither pro-West nor pro-East, neither left nor right, could argue on the basis of national interest, develop policy options without having to access governmental information, bring together serving and retired bureaucrats, political leaders, senior editors, reporters and businessmen, and create facilities for any one to develop the skill for gathering open source intelligence.

THE CHANGING INSTITUTIONAL BALANCE

When Subrahmanyam started writing for newspapers as the director of IDSA in the 1960s, there was barely concealed condescension from the traditional international relations community. The prevailing view was that 'serious scholars don't write in newspapers'. While the Indian academic attitudes towards media might not have changed significantly over the last four decades, the power of the public forum has dramatically increased in the intervening period. As the Indian democracy matured, the media began to acquire greater visibility if not influence on policy making. The area of foreign and national security policies was no longer immune to the impact of the media.

One of the unintended consequences of Indira Gandhi's short-lived Emergency Rule during 1975-77 was a palpable increase in the power of the print media and its new self-assurance. That the rulers of Delhi could be overthrown in elections helped generate a more equal two-way relationship between the print media and the government.

If the 1980s saw the steady accretion of the print media's power in the country, there has been a dramatic surge in the power of the private electronic media since the late 1990s. This in turn has had a significant impact on the national security and foreign policy discourse within India. That the Indian media could be treated as a hand maiden of the foreign office bureaucracy was a commonly held view within the South Block.

This perception might have been valid when a small but docile group of foreign office 'beat' correspondents would deferentially take dictation from mid-level bureaucrats in the foreign office. Those days, however, are long gone, as a number of factors have altered the equations between media and the officialdom. The class background, educational qualifications, and the pay of the media personnel has dramatically evolved during the 1990s, and they no longer have a reason to acknowledge the presumed superiority of the officer class, nor are the new generation of journalists dependent on a variety of favours dispensed by the state machinery. The media's access to political leaders within and outside the government has become closer over the years and many journalists themselves have effortlessly moved into political parties and the parliament. The tabloidisation of the media meant it is constantly on the lookout for juicy human interest stories about the foreign office and the rest of the bureaucratic system; it could make or break personal reputations of senior officers.

From being a one-sided relationship, the media-foreign office relationship is a two-way street of mutual give and take. Even more significant was the weakening of New Delhi's power structures after 1989. The replacement of one party or one family rule by weak coalition governments meant the political classes were less domineering and more eager to please the media. Just as a host of other institutions, including the judiciary and the election commission to name a few, asserted themselves in the last two decades, the fragmentation of political power in the centre strengthened the media's clout. If the politicians needed good press, the bureaucrats were quick to adapt in the 1990s as they sought to leverage the press for their own individual advance or in winning policy battles within the government. The media scene in Delhi began to resemble that in Washington, where different sections of bureaucracy routinely leak information on a selective basis to shape public opinion.

Weak governments and strong media meant the press and television could whip up popular passion and utterly complicate the functioning of the government in such crisis situations as the hijacking of the Indian airliner IC814 at the end of 1999. Even more significant was the fact that focused arguments in a section of the Indian English media turned the Indian government from an active supporter of the international negotiations on the Comprehensive Test Ban Treaty (CTBT) during 1993-95 into a ferocious opponent during 1995-96. Central to this turnaround was the massive mobilisation of the nationalist sentiment against the CTBT in India in a short period of time.

Since the turn of the millennium, the media has become the principal theatre for intellectual and policy contestation on the direction of Indian foreign policy. This was most visible in the passionate discourse on the Indo-US civil nuclear initiative that saw the left parties withdraw support from the Singh government, which in turn had to go to the floor of the parliament to demonstrate majority support in July 2008 different sections of the media root for different directions of change, the media does not simply neutralise itself; it has become a potential brake on new initiatives as well as a facilitator of new moves by the government. This in turn has put a new premium on the political classes and the security establishment reaching out to the media and leveraging its influence.

The media is not the only new actor shaping India's foreign policy in the last two decades. As India moved towards a state-led socialist economic path, its business community too became marginal to the foreign policy of the nation. Although businessmen were occasionally employed for specific diplomatic purposes, Mrs. Gandhi used the Hindujas to reach out to the Shah's Iran in the 1970s. Similarly, Vajpayee tapped the Hindujas to reach out to the British Prime Minister Tony Blair in the wake of Pokharan nuclear tests of May 1998. The objective was to soften the reaction within the G-8 that Britain was chairing and facilitating meetings between the National Security Adviser Brajesh Mishra and top officials of the Western nations. Since the launch of the economic reforms, the business community has become an important influence in shaping relations with other nations as well as influencing the domestic public opinion and media on a range of political issues including those on foreign policy.

Large individual business houses like the Tatas and Ambanis, as well as business associations like the Confederation of Indian Industry (CII) and the Federation of Indian Chambers of Commerce and Industry (FICCI) have become recognisably important in diplomacy as well as national discourse on foreign policy. The British businessman, Laxmi Mittal was tapped by New Delhi in this decade to facilitate India's search for equity oil around the world, especially in Central Asia. During his visits abroad, it has become customary for the Prime Minister to take with him large business delegations. Joint forums of Chief Executive Officers have become an important vehicle for moving crucial bilateral relations forward and pressure points for internal bureaucratic change. Given the weakness of the universities and the think tanks, the CII and FICCI have also appropriated some of their functions, for example developing Track Two and Track One and a Half dialogues and often acting as think tanks on specific policy issues. Some of these initiatives did become rather consequential. Initiated in early 2002, the CII-Aspen Indo-US strategic Dialogue has met every six months, brought together influential voices in both countries and cleared the ground for major new bilateral initiatives. One of its rounds in Jaipur in early 2005 helped generate a mutually acceptable framework for resuming civil nuclear cooperation. The essence of this understanding was reflected a few months later in the Bush-Singh nuclear deal. While some see this as a positive development, others see it negatively.

The new forces shaping public opinion and influencing foreign policy are not limited to the national theatre. There is no doubt that different regions of India had always had some influence on the nation's foreign policy towards some of the neighbouring and ethnically kindred countries. The influence of Tamil Nadu politics on India's policy towards Sri Lanka is well known influences on the making of foreign policy, traditionally a 'national endeavour', have steadily increased during the last two years thanks to the emergence of coalition rule at the centre, in which regional parties have become critical components. This 'municipalisation' of foreign policy, interestingly, has not always led to the 'regional' prevailing over the 'national', as the local forces acquired high stakes in federal power structures. Nevertheless, the growing impact of local interests on India's foreign policy in recent years could be seen as the successful result of a campaign of the Sikkim government in New Delhi to open up trade with Tibet. Equally important has been the growing contact between the chief ministers of the two Punjabs across the Radcliffe line and the attempt to promote the shared cultural identity of 'Panjabiyat'.

Among the other forces that have emerged in recent years has been the military. After years of enduring the jack-boots of civilian control, the armed forces have begun to find their voice on national security. Organisations such as the United Services Institute have been revived, many retired members of the armed forces are now a regular fixture in the public discourse and have joined political parties. All three Indian services have now established their own think tanks that have begun to develop capabilities for research on foreign and national security issues and intervene in the public debates. Equally important has been the rise of what might be called the Track Three that has sought to mobilise activist groups across the nation on critical foreign policy issues. Unlike the Track Two process that involves experts and retired diplomats and soldiers, Track Three reaches out into the wider civil society and has been fairly effective in making points on war and peace issues in the region. Civil society leaders like Nirmala Deshpande, not generally known to take an interest in foreign affairs, played a key role in promoting Indo-Pak dialogue and reconciliation in the post Kargil phase.

Meanwhile, the strongest force in the making of Indian foreign policy, the bureaucracy, has had to adapt to the rising power and influence of the new institutions. In all those democracies that feature a permanent bureaucracy, universities and think tanks tended to be relatively less important in shaping foreign policy. In Britain and France, small collegial bureaucratic elites have dominated the making of foreign policy and selling it to the political classes as well as the public. The absence of such a bureaucracy in Washington and the ease of moving in and out of government have allowed the emergence of a wide and deep foreign policy establishment in the United States. It was but natural that the Indian model would look a lot similar to that of Britain and France in this respect. Given the extraordinary task of managing a large and diverse country, the weight of the permanent bureaucracy in making national security policies seemed to steadily increase. The Indian Foreign Service did inherit some of the finest traditions of its precursor, the Indian Political Service.

Many of the early civil servants retiring from the Foreign Service made their reputation as scholars and publicists profoundly influencing the national discourse on foreign policy. The writings of Sardar K. M. Panikkar and K. P. S. Menon Sr. readily come to mind. With his prolific writing after his retirement in the early 1990s, J. N. Dixit seemed to carry on that tradition until his death in 2005.

When it came to the making of foreign policy, however, the South Block was a closed shop. Thanks to Nehru's leadership of the Ministry of External Affairs in the first years of the Republic and the sustained interest in foreign affairs demonstrated by Indira and Rajiv, the Indian Foreign Service also enjoyed a measure of autonomy from the growing dominance of the Indian Administrative Service. While outside experts made inroads into the economic and technical ministries, the national security ministries remained thoroughly insulated from external 'penetration'. The Indian Foreign Service would not even make room for other services let alone outside experts, even on a temporary basis, into its fold. The monopoly on information on world affairs, and the development of sophisticated cadres in Russian and Chinese affairs reinforced the condescension in South Block that they have little to learn from outsiders. But nearly two decades of globalization, the emphasis on commercial diplomacy, the information revolution, an irreverent print and electronic media, the emergence of Track Two and Track Three formations, and above all the fragmented structure of power in New Delhi have meant the South Block had to cope with a very different template. If the imperative of adjustment has been relentless, not all in the Foreign Office and diplomatic corps have managed to adapt. Those who did have been far more effective in driving Indian foreign policy in new directions.

INDIA'S QUEST FOR BALANCE

The US National Security Strategy of 2002 had acknowledged India as a "growing world power with which we have common strategic interests." It was not until the second Bush term in March 2005 that the US made a conscious decision to raise the stakes and decide to "help India become a major world power in the 21st century." The first step in this direction was the New Framework for the US-India Defence Relationship signed in June 2005, which included a clause stating that "our defence establishments shall collaborate in multinational operations when it is in their common interest."

The nuclear agreement, which followed three weeks later, calling for the separation of India's nuclear facilities into civilian and military, and bringing India's civilian facilities under international safeguards in exchange for nuclear energy cooperation, demonstrated the growing strategic convergence between the two countries. Domestic political considerations have come in the way of the Indian government operationalising the nuclear deal. That notwithstanding, the deal was widely welcomed in India because it opened the doors for India to participate in civilian nuclear commerce with members of the NSG while allowing it to retain its nuclear weapons programme despite being outside the NPT. The Indian media has overwhelmingly supported the nuclear deal. A frequent theme in the coverage of the India-US strategic convergence is the suggestion that this is intended as a potential counterweight to China.

Rice elaborated on the role of the US-India relationship vis-a-vis China in a speech in Japan in 2005: "I really do believe that the US-Japan relationship, the US-South Korean relationship, the US-Indian relationship, all are important in creating an environment in which China is more likely to play a positive role than a negative role. These alliances are not against China; they are alliances that are devoted to a stable security and political and economic and, indeed, values-based relationships that put China in the context of those relationships, and a different path to development than if China were simply untethered, simply operating without that strategic context."

China's concerns over the emerging India-US relationship are apparent from its opposition to the nuclear agreement. While this has been expressed in a relatively guarded manner, China has also held that US-India nuclear cooperation must conform to the rules of the global nonproliferation regime, which should not be weakened by exceptions. The strategic partnership with the US now provides India with greater leverage over China although India will be cautious in exercising it. India does not view its relations vis-a-vis the US and China as a zero-sum game. The challenge before it lies in being able to build favourable relationships with both the US and China.

The collapse of the Soviet Union and the collapse of the Indian economy in the beginning of the 1990s forced India to reposition itself strategically. The Soviet Union had provided India with a massive security net, the sudden withdrawal of which meant that India had to reassess its security policy and especially its relationship with the US, the sole remaining superpower.

Simultaneously India also had to reassess its economic policy in the wake of the near bankruptcy of the economy resulting from the failed socialist policies of the past. As C Raja Mohan notes, "fundamental changes in foreign policy take place only when there is a revolutionary change either at home or in the world." Although economic reforms had begun on a smaller scale in the 1980s, the more systematic reforms initiated by the Narasimha Rao-Manmohan Singh duo in 1991 were crucial in taking India away from the old slow rate of growth and advancing its claims as a major power

Since 1998, successive Indian governments have worked hard to obtain a measure of nuclear legitimacy for the country's possession of nuclear weapons. India's refusal to join the NPT arose wholly out of its belief that the treaty was discriminatory in perpetuating the 'right' of a few states to possess nuclear weapons. Yet, India has followed all the essential responsibilities of a NPT member. Indian authorities claim, not without considerable justification, that India's record in nuclear export control discipline has been better than that of nuclear weapons states. Indian nuclear doctrine defines the limits placed on the use of nuclear weapons. The nuclear doctrine is based on the principle of No First Use. This is explained as a policy of not using nuclear weapons, unless India is first attacked with weapons of mass destruction. India has chosen not to make tactical nuclear weapons, because it does not intend to use nuclear weapons for war fighting. Nuclear weapons are thus only to be used as instruments of deterrence. India seeks recognition for its nuclear legitimacy through its record on non-proliferation of nuclear technology, its democratic political system and firm civilian control over its strategic assets, and is willing to bind itself into all nuclear regimes and their stipulations, as proof of its determination to play a greater global role. India by its emerging major power potential and commitment to nuclear disarmament, should be a solution to the challenges of proliferation, since it has never been a part of the proliferation problem.

There is a peace process in place between India and Pakistan; a ceasefire on the Line of Control in Jammu and Kashmir has held for nearly four years. There is significant increase in people to people contacts across the borders and the LoC. A military conflict is furthest from the perceptions of the people and leadership of both nuclear powered opponents. India and Pakistan have both formally recognized each other's need for nuclear weapons as strategic assets rather than a war-fighting instrument. Nuclear confidence building measures, albeit limited in nature, are in existence and more are being negotiated. There is also a continuing effort by both countries to improve nuclear delivery means, build credible nuclear command and control facilities and increase the size of nuclear arsenals. Yet, there is an acceptance between India and Pakistan of the need for resolving the regional conflict through negotiations. These are momentous outcomes consequent to the presence of nuclear weapons within a regional conflictual situation.

The nuclear isolation of India that had held its relations with US hostage for decades had to be ended. This realization in Washington and New Delhi was a major strategic turning point in the history of India-US relations. It was in fact the culmination of the process of re-positioning India, that had started after the collapse of Soviet Union and India's own near economic collapse. This repositioning with its strategic and economic shifts had been started by Narasimha Rao and Manmohan Singh. Atal Bihari Vajpayee and Jaswant Singh stayed on that course. It is in a way apt that Manmohan Singh brought that process of repositioning India in the new international order to its present juncture although domestic opposition to the nuclear agreement in India has prevented it from reaching fruition. Today, India is in the enviable position of having stable relations with all major military and economic powers. It is a condition that had been five decades in coming and one that is to be valued and sustained.

As a swing state being courted by all other major powers, India has to perform a balancing act. The India-US strategic partnership cannot be entirely free from the context of the Sino-US relationship, which will act as a cloud on India's relationship with the US because India has no control over US policies and China's responses to those policies. This will in turn be influenced by the flux in the global strategic calculus, which is shifting rapidly both due to changing power equations as well as leadership changes. The challenge before India lies in managing these two bilateral equations under this state of uncertainty and being able to build favourable relationships with both the US and China. India will be cautious in playing the US card against China since it does not view its relations vis-a-vis both countries as a zero-sum game. This would also be in US interests according to Robert Sutter who suggests that "US government leaders should seek to advance US interests in Asia without overt competition with China that would try to force Asian governments to choose between Washington and Beijing."

India is participating in a trilateral dialogue with China and Russia, which met for the first time at Foreign Minister level in 2002. In May 2008, Russia hosted a stand alone meeting of the Foreign Ministers of the BRIC countries which includes Brazil in addition to the other three. A joint communique released on the occasion stated that "Building a more democratic international system founded on the rule of law and multilateral diplomacy is an imperative of our time."

India is also a member of the IBSA which is a trilateral forum including Brazil and South Africa. As Pranab Mukherjee has said, "We are no longer bound by the Cold War paradigm where good relations with one power automatically entailed negative consequences with its rivals."

Bibliography

Ahmad, Imtiaz: *State and Foreign Policy: India's Role in South Asia,* New Delhi, Vikas, 1993.

Anthony, J. Parel : *Hind Swaraj or Indian Home Rule,* Cambridge University Press, 1925.

Ashton, S.R.: *British Policy Towards the Indian States, 1905-1939,* London: Curzon, 1982.

Atri, Ajit : *Gandhi's View of Legal Justice,* New Delhi, Deep and Deep Pub., 2007.

Barber B.R.: *Strong Democracy. Participatory Politics for a New Age.* Berkeley, University of California Press, 1984.

Budge I: *The New Challenge of Direct Democracy,* Oxford, Polity Press, 1996.

Gehlot, N. S.: *Indian Government and Politics.* New Delhi: Rawat Publications, 1996.

Ghosh, Arun : *Indian Industrialization: Structure and Policy Issues.* New York: Oxford University Press, 1992.

Imtiaz, A.: *State and Foreign Policy: India's Role in South Asia,* New Delhi, Vikas, 1993.

Jha, Prem Shankar: *India: A Political Economy of Stagnation,* Bombay, Oxford University Press, 1980.

Mathur, Krishan D.: *Conduct of India's Foreign Policy.* New Delhi: South Asian Publishers, 1996.

Mclean, I.: *Democracy and New Technology,* Cambridge, Polity Press, 1989.

Metcalf, Thomas R.: *Land, Landlords and The British Raj: Northern India in the Nineteenth Century,* Berkeley, UCP, 1976.

Morris-Jones, W.H.: *The Government and Politics of India,* London, Hutchinson, 1971.

Narula, Sanjay : *Indian Politics,* New Delhi, Murari Lal and Sons, 2007.

Patnaik, Naveen: *A Second Paradise: Indian Courtly Life, 1590-1947,* Garden City, New Jersey, Doubleday, 1985.

Prasad, Lal Bahadur : *Indian Political System and Law*, New Delhi, Shree, 2005.

Prem Shankar: *India: A Political Economy of Stagnation*, Bombay, Oxford University Press, 1980.

Probyn, Mr. : *Indian Coinage and Currency*, Effingham Wilson, London, 1897.

Ram, S. and R. Kumar : *Encyclopaedia of Indian Freedom Struggle*, Commonwealth Pub., New Delhi, 2008.

Saksena, N.S.: *India: Towards Anarchy, 1967-1992*, New Delhi, Abhinav, 1993.

Seligman, E. R. A. : *Currency Inflation and Public Debts*, New York, 1922.

Tomlinson, B. R.: *The Economy of Modern India, 1860–1970*. New York: Cambridge University Press, 1993.

Vohra, Ranbir. *The Making of India: A Historical Survey*. Armonk, N.Y.: M. E. Sharp, 1997.

Yasin, Mohammad : *Indian Politics : Processes, Issues and Trends*, New Delhi, Kanishka, 2004.

Zaidi,A.M. and S.G. Zaidi: *The Foundations of Indian Economic Planning*, New Delhi, 1979.

Index

A

Asean Cooperation in Services, 218.

B

BRICS Summit, 10, 27, 35, 48, 56, 178.

C

Climate Change, 46, 49, 122, 123.

Cold War, 52, 54, 60, 62, 63, 64, 65, 68, 72, 195, 199, 209, 219, 230, 231, 264, 265, 266, 276, 277, 278, 285, 286, 292, 297, 305, 307, 313, 314, 332.

D

Diplomacy, 21, 24, 33, 39, 41, 43, 69, 70, 75, 129, 163, 171, 189, 196, 197, 231, 234, 255, 280, 301, 302, 303, 304, 305, 306, 307, 308, 309, 320, 321, 325, 328, 332.

F

Foreign Policy Approach, 10, 26, 70, 200.

Foreign Policy Opportunities, 6.

Foundations, 53, 77.

G

Global Power, 72, 86, 199, 246, 279, 281, 282, 311, 312, 313, 314.

Government Organizations, 190.

I

Investment, 4, 5, 6, 15, 16, 18, 20, 24, 25, 27, 32, 34, 35, 36, 37, 41, 45, 48, 116, 117, 153, 154, 155, 156, 157, 185, 189, 192, 203, 207, 210, 211, 212, 217, 219, 220, 221, 222, 224, 227, 252, 253.

M

Maoists Rhetoric, 149.

N

Narendra Modi Government, 28.

National Policy, 309, 310, 311.

Nuclear Doctrine, 294, 295, 296, 297, 298, 299, 300, 330.

Nuclear Option, 67, 70, 197, 286.

Nuclear Proliferation, 70, 197, 286, 287, 289, 290, 291, 292, 293, 294.

O

Organizations, 110, 126, 130,

135, 149, 190, 201, 203, 226, 321, 324, 325.

P

Policy, 1, 2, 3, 5, 6, 7, 9, 10, 11, 12, 13, 17, 18, 21, 22, 23, 24, 25, 26, 27, 28, 29, 30, 32, 33, 35, 36, 37, 39, 48, 50, 53, 54, 55, 56, 57, 58, 59, 60, 61, 62, 63, 64, 65, 66, 67, 68, 71, 72, 73, 74, 75, 76, 77, 78, 83, 87, 88, 93, 94, 105, 106, 107, 108, 109, 116, 126, 136, 148, 153, 154, 155, 156, 157, 162, 163, 166, 174, 175, 177, 178, 181, 190, 191, 192, 194, 195, 196, 199, 200, 201, 202, 211, 215, 217, 223, 224, 225, 229, 230, 231, 233, 234, 235, 236, 237, 238, 239, 240, 241, 242, 244, 245, 249, 250, 252, 269, 270, 271, 272, 273, 274, 275, 276, 277, 278, 279, 280, 281, 282, 284, 285, 286, 287, 288, 289, 290, 291, 292, 293, 294, 296, 297, 298, 299, 300, 301, 302, 303, 304, 305, 307, 308, 311, 312, 313, 314, 315, 316, 317, 321, 322, 323, 324, 325, 326, 327, 328, 329, 330, 331, 332.

Proliferation, 78, 81, 82, 83, 84, 85.

Public Diplomacy, 304, 305, 306, 307, 308.

R

Recognition, 78.

S

SAARC Satellite, 30, 87, 89, 90, 91.

South Asian Association for Regional Cooperation, 56, 88, 94, 97, 108, 110, 119, 121, 172, 179, 184, 201, 279.

T

Trade Area, 56, 114.

W

Weapons, 79.

□□□